Subediting and Production for Journalists

The new edition of *Subediting and Production for Journalists* is a concise, clear and contemporary introduction to the skills required for subediting newspapers, magazines and websites. Tim Holmes describes how subediting has developed, from the early days of print to the modern era of the internet browser and social media, and explores the many challenges for the sub working today.

Using numerous practical examples drawn from print and online, *Subediting and Production for Journalists* introduces the various techniques employed by the sub to help make the written word stand out on the page, including:

- subbing news and features for sense and style
- writing headlines and sells
- making copy legally safe
- understanding production, using software packages and content management systems
- editing and rewriting stories for online publication
- creating suitable page furniture for websites
- handling and sizing pictures digitally
- handling audio and video.

Subediting and Production for Journalists is the perfect guide for all those with an interest in subbing in today's multimedia environments, as well as anyone wanting to see their words come to life.

Tim Holmes is Associate Director of the Centre for Journalism at the Cardiff School of Journalism, Media and Cultural Studies, Cardiff University, UK. He teaches on the MA in Magazine Journalism, the MBA in Media Management and the BA in Journalism and Communications. He is co-author (with G. G. Mottershead and S. B. Hadwin) of *The 21st Century Journalism Handbook: Essential Skills for the Modern Journalist* (Routledge, 2012), and editor of *Mapping the Magazine: Comparative Studies in Magazine Journalism* (Routledge, 2008).

Media Skills

EDITED BY RICHARD KEEBLE, LINCOLN UNIVERSITY
SERIES ADVISERS: WYNFORD HICKS AND JENNY MCKAY

The *Media Skills* series provides a concise and thorough introduction to a rapidly changing media landscape. Each book is written by media and journalism lecturers or experienced professionals and is a key resource for a particular industry. Offering helpful advice and information and using practical examples from print, broadcast and digital media, as well as discussing ethical and regulatory issues, *Media Skills* books are essential guides for students and media professionals.

Designing for Newspapers and Magazines
2nd edition
Chris Frost

English for Journalists
Twentieth Anniversary Edition
Wynford Hicks

Ethics for Journalists
2nd edition
Richard Keeble

Feature Writing for Journalists
Sharon Wheeler

Freelancing For Television and Radio
Leslie Mitchell

Interviewing for Journalists
2nd edition
Sally Adams, with Wynford Hicks

Interviewing for Radio
2nd edition
Jim Beaman

Magazine Production
Jason Whittaker

Programme Making for Radio
Jim Beaman

Production Management for Television
Leslie Mitchell

Researching for the Media
2nd edition
Adèle Emm

Reporting for Journalists
2nd edition
Chris Frost

Subediting and Production for Journalists
2nd edition
Tim Holmes

Writing for Broadcast Journalists
2nd edition
Rick Thompson

Writing for Journalists
2nd edition
Wynford Hicks with Sally Adams, Harriett Gilbert and Tim Holmes

Subediting and Production for Journalists

PRINT, DIGITAL, SOCIAL

SECOND EDITION

Tim Holmes

Routledge
Taylor & Francis Group

LONDON AND NEW YORK

Second edition published 2016
by Routledge
2 Park Square, Milton Park, Abingdon, Oxon OX14 4RN

Simultaneously published in the USA and Canada
by Routledge
711 Third Avenue, New York, NY 10017

Routledge is an imprint of the Taylor & Francis Group, an informa business

First published 2002 as *Subediting for Journalists* by Routledge

British Library Cataloguing in Publication Data
A catalogue record for this book is available from the British Library

Library of Congress Cataloging in Publication Data
Holmes, Tim, 1953–.
  Subediting and production for journalists/Tim Holmes. – Second edition.
  pages cm. – (Media skills)
  "First published 2002 as *Subediting for Journalists*"–Title page verso.
  1. Journalism – Editing. I. Hicks, Wynford, 1942–. Subediting for journalists.
  Based on (work): II. Title.
  PN4778.H48 2015
  070.4′1 – dc23
  2014047230

ISBN: 978-0-415-49200-3 (hbk)
ISBN: 978-0-415-49201-0 (pbk)
ISBN: 978-0-203-14354-4 (ebk)

Typeset in Goudy and Scala Sans
by Florence Production Ltd, Stoodleigh, Devon, UK
Printed in Great Britain by Ashford Colour Press Ltd

MIX
Paper from
responsible sources
FSC
www.fsc.org   FSC® C011748

Contents

Figures

Acknowledgements

There are many people who contributed to the making of this book but I would like to thank the following in particular:

First and foremost must come Wynford Hicks, co-author of the first edition, the person who brought me into the project and from whom I have inherited it. I hope this new edition meets his exacting standards.

The many students who have bought, borrowed or otherwise used the first edition and their tutors, who put it on reading lists and gave me kindly and positive feedback.

Students on the MA in Magazine Journalism at Cardiff University on whom I have road-tested much of the new material.

My colleague Glyn Mottershead for his contribution to Chapter 3 and his insights into digital publishing.

Professor Duncan Bloy of the Cardiff School of Journalism, Media and Cultural Studies for his material help and careful guidance in matters of law as they affect journalists. Chapter 9 would not have been possible without his unstinting assistance.

Niall Kennedy, who spotted that 'Super Cally' should in fact be 'Super Caley' when referring to his football team of choice, Inverness Caledonian Thistle. Niall's unending patience saw the book through several upheavals and brought it safely home.

Sue Leaper and her colleagues at Florence Production for taking such care with proofing and corrections.

Finally, to my wife Rebekka Smith and my son George Smith Holmes, thank you for tolerating the ups and downs of authorship. It wouldn't mean anything without you.

Tim Holmes
Holmesta@cardiff.ac.uk

Text acknowledgements

'Who needs sub-editors? Read David Montgomery's 2,200-word missive on the future of Local World in full' by Axegrinder. Courtesy of *The Press Gazette*.

'Standard Chartered share price falls 16%, wiping £6BILLION from its value, after claims the UK bank laundered billions for Iran and Hezbollah' by James Salmon. Courtesy of *The Daily Mail*/DMG Media.

'Huge data blunder by the Serious Fraud Office sees 32,000 pages of evidence in BAE Systems bribery case released by mistake' by Matt Chorley. Courtesy of *The Daily Mail*/DMG Media.

'UK has had the fastest growing population in Europe for a decade' by John Bingham, 26 June 2014. © Telegraph Media Group Limited 2013/2014.

'Children of Paradise' by Todd S. Purdum, originally published in *Vanity Fair*. Courtesy of Todd S. Purdum.

Text from *This Is The Order*, Issue 3. Courtesy of Ross Cairns/Vince Medeiros.

'The Grande Dame of Charing Cross Road', first featured in *Riposte*, Issue One. Courtesy of *Riposte*.

'Walls of Death, Wheels of Life'. Courtesy of *Boneshaker Magazine*.

'The Desert Stage' by Buzz Bissinger/*Vanity Fair*/© Conde Nast.

Text from *Autocar*, 15 January 2014. Courtesy of Haymarket Media.

'How to Pass the Xavi Way', SportsDirect.com magazine. Courtesy of Haymarket Media.

Text from Creative Review's *London Underground 150* commemorative issue, March 2013. Courtesy of Creative Review.

Alexander McQueen and Vivienne Westwood collection summaries, *Marie Claire Runway*, Spring/Summer 2014. Courtesy of Time Inc. (UK).

'The nine lives of Felix' by Sean O'Hagan. 2 June 2013, originally published in *The Observer Magazine*. © Guardian News & Media Ltd 2013.

'How to Spend Time Alone'. The article first appeared in the March 2015 issue of *Red Magazine*. Courtesy of Red Magazine/Hearst Magazines UK.

Extract from Buck Owens's memoirs, featured in *Country Music* magazine. Courtesy of Team Rock publishers.

'Definitive guide to using important meta-tags' by Shaun Anderson [Hobo]. Available at: www.hobo-web.co.uk/seo-blog/. Courtesy of Shaun Anderson.

'TwoTwentyTwo is a landmark of bad taste' by Marina O'Loughlin. Originally published in *The Metro*, 23/7/2009. Courtesy of Solo Syndication.

Preface to the second edition

When the first edition of this book, then called *Subediting for Journalists*, appeared in 2002, the world of magazines and newspapers was on the cusp of a publishing revolution that has had effects as far reaching as that of Johannes Gutenberg when he perfected the printing press and moveable type in 1439.

In 2002 the internet had already been invented for some time and publishers had begun to use the world wide web to supplement their printed material. Thirteen years later the situation has been reversed – increasing numbers of publications are moving to a digital first policy and even though print still brings in a substantial proportion of revenue, publishers with foresight have begun to manage print for profit and digital for growth. In other words, they will squeeze as much money as they can from print for as long as possible while looking to digital for future prospects.

One thing I am certain about, however, is that whatever its substrate, text-based content has to be as pleasurable to read as possible and the only way to ensure that is to have professionals whose job is to attend to spelling, punctuation, factual accuracy and presentation. These professionals are subeditors and production journalists and they will be needed as long as there are people who want to read. In the fifteenth century Johannes Froben observed, 'the buyer of a book full of misprints does not really acquire a book but a nuisance': it was true then, it is true now and it will be true in 500 years time.

Changes in publishing practice have, of course, brought changes in working practices and production flows. Subs may not work exclusively for a single publication, they may be situated scores or hundreds of miles away from where the editorial content is created, they may operate under a different job title, they will almost certainly have to work across print and digital, they are very likely to require the skills to find and edit still or moving images, they may be involved in managing social media and user generated content – but when all is said and done, these professionals are doing the job of a subeditor.

So although the book has been changed to incorporate all those elements, and the content has been almost completely rewritten to acknowledge the fact that digital production runs alongside print (also reflected in the numerous hyperlinks that will only really make sense in a digital edition), its title still leads with the word 'subediting' and still focuses on the primary tasks of a subeditor – to make the reading experience as pleasurable, profitable and perfect as possible.

Abbreviations

B2B	business to business
DMGT	Daily Mail and General Trust
dtp	desktop publishing
HCI	human computer interaction
HTML	hyper text mark-up language
MIN	Midland Independent Newspapers
MMR	Measles, Mumps and Rubella
NATSOPA	National Society of Operative Printers and Assistants
NGA	National Graphical Association
PA	Press Association
QPS	Quark Publishing System
SEO	search engine optimisation
SLADE	Society of Lithographic Artists, Designers and Process Workers
SOGAT	Society of Graphical and Allied Trades
UPN	United Provincial Newspapers
wysiwyg	what-you-see-is-what-you-get

1
Introduction

When Tom Crone and Colin Myler were being quizzed by MPs (7 September 2011) about the *News of the World* phone tapping scandal, they said a lot of interesting things, one of which was about subediting. The context was whether Clive Goodman, who had been jailed for tapping into phones belonging to members of the royal family, had been promised a role at the paper after he had served his sentence. Crone, who looked after legal affairs, suggested that Andy Coulson (the editor) thought this would be appropriate:

> when [Clive] had served his sentence, paid his fine, done community service ... Mr Coulson, was hoping he could persuade the company that Clive Goodman could come back and work at the company, all be it [sic] not in a reporting capacity, perhaps as a sub-editor or a book filleter.
>
> (http://bit.ly/goodmansub)

A 'sub-editor or a book filleter' rather than a reporter! What a fall from grace this was clearly intended to convey – no longer allowed to don the sacred mantle of 'reporter', but only allowed to do a job that was on a par with 'filleting': from top chef to fish market skivvy at one fell swoop.

This book sets out to remedy that perception. Subediting is an essential part of journalism and something that all journalists – reporters, writers, even executives – need to know how to do. Structural changes in newspaper, magazine and online publishing not only make it essential to know how to subedit well but also put subbing ever closer to the heart of those businesses. How so? When Mel Exon of BBHLabs wrote about his visit to Telegraph Media Group's hub-and-spoke newsroom he explained the background to the new way of working. Will Lewis (who became editor in chief before moving on to News International) had spent five months working on a pilot scheme, called Project Victoria, to establish the most effective ways for working for a newspaper that wanted to integrate print and online without replicating the old protocols of news production. Exon wrote:

> Project Victoria's aims were straightforward: could they move to a model where more content was produced, more often, by fewer people . . . across more platforms . . . Whilst maintaining the quality of journalism? Without increasing errors? . . . the net result was more content, of equal if not higher quality, for less.
>
> (http://bit.ly/projectvictoria)

With three to four pairs of eyes looking at content instead of 11, each of those pairs has to belong to someone who is totally aware of the need for clearly written and accurate stories that are legally sound and presented in a way that will attract readers – someone with the skills of a subeditor, in fact.

When the first edition of this book was published (all the way back in 2002) subediting was still a distinct role in its own right – newspapers and magazines had subeditors who did nothing but sub. In the intervening decade, the number of people who do subbing pure and simple – subbing of the kind a true Fleet Street journalist would recognise – has declined as the task has been absorbed into a broader production role. This reduction in the number of specialised subeditors, combined with changes in production processes and widespread digitisation of journalism generally, has thrown more responsibility for subbing onto writers. This has three effects:

- the people formerly known as subeditors have more to do;
- journalists not previously expected to undertake subbing duties are now likely to have to do some;
- many writers will be left to their own devices so had better get up to speed with subbing and production.

Why I changed the title

For these reasons the title of the book has been changed to *Subediting and Production For Journalists*, to reflect the new reality, while the content has been substantially revised to take account of the skills and knowledge needed to fulfil the new-look job. The need for these changes is real but the core purpose of the book remains the same – to help journalists publish accurate stories that attract as many readers as possible in print and online. Job titles change, job descriptions change but the need for subbing continues, as we shall see.

To return to the situation at the *News Of The World*, perhaps the very attitude displayed in the quote above helped to destroy the 168-year-old newspaper that Goodman might or might not have been allowed to creep back to. Perhaps because the view that anything less than 'reporter' was unworthy of recognition as a 'real' journalism job fuelled the mania that led to such widespread unethical behaviour – behaviour that also tainted the police and politicians – the proprietor saw no option but to close the publication immediately, taking with it reporters, subeditors, filleters and all. Perhaps, in fact, if the subeditors had been looked to as role models, the unethical behaviour might have been checked and the newspaper might have survived.

This sounds fanciful but it can be justified. The distinction between reporting jobs and subediting jobs has been evident since the mid-nineteenth century, when print production became an industrialised process that demanded a classic division of labour within its workforce: journalists wrote, subeditors organised and improved, typesetters set type, printers printed and so on. Eventually the distinctions became hardened into demarcated roles jealously guarded by craft bodies and trade unions such as the National Society of Operative Printers and Assistants (NATSOPA), the National Graphical Association (NGA), the Society of Graphical and Allied Trades (SOGAT) and the Society of Lithographic Artists, Designers and Process Workers (SLADE).

Adam Smith would have recognised this set-up. Perhaps the most well-known and most frequently cited example from his 1776 work *An Inquiry into the Nature and Causes of the Wealth Of Nations* is the division of labour in a pin factory, wherein:

> One man draws out the wire, another straights it, a third cuts
> it, a fourth points it, a fifth grinds it at the top for receiving
> the head; to make the head requires two or three distinct oper-
> ations; to put it on, is a peculiar business, to whiten the pins
> is another; it is even a trade by itself to put them into the

paper; and the important business of making a pin is, in this manner, divided into about eighteen distinct operations, which, in some manufactories, are all performed by distinct hands.

(Book 1, Chapter 1, I.1.3 http://bit.ly/
pinfactory)

The *News of the World*, a good example of an industrialised newspaper, was founded in 1843 at a time when developments in Victorian technology – steam-driven printing presses of various types, new type-founding processes, the electric telegraph, photo-mechanical reproduction – were starting to demand specialised knowledge to operate the necessary machinery or manipulate its output. It made sense to have these roles performed by different people, and it continued to make sense until the 1970s, when the use of labour reached a point of potential unification rather than division. This was when personal computers reached a stage of development that made them commercially viable. As their numbers proliferated, their reach began to extend into all areas of commerce including previously craft-based sectors. Typesetting on a desktop computer became possible in the late 1970s with the TeX programme; full what-you-see-is-what-you-get (wysiwyg) desktop publishing arrived in 1985 with MacPublisher on the Apple Macintosh, rapidly followed by Ready, Set, Go! and Aldus Pagemaker. Non-Apple computers joined the desktop publishing (dtp) revolution with Ventura Publisher in 1986. Since then QuarkXPress and Adobe InDesign have come to dominate the market for this type of software.

The point here is that processes of labour previously divided by necessity, and then tradition, could be unified within a single machine, operated by a single person. The full effects of this potential were realised in 1986 when News International moved production of its British newspapers from Fleet Street, the traditional centre (or hub) of the newspaper industry, to Wapping, defying the craft and trade unions with a vested interest in doing things the old way and causing considerable social unrest.

Since then just about everything in journalism has been up for an overhaul and of all the elements of labour in the magazine and newspaper industries, it is production journalists who have had their roles expanded most significantly, not just because print processes have changed but also because digital processes have been added to the mix. Furthermore, even reporters are routinely expected to be able to fulfil what would previously have been categorised as production tasks – writing straight onto a page, for example.

Changes of this nature have gone so far that there are now voices debating whether production journalists, and particularly subeditors, have a distinctive role to play within specific publications at all. Roy Greenslade, for example, got into a bit of a comment war on his blog:

> subbing numbers could be drastically reduced . . . subbing can also be outsourced in order for hard-pressed newspapers groups to reduce their overheads . . . publishers [might] consider whether to cut costs by having the task done by a centralised collective of skilled journalists elsewhere, be it in Australia or India.
>
> (http://bit.ly/greensladesubs)

In one sense he is right: many jobs in journalism can be centralised or outsourced. Reporting – that sacrosanct role – provides some excellent historical examples of this. Julius de Reuter founded his eponymous news agency in 1847 and began to supply British newspapers with foreign news in 1858; the Press Association (PA), a co-operative news gathering organization for provincial papers intended to allow them timely coverage of general and parliamentary news, was founded in 1868; the Central News agency began supplying reported material in 1870. What did all these bodies have in common? They reduced the number of journalists a paper had to employ, they centralised the news gathering process, they outsourced reporting to a 'collective of skilled journalists elsewhere'.

If subeditors are now going down the same road, it is a road that has been well trodden by reporters. What this evolutionary process does not do, however, is remove the need for subeditors and production journalists from newspapers, magazines and digital publications. An earlier contributor to the debate about the future of subbing, which has been rumbling on since at least 1996, was reported by *Press Gazette* on April 12 of that year:

> This move inspired a riposte from the chief sub-editor of *The Health Service Journal* which neatly encapsulated all the benefits a good sub-editor can bring to a title. To summarise, subs

> can help to keep readers reading, improve dull stories, pick up
> errors, spot libels and, in short, act as 'a reporter, an editor, a
> designer and a proof-reader all rolled into one.' As the buffer
> between writer and reader they should be 'the lynchpins of
> the modern editorial process'.
>
> (PG 12/4/96)

Interestingly, the traditional buffer analogy can also be applied to one of
subbing/production's more recent responsibilities, social media management – the moderation of comments on blog posts, the safeguarding of
reputation on Facebook or Twitter. This is, of course, a very different
task from the all-in-one skillset proposed above but, inevitably, things
have been moving in that direction. For a while after the internet had
become a ubiquitous facility, print and the web were understood almost
as binary opposites and job set-ups reflected the idea that people with
print skills could not be expected to practise online skills and vice versa.
Now it is recognised that while separate skills are involved, they are
closely related and production journalists are routinely expected to
perform both.

A good example of this phenomenon can be found in RBI (Reed Business
Information) a major publisher of b2b titles that has invested heavily in
digital journalism over a long period – all of its print magazines have a
strong web presence and journalists are encouraged to blog, tweet and
generally raise their online profiles. An important part of that investment has been directed towards increasing transparency not just between
publication and reader but also within the organisation. Karl Schneider,
RBI's editorial development director, used his blog *Falling Off A Blog* to
raise issues that were affecting the workforce and invited debate from
them. In February 2009, around the same time as Roy Greenslade was
dismissing the need for subeditors in his *Guardian* blog (see above),
Schneider posted a piece about the development of production because
although RBI had done a considerable amount of work with writers, 'so
far we haven't talked very much about the future for the people who
work on our production desks'.

> In the print world these are the people who process/check/
> improve individual lumps of content (articles, headlines,
> images, captions etc) and combine them to create compelling,
> effective pages. They are the custodians of quality and

consistency on our magazines and they have a huge impact on the overall package presented to readers.

We already have people doing things on our websites that fall into the same sort of category. As well as editing copy, we have people editing video, aggregating feeds, uploading podcasts, updating 'slots' on home pages, tweaking HTML and embedding widgets.

(http://bit.ly/schneider1)

The post attracted a lot of comments. One from John Snuggs pointed out that *Farmers Weekly* had already gone a long way down this road:

We have five subs, two artists and a picture editor producing 4000-odd pages and 6000-odd web stories a year.

Eighteen months ago, we had a dedicated online sub and web production took up about 30% of our time, most of that work being done by the online sub. Now, all five subs work both in print and online, and web production accounts for more than 50% of our work.

We've had to learn a lot of new techniques, change our mindset to treat all copy as web-first (or to be more accurate, 'web at about the same time') and arrive at a way of doing all this without working all the hours there are. We've just about managed it.

But the job of the sub has remained the same – that is, to present copy and pictures to the reader in an attractive package, checked and where necessary enhanced for sense, legality, clarity, writing style, spelling and grammar, and above all, to make sure it gets read.

A few comments below this, SueP (who noted "I've been a sub for about 25 years – since the paper and pencil, casting off [1] headlines days") reinforced the point that change has already happened:

I work on an integrated team (has been since I joined it in Dec 04) where we deal with three monthlies, a weekly news led mag and the associated website – which now dominates. We have been publishing web-first for about a year, and the only difference between the skills used across the range of products is that (at the moment) we can't do layouts on the web. But it is a dynamic medium and I have no doubt that will change as the technology becomes more user friendly.

In addition to traditional subbing tasks we add value by checking and adding links; checking the searchability of key terms; making sure SEO [search engine optimisation: the process of improving the visibility of a website or a web page in search engines] best practice is observed, blogs and related links established; sourcing, sizing and uploading pictures; and driving the rest of the team to support the web-first approach.

The debate sparked by this post encouraged Schneider to develop his theme in a second post that also brought a healthy response from the people working in his company. SueP came back with a comment that is worth quoting at some length as it encapsulates a lot of what this book covers:

It's important not to see any of the creative team – writers, designers, subs – as superfluous to the process of delivering a product that will meet the needs of readers/users, and provide a strong brand against which the company can sell. The requirements of online publishing are different to those of print, but only in terms of the detail, not the bigger picture, and the skills and experience acquired by journalists belonging to each of these three disciplines will continue to be just as important to producing a unique and valuable online product as they have been in print.

When desktop publishing arrived subs stopped using the skills of casting off headlines and copy, measuring and sizing photographs for scanning, and so on – developing instead the skills of the typesetter and benefiting from the wysiwyg potential of DTP, which gave them the opportunity to experiment with headlines to find the best balance between impact and fit, to move pictures, other graphics and text boxes around to find the ideal combination of ingredients. But the intellectual process required to arrive at that solution remained, just using different tools to achieve the same ends.

Currently web publishing tools . . . make the web environment less flexible, so that this sort of intervention is less common, but this need not be the case, and in the longer term, as tools become more user-friendly, layout subs will resume the practice of adjusting standardised pages to improve their impact.

The pace of change has accelerated as online offerings morphed rapidly from straightforward uploaded magazine content to blogs, forums, podcasts, videos and tweets delivered through a multitude of devices. The skills to deliver optimised content will similarly morph, but the ability of experienced subs to understand the requirements of these new media and devices will draw on their knowledge of past production processes, adapting them to the new requirements.

RBI still has people called 'subs' but even in companies where production roles have been combined and job titles have been changed, subediting is still an essential part of the overall process. At Future Publishing, Cat Hackforth explains:

We don't have anyone with the job title 'subeditor' – we have production assistants, production editors and operations editors. I'm an operations editor, which means I'm responsible for subbing raw copy and fitting InDesign documents, as well as commissioning and editing the news section.

Emma Davies is a production assistant in the editorial production studio at the same company. She notes:

Most of my work involves laid-out InDesign pages. We're obviously never expected to lay anything out for ourselves . . . but having a decent knowledge of the program does help. I sometimes do some raw copy work, but it really depends on the stage at which the mag is in their production cycle. As we're normally brought in to help in the week or two leading up to deadline, though, raw copy is only about 25% of what I do, tops. I can't say that I've ever really thought about the distinction between subbing and production; my role is a production one, but I tend to refer to the work itself as subbing. I suppose I think of the words as interchangeable

. . . [knowing] InDesign is useful because we do a lot of subbing directly on to the pages – I only really work on paper if it's raw copy or if I'm giving something a final read-through. It's also just nice to know how to go about moving stuff about if needed, although some art editors are more precious about that than others. Also, if there's a problem on a page, I'm quite likely to know how to sort it out.

Who this book is for

As should have become obvious from the foregoing, it is my firm belief that *Subediting and Production for Journalists* is for everyone involved in the production of journalism. One reason is the three effects noted earlier:

- the people formerly known as subeditors have more to do;
- journalists not previously expected to undertake subbing duties are now likely to have to do some;
- many writers will be left to their own devices so had better get up to speed with subbing and production.

The book will also be invaluable to journalists at different stages of their careers:

- Beginners – if you are at the start of your career, use it as a text-book. You will gain a valuable overview of the production role and will be able to pick up many useful basic skills and shortcuts from the content and case studies.
- Developers – if you have been working as a journalist for a while you can use the book to judge your progress and learn about new, different or more advanced ways to do the job.
- Refreshers – if you have been in the job for a while it may be that you are in need of a little professional development, in which case the book will give you new insights and allow you to see where your skills need to be reinforced.
- Out of office freelancers – if you are working from a remote site there are probably times when you feel a little out of the loop or behind the curve; this book will bring you bang up to date.

Subediting and Production for Journalists will also be useful to a number of classes or types of journalist:

- subeditors – will be able to ensure they are au fait with the latest techniques as well as seeing where their specialisation fits into the bigger picture;
- production journalists – will be able to understand how subediting fits into the wider process, and why it is so important to a quality publication;
- writers – will gain valuable insights into the processes that their work goes through;
- editors/section editors – will get a clear picture of processes within their purview that sometimes get lost or overlooked in a complex and highly pressured situation.

All of the above will be able to update their knowledge and hone their skills, as well as gain a greater understanding of and insight to the whole vital field of production. In addition, case studies and examples from different companies will allow comparison of techniques and perhaps the adoption of more efficient or effective ways of doing things.

Finally, never let anyone tell you that if your first job is as a subeditor you'll never be able to move into a writing role. This is one of the enduring myths of journalism and it is a myth for the simple reason that working as a subeditor gives you a much clearer understanding of how to write well.

Jon Severs has taken the sub-to-writer route, starting as a subeditor on *PrintWeek* before working on the features desk of the same title and then moving to *TES* (formerly the *Times Education Supplement*) as a commissioning editor. Not only did he find it possible to make the move, he is certain that his initial stint as a sub has helped his development as a writer:

> Starting out as a subeditor was not the beginning to a career in journalism I had envisaged – I was told once I had spelling blindness – but I can honestly say it has been integral to pursuing a career as a features editor and freelance features writer. This is not purely because under the frightening guidance of an old editing stalwart my spelling and grammar improved immeasurably – though these are of course crucial

skills for any writer and editor – it was actually that my ability to write, edit and structure was transformed.

It's partly because you read such a volume of work that you quickly build up an expertise as to what works and what doesn't. This volume of reading and editing also helps you realise an appreciation of individual writing styles and you learn how to maintain that individual voice when trying to channel it through the tones and cadences of the overall voice of the magazine you work on – when writing, this ability to bend your writing to a magazine is crucial.

Subediting also makes you approach journalism as a reader, not a writer. When a writer reads they judge each decision in isolation and consequently their reading can be microscopic, missing the larger irregularities. As a subeditor, you read with a much wider, less connected, view, so you can spot structural irregularities, mismanaged information, broken or weak themes, mismatched introductions or endings, ramblings that need shortening and contractions that need expanding. A writer is too immersed in his topic to see these things – with subediting experience, however, the writer can take a step back and is happier to self-edit and criticise their own work in an impartial way.

Note

1   Also known as casting up or copy fitting, this is the name for the pre-digital process of determining the space needed for a given amount of copy. The total number of pages could be estimated by dividing the word or character count by the word or character count per page for the specified text typeface. This could be performed mentally or by using special casting off tables issues by print foundries. Once desktop publishing became widespread casting off became a lost skill since wysiwyg allowed subs and designers to see exactly how much space the copy occupied.

2

How to be a modern subeditor

Wanted: subeditor. Must have traditional subbing skills, excellent spelling and grammar, be great at rewrites and converting to house style, capable of coming up with creative headlines, sells and captions, generally computer literate but an expert at layout using InDesign, with management skills and the expertise to oversee the entire production process from raw copy to final pages. Experience of online journalism, web pages and content management systems essential, as is the ability to write news and features and edit audio and video. Must be fast, accurate, competent in media law and able to remain calm and positive under extreme pressure.

Oh, and must not mind being invisible in the final product, having the job dismissed as desk-bound drudgery or being blamed when everything goes wrong.

It seems like a lot to ask of one job – and it is. Yet all of these desired qualities (and more) were derived from advertisements for subediting and production jobs; if nothing else, this demonstrates that the list of skills required of a subeditor is broad and still growing. Furthermore, the strictly defined traditional role of 'subeditor' has come under intense pressure – and in some instances the threat of outright abolition – from powerful players in the publishing industry.

Looking at these trends might lead to the supposition that a subeditor's job is both highly demanding and precarious in the extreme but the reality is that subediting and production is not only more crucial to the publishing process than ever before, it has also become considerably more creative – a quality that is called for in an increasing number of job advertisements.

If we take all of the points above and look at them as opportunities rather than threats, there is probably more scope than ever before for anyone who wants to enter the world of subediting and production. Research for this book, for example, showed not only that b2b title *Farmer's Weekly* needed a multimedia subeditor who could provide 'new ideas and solutions to problems and issues as they arise' but also that top-end consumer title *Tatler* wanted a production editor who would 'become the team expert on the digital production process'.

The question is not whether subeditors are still needed, because the evidence shows clearly that they are and, for as long as there is a publishing *process*, always will be. The real question is – how did a job that was long seen as a dull backroom speciality come to be so inclusive and creative?

Background

Leslie Sellers begins his classic 1968 work *The Simple Subs Book* by deprecating the practice of starting such books with a historical overview. 'Sub-editors', he wrote, 'haven't any history to speak of. Their arrival on the scene is due to two factors – the size and complexity of modern newspaper organisations, and the increasing concentration on both readability and design.'[1]

Thirty years earlier F. J. Mansfield had begun *Sub-editing: A book mainly for young journalists* (1931) in a very similar way: 'The sub-editor has little "historical background." ... This sub-division of editorial labour could only have occurred with the growth and organization of newspapers into larger and more elaborate entities.'[2] Despite this he supplies a very elegant history of the subeditor's role as he sees it, quoting from Ben Jonson (1573–1637), Thomas Carlyle (1795–1881) and William Makepeace Thackeray (1811–63), among others, to prove his point.

As good as those books by Mansfield and Sellers were in their day, in this particular they were wrong on two counts for the subeditor's craft can be traced from the birth of modern printing processes, through the birth of dtp to current content management systems for digital journalism, a period of nearly 600 years. And since they were written there have been numerous technological advances, each of which has added a new layer to the production process as well as radically altering the commercial and economic basis of the publishing industry.

This cumulative development makes it difficult to pin down what exactly is expected of a subeditor. Although most journalists will have a general idea of what the name means it has never been a universal and specific job title. In his landmark series of training manuals *Editing and Design: A Five-Volume Manual of English, Typography and Layout* (1972) Harold Evans decided to use American nomenclature in the first volume which is why you will find very few references to subeditors in *Newsman's English* and a great many to 'copy readers', 'desk editors' and 'deskmen'. Nor is the job description static; look at the job ads on Gorkana.co.uk and see for yourself.

As for what subs do, there has, as one author noted in 1963, long been confusion over this: 'I can remember when schoolmasters used to approach newspapers for holiday jobs as subeditors. They thought the work would involve no more than correcting errors of grammar and spelling. Would that it were so easy!'

A subeditor certainly must correct spelling and grammar, but must also check factual accuracy, rewrite copy to make it better or to conform with a house style, seek out potential libels or other legal pitfalls and remove them, fit copy into a layout, devise headlines, standfirsts and captions, and then, more than likely, lay that copy out in page templates for print *and* online editions, having selected, cropped and sized the illustrations or photographs *and* edited and uploaded audio or video files.

Although even the anonymous author quoted above didn't have all of these processes in mind, his assertion that subediting 'consists of taking the written raw material and moulding it into the form in which it will appear in print' is spot-on, though it's not just for print now. All of this will probably be done at a computer screen using a range of software packages, each of which the subeditor must be able to use proficiently.

This very condensed summary of a subeditor's tasks does not reflect the relative complexity of tasks because they are all important; ensuring that a piece of copy is spelled correctly is at least as important as putting that copy into a layout or content management system – and it was with spelling that the job started.

The subeditor's role had its beginnings around 1450, when Johann Gensfleisch zum Gutenberg successfully developed the use of moveable type. Contrary to popular opinion, the German goldsmith did not invent printing as such. According to the great historian of print S. H.

Steinberg, 'What was epoch-making in Gutenberg's process was the possibility of editing and correcting a text which was then (at least in theory) identical in every copy; in other words, mass production preceded by critical proof-reading' (Steinberg 1996: 6). It is also worth noting that Gutenberg simultaneously invented typography, the art of making and using type faces and a topic in which subeditors will have a natural interest.[3] Creating two modern industries with a single development is remarkable enough, but a third was also made possible, and it was the one that is of most interest to us as professional journalists. Steinberg (1996: 7) continues:

> At the same time, when Gutenberg made it feasible to put on the market a large number of identical copies at any given time, he thereby foreshadowed the possibility of ever increasing the number of copies and ever reducing the length of time needed for their issue ... Thus Gutenberg can be acclaimed also as the progenitor of the periodical press.

Once the possibility of making corrections to texts had been established, the subeditor's role could begin in earnest, and with some academic prestige attached to it. In the 1470s, Johann Amerbach saw to it that his books were 'edited with care and accuracy ... professors of Basel university served Amerbach as editors and proof-readers' (Steinberg op. cit.: 21). Subeditors everywhere should take to heart the words of Amerbach's successor Johannes Froben: 'the buyer of a book full of misprints does not really acquire a book but a nuisance.'

With proofreading established, the next step was to ensure uniformity in the use of language – the beginnings of a house style and tone of writing. William Caxton decided to adopt the dialect of London and the Home Counties for books such as *The Canterbury Tales* (1478), and his successor Wynkyn de Worde (a true subeditor's name if ever there was one) developed the process to such an extent that he could, says Steinberg (op. cit.: 58), 'put forward a modest claim to having inaugurated what we now call the house style of a printing or publishing firm, which overrides the inconsistencies of individual authors'.[5]

Technical advances in printing and typography changed the way books, pamphlets, circulars, periodicals and newspapers looked, but the next major advance came with John Bell, a printer, publisher and journalist of the eighteenth century. Not only did he design at least one classic typeface (the eponymous Bell), he also:

revolutionised the whole typography and display of the English newspaper . . . Bell was the first printer to realise that a newspaper is read at a speed and for purposes different from the reading of a book; and he drew the typographical conclusions. His newspapers broke up the solid setting of the book-page and gave prominence to the paragraph as the unit on which the newspaper-reader's interest is centred.

(Steinberg, op. cit.: 113)

Bell started numerous newspapers, including the *Morning Post* which lasted from 1772 to 1937. Publishing clearly ran in the family blood; his son John Browne Bell also founded a number of papers, the best known of which was undoubtedly the *News of the World*, born in 1843 and killed off in 2011 by a rash proprietor looking for redemption after a massive phone hacking scandal.

So, by the beginning of the nineteenth century the subeditor's domain already incorporated spelling, grammar, house-style and eye-catching layout even if the job title had not become common currency. Well before Mansfield's 'elaborate entities' or Sellers's modern newspaper organisation, there was a concentration on accuracy, readability and design.

The rise of the subeditor

Listen to the mythologists of journalism history and it is easy to think that newspapers became 'elaborate entities' in some kind of truth-seeking, public-educating, polity-influencing, fourth-estate, organic evolutionary process. The truth, however, is more complicated than that – never pure and far from simple.

In the eighteenth and nineteenth centuries newspapers were often owned by printers and were expected to make a profit – that was their purpose. As Alan Lee observes:

the Victorian newspaper was not just, or even primarily, a vehicle of national education or of political democracy. It was for those who ran it first and foremost a business, and had long been recognised as such . . . There can be little doubt that the proprietors of early Victorian newspapers ran them in the vast majority of cases in order to make a profit.

(Lee 1976: 49)

There are two main sources of income, and therefore potential profit, for a product such as a newspaper: those who buy the product itself and those who advertise in the product in order to attract those who buy the product to buy *their* products. In short, readers and advertisers – and subeditors, or what subeditors do, became increasingly important in attracting or retaining both streams of revenue.

The first newspaper-like publications, the corantos and mercuries, were laid out in a very plain style such as books or pamphlets in runs of eight, 16 or 24 pages. As the number of publications increased, all looking very similar, publishers began to experiment with ways of drawing attention to their products and readers increasingly had to be tempted by attractive layouts. The origins of this can be traced back at least to 1642, when the *Mercurius Civicus*, an early news-sheet, began to make regular use of headlines and illustrations, such as a portrait of the King or Queen, but it was the *Oxford Gazette* of 1665 that really established a new format:

> In the history of journalism its significance lies in the fact that its single-leaf form . . . with its pages divided into two columns, broke away from the news-pamphlet form to a style that is a recognizable link with the newspaper as we know it today . . . The two-column layout which it inaugurated became the standard for the new publications of the next few decades.
>
> (Herd 1952: 33)

This set a new standard for newspaper layout, dividing the pages and making blocks of text easier to read by reducing the length of each line. As noted above, John Bell was one of the publishers who understood the need to create elegant, easy-to-read pages but there were plenty who just crammed in more and more text, until:

> The end of the nineteenth century found some of the leading British newspapers in a precarious condition . . . Much ingenuity and large sums of money had been expended on improving the mechanical equipment of the newspaper; great enterprise had been shown in speeding up the collection of news and the distribution of the paper; but not since the days of John Bell and other designers of elegantly composed eighteenth-century journals had anyone been interested in making the newspaper agreeable to look at and pleasant to read.
>
> (Herd 1952: 222)

As Herd's quote indicates, external technologies and socio-economic developments also had an effect on the way newspapers were created and distributed. Steam-driven presses – pioneered in the UK by the *Times*, which installed a Koenig & Bauer steam-driven press, first used for the issue dated 29 November 1814 – allowed production to be speeded up and expanded enormously. Steam-driven railway trains delivered the papers to all corners of the kingdom at previously undreamed of speeds, expanding the reach and potential readership of daily national newspapers enormously, and entrepreneurs such as John Menzies and William Henry Smith developed newsstands (Smith's first was at Euston station in 1848) to make finding and buying the papers quick and simple.

The same spirit of innovation drove the development of the electric telegraph, which soon became an essential news-gathering tool for newspapers: not only could the physical paper be delivered from London to Edinburgh before the working day began, news from the other side of the world could be delivered on a current of electrons. As Alan Lee notes, 'The communications revolution which so deeply affected nineteenth-century society enabled news to be gathered, processed and distributed at a pace and on a scale which became almost an obsession of the Victorians' (Lee 1976: 59).

If the telegraph brought a constant stream of news it also brought the need to capture that flow and then expand on it, for telegrams are by their very nature brief and epigrammatic. Someone had to be in place to stitch together these nuggets of news and rewrite them into a comprehensible narrative – the subeditor.

But it was not just telegrams that brought news. London in the nineteenth century boasted a large population of freelance journalists, then called 'penny-a-liners' for the simple reason that they were originally paid a penny for every line of copy that was published. James Grant in his social study of London, *The Great Metropolis* (1837), devotes considerable space to analysing this group, descendants of Grub Street's infamous residents,[6] whom he describes as:

> altogether a singular race; they are a class, in a great measure, by themselves; they live by the press, and yet they do not, strictly speaking, belong to the press. They have no regular sum for their labours; sometimes no sum at all . . . Sometimes they will fag away without a moment's intermission for seven

or eight hours, writing in that time as much matter as would
fill from a column to a column and a half of a morning newspaper, walking, it may be, in addition, five or six miles, and
yet not receive one penny, notwithstanding all their enter-
prise and exertion. No paper is bound to use the matter, or
any part of it, which they furnish [. . .]

(http://bit.ly/greatmetropolis)[7]

If hopeful penny-a-liners were flooding the newspapers with copy, offering as many lines as possible in order to secure a good flow of pennies,
there needed to be someone in place to monitor, arrange and if necessary
correct or rewrite the lines – the subeditor. Historian Alan Lee believes
the subediting role burgeoned as the press, like most other manufacturing
processes in the nineteenth century, underwent the transformation
from craft to industry: '[Subeditors] had probably been first introduced to
control the penny-a-liners, but it was the telegraph which made them
indispensable, with their scissors and paste-pots' (Lee 1976: 110).

For a while the novelty and stimulus of increasingly current national and
international news was sufficient in itself to ensure the success and profitability of newspapers but as we have seen from Harold Herd above,
little attention had been paid to 'making the newspaper agreeable to
look at and pleasant to read' – nor to expanding its base of readers from
the metropolitan elite, the kind of reader served so well by the *Times*:
well-educated, serious, responsible and, to judge by the look of their
newspaper, just a bit dull.

Towards the end of the century this now-traditional approach to newspaper production was rejected by a number of forward-thinking editors
and publishers; there was no consciously planned movement but the
results have been banded together retrospectively under the heading 'new
journalism' (not to be confused with the later 'new journalism' of Tom
Wolfe and Hunter S. Thomson). Established papers, or those of the
Establishment, were quick to criticise what they saw as a lowering of
standards: 'the journalism of the *Daily Telegraph* and the *Pall Mall Gazette*
created a furore because they had broken with the staid traditions suppos-
edly set by the *Times*, although neither was trivial or frivolous in its
treatment of the news', Alan Lee notes.

These strains were to be the common accompaniment of the
'new journalism' in the 1880s, which can best be described as

> a mixture of journalistic and typographical devices, which taken together constituted a new style of journalism, a style which reflected a changing relationship between the newspaper and its readers.
>
> (Lee 1976: 120)

The relationship between newspaper and readers Lee refers to here can be characterised as 'giving the readers what they want'. This may now be the motto by which magazines and newspapers live but in the 1880s many saw it as too radical by half – just how, the prominent figures of the establishment asked, were the semi-educated, barely literate masses supposed to know what they wanted or what was best for them? A large number of people were not even allowed to vote – universal male suffrage was not introduced until 1918 and women did not have the same voting rights as men until 1928. These people could not possibly be expected to understand the news unless it was carefully explained to them and they were in no position to demand any kind of content just because they wanted it.

Many journalists were none too happy with these developments either; their role was either to report, at great length, parliamentary proceedings or pontificate, at equally great length, on the implications of those proceedings. Thus when

> innovators came along in the 'eighties and 'nineties who strongly urged that the primary task of a newspaper was to get itself read, and that there was a whole range of human interests that found no reflection in the columns of existing journals, the reaction of the majority of journalists was violently unfavourable.
>
> (Herd 1952: 223)

The trouble was, once the genie was out of the bottle there was no way to put it back. As is the case with any widely and rapidly adopted cultural or technological advance, from pop music to Twitter, it is impossible to uninvent it. Newspapers such as the *Pall Mall Gazette*, which emphasised human interest stories, and magazines such as *Tit-Bits* (the British weekly magazine founded by George Newnes in 1881 that was literally a collection of short tit-bits) increased the potential popularity of the press – and the need for subeditors to marshal and present all this content in an attractive way.

The railways that had allowed national distribution of newspapers also provided an enormous potential readership as cities developed suburbs and workers began to commute to work – they wanted something to help pass that time, something that would ideally entertain and inform them. As Brian Lake writes:

> The potential was there. *Tit-Bits* showed the popularity of the short, simple paragraph combined with gimmicks such as prize competitions and free accident insurance; the 'New Journalism' of the *Pall Mall Gazette* and *The Star* of 1888, provided the topical news element.
>
> (Lake 1984: 74)

All that was missing was a way to make it affordable for the masses, and it was only a matter of time before a business-minded publisher picked up the type of content embraced by the *Pall Mall Gazette* (but not its layout, which was conventional[8]) and applied them to a truly mass-market newspaper. That publisher was Alfred Harmsworth, whose magazine *Answers To Correspondents* had followed *Tit-Bits* to success, and the newspaper was the *Daily Mail*, launched on 4 May 1896. The paper's motto was 'A penny newspaper for a halfpenny', it styled itself the 'Busy Man's Journal' and it embraced the modern world wholeheartedly. The first issue contained a piece that predicted the rise of the automobile and had a page for women, at a time when most established newspapers ignored women, who didn't have the vote and never seemed likely to.

Lord Salisbury, the prime minister and also incidentally one of the pontificators of the established press, dismissed the *Daily Mail* as a newspaper written by office boys for office boys, but he had clearly failed to notice the number of office boys who wanted a newspaper of their own, because the first issue sold out a 397,215 print run. It is still, at the time of writing in 2015, an enormously successful publication, whereas Lord Salisbury is best remembered, if at all, for resigning over the introduction of Benjamin Disraeli's Reform Bill that extended the suffrage to working-class men and (allegedly) hushing up a homosexual scandal that involved a member of the royal family.

Alfred Harmsworth later became Lord Northcliffe and his name and his newspaper empire live on as Northcliffe Media, until 2012 part of the Daily Mail and General Trust (DMGT) group. His title was also adopted as shorthand for a shift in the way newspapers were produced and the way they looked – the Northcliffe Revolution required copy to be well edited, written in a tone that the general reader would find familiar, and presented in carefully planned and well laid out pages with a liberal use of pictures and illustrations. According to R. McNair Wilson, quoted in Mansfield's book about subediting:

> [Northcliffe] saw associations between typesetting and author-ship, between the nature of an article and the manner in which it was presented. He began to understand the immense power of suggestion which rests in headlines and cross-head-ings. He began to think in pages as well as columns and lines.
>
> (Mansfield 1931: 132)

In short, the Northcliffe Revolution ushered in the era of the subeditor, making production the equal of reporting and writing. Furthermore, the revolution has now affected the way all newspapers are produced, from red top tabloid to the quality broadsheets and former broadsheets. In 1952 Harold Herd observed:

> Cautious adaptation of the Northcliffe formula has brought fresh vitality to serious newspapers. Not only is the modern 'quality' journal, with its clean, well-designed pages, a better job technically than in 1901, but it is also better written. Modern journalism has responded to the accelerated pace of life and the general trend towards simplicity by evolving a more lucid and direct style of expression in both news and comment.
>
> (Herd 1952: 279)

None of these changes to the editorial aspects would have been possible without subeditors – but this is to consider only one side of the revenue equation mentioned earlier. If newspapers found themselves having to cater for what readers actually wanted in order to get them to buy the product, they also had to make major concessions to the advertisers who wanted to attract those readers. The increasing importance of advertising revenue to profitability became another genie out of the bottle, a rather demanding genie. Harris and Lee remark on the physical change that display advertising brought to page layouts:

From the 1870s the demands of advertising, the most potent commercial force at work on the press, involved the introduction of an increasing amount of pictorial material as well as the breakup of the inflexible columns in ways which were soon reflected in other areas of content.

(Harris and Lee 1986: 110)

This demonstrates how sensitive newspapers and other publications had to become when responding to the demands of both readers and advertisers, a point reiterated by Terry Nevett in an essay on advertising and editorial integrity: 'Gradually publishers were forced to allow advertisements which were several columns in width, breaking through the column rules which had traditionally contained them, and to permit the use of bold display types and eventually of illustrations' (Nevett in Harris and Lee 1986: 153).

And who made sure those columns could be broken, the right typefaces would be used, the illustrations appeared in the right place? Subeditors.

Focus on . . . What employers look for in a subeditor

The following lists are taken from job advertisements for subeditors and production editors. No single advert asked for all of these but most asked for a significant combination from each category.

Editorial skills
- Ensure quality is maintained in right style
- Ensure creativity and quality of copy
- Ensure ideas are in line with strategy and written to tone
- Ensure print and online content meets quality standards
- Strong writing and rewriting skills
- Create pages that bring stories, graphics and data together in compelling layouts
- Write attention-grabbing headlines, standfirsts and captions
- Proofreading
- Fact checking
- Understand SEO
- Understand editorial use of social media

Technical skills
- Proficiency in InDesign (or QuarkXPress, though none of the adverts in this small research exercise mentioned Quark)
- Proficiency with Content Management Systems
- Know how to handle words, pix, video, graphics
  - editing
  - sizing
  - uploading
- Know how to create online landing pages to template
- Know how to create print pages to template
- Ensure online content is linked and tagged
- Ability to update flatplan and manage copyflow
- Ability to moderate a publication's community forum
- Manage site's presence on social media

Personal characteristics
- Attention to detail
- Ability to learn quickly
- Remain calm and positive under pressure
- Work quickly and accurately to tight deadlines
- Excellent communication skills
  - with production studio
  - with writers
  - with management
- Organisational and administrative skills
- Flexible attitude to last minute changes
- Able to work quickly and accurately to tight deadlines
- Able to co-ordinate publishing schedules
- Able to co-ordinate multiple projects
- Keep pace with hectic production schedule

Experience, knowledge and understanding
- Knowledge of media law
- Understand repro and production

Development – training, learning, innovation
- 'Providing new ideas and solutions to problems and issues as they arise' – Multimedia subeditor, *Farmers' Weekly*, RBI

- 'Become the team expert on the digital production process' – Production Editor, *Tatler*, Condé Nast

Subediting news stories

Well could F. J. Mansfield write, 'The rise of the great modern news-paper has produced, possibly as the most characteristic creation in its domestic economy, the skilled sub-editor' (op. cit.: 7). The answers in Alfred Harmsworth's eponymous magazine were short, snappy and factual, and there were plenty of them, mixed in with competitions to attract and keep readers. This technique found its way into the *Daily Mail*, where, as Matthew Engel observes in his history of popular jour-nalism: 'The little one-paragraph items that had dominated . . . *Answers* were now adapted to the business of news' (Engel 1996: 60).

Clearly it is a skilled job to condense news reports (or any report) into bite-sized chunks that will still tell the story accurately, and this is when the newspaper subeditor began to come into his own (and in those days it was almost certainly a him on newspapers; magazines were different in that they employed significant numbers of women). The *Times* or *Daily Telegraph* had been content to run columns and columns of verbatim reports from Parliament or the courts (as much as 61,500 words on occa-sion, Engel, op. cit.: 24), leading to copy that was almost impossible to read – assuming anyone wanted to read it in the first place.

The *Daily Mail* cut through all this to present news in a format that could be easily taken in by people commuting into London, Birmingham or Manchester on recently established railway lines from the newly built suburbs. It was intended to appeal to everyone, and one consequence was that the power to publish passed from long-winded reporters to subedi-tors who could literally cut their prose down to size. The saying that 'reporters have all the glamour but subeditors have all the power' might well be traced back to the *Mail*'s launch.

For the next 100 years, the characteristics of a subeditor could more-or-less be taken for granted. The attributes that Alexander Nicol listed in 1950 for his contribution to *The Kemsley Manual of Journalism* had been accurate for 50 years and would remain pretty accurate up to at least 2000 when Harold Evans's book *Newsman's English* was revised and republished as *Essential English for Journalists, Editors and Writers*. There was even a general agreement that a good subeditor should be physically fit 'for a trying, sedentary life which takes its toll of nerves, sight and digestion'.

What are those attributes? Nicol thought that the subeditor must have:

> a nimble intelligence ... an extensive vocabulary, a sound understanding of English grammar and of the 'atmosphere' of words. He should keep cool when hours of concentrated work are made useless by later developments ... he should have a comprehensive technical knowledge of newspaper production. In addition to those qualities, he must possess the unusual attribute of seeing both sides of an argument and an understanding of the human elements in life.
>
> (Nicol, 1950: 99)

According to another authority, 'Nearly everyone puts accuracy first ... A good current affairs background is needed, an analytical mind and an ability to visualise not only how a story may be developed, but its impact on the readership' (Dicker: 164–5). The only thing that Evans adds, or perhaps just expresses differently, is 'Conscientiousness, keenness and ruthlessness, rightly directed' and, of course, 'Knowledge of the main principles of the laws of libel, contempt and copyright' (Evans 2000: 11).[32]

Useful though these descriptions are, they do not really describe how the role fits into the overall scheme of things. Australian journalist Arthur Polkinghorne put the latter very succinctly when he wrote:

> The editor, within the framework of policy set down by the management, determines the personality of the paper; the chief subeditor, in consultation with the editor, attends to the components of this personality; and the subeditors attend to the final tailoring of these components.
>
> (Polkinghorne 1965: 97)

As for what a sub actually does, Ian Mayes provided a comprehensive analysis during his stint as the *Guardian*'s Readers' Editor:

> It is the subeditor who checks the reporter's copy for grammatical and ... factual errors ... It is the subeditor who cuts

> copy to the required size . . . writes headlines and captions and, in certain cases, who lays out the page, articulating the headings, stories, pictures and graphics.
>
> (*Guardian Saturday Review*, 18/9/99, p. 7)

Missing from all these definitions is the fact that successful execution of the job routinely requires computer skills and knowledge of an increasing number of software applications. Subs on the *Guardian*, for example, have to prepare two versions of stories – one for print, the other for the web – from the same source material. Each version of the story has different requirements, for example the online version will publish immediately and so refers to the events of 'today', while the print version must refer to 'yesterday'. The lengths will also be different as print versions must fit a specific space on the page, while online stories can run longer. In 2012 Charlotte Baxter described the various tasks a sub on the *Guardian* has to perform in a post on the paper's 'Comment is free' section (http://bit.ly/guardsub).

As her piece makes clear, the print/online sub also has to source accompanying pictures and make sure they fit. Increasingly subeditors and production editors are also expected to be able to edit audio and video files in addition to the usual range of word processing, image manipulating and page make-up documents.

Subediting features

One notable way in which newspapers have changed over the decades has been the inclusion of more 'magazine-y' material – and indeed more actual magazines as part of Saturday and Sunday packages. Media historians have commented on this process: John Tulloch (2000) identifies magazines as 'the main source of the innovations in the publishing industry that created the modern popular press' (139), while Martin Conboy (2004) flags up 'the ability of magazines to influence the mainstream of journalism' (162), the 'cross pollination' process by which newspapers have appropriated magazine formats and genres – the transmission of aesthetics (163) – and acknowledges that magazines have been 'heralds of social and cultural change' (163). In a discussion of tabloidisation and dumbing down, Dick Rooney (2000) goes so far as to suggest that 'tabloidisation' might in fact amount to a 'magazinization' (107).

Whatever the historical viewpoint, it is true to say that if newspapers have changed, magazines led the way – and this has had a significant effect on the subeditor's job. Up to this point the main focus has been the role of the news subeditor, which would apply equally to news-oriented periodicals, especially trade or business to business (b2b) weeklies or their always-on websites. Features, however, require different treatment. To take two possible extremes, the words may have been commissioned from a writer who has a great style but no in-depth knowledge of the subject, or, conversely, from an expert with no writing skills. Either scenario is entirely possible, as acknowledged by John Morrish in his book *Magazine Editing*: 'The craft of the subeditor is absolutely vital to successful magazine journalism, which increasingly relies on the seamless incorporation of copy from many different writers' (Morrish 1996: 140).

He then specifies the magazine sub's role:

> Subediting has three strands: a kind of quality control, ensuring that everything is accurate, well-written and likely to be legally safe; a production function, ensuring that everything fits and that deadlines are kept; and a key role in the projection of material, through the writing of appropriate and attention-grabbing headlines, standfirsts and captions.
>
> (Loc. cit.)

Exactly the same range of tasks applies to subediting features for newspapers and the skills needed to do them will be examined in more detail in the following chapters.

Developments in newspapers

Press Gazette, the online news source for journalists, regularly runs stories about subediting and production, most of them about cuts or centralisation. A selection taken at random while this chapter was being written ran from *Strike vote over 'illogical centralisation' at Newsquest* (about several newspapers and magazines merging their production facilities: 13 April 2011) via *Johnston Press plans 'hub' to sub all its southern titles* (plans to create a subbing hub for all its papers in the south of England raise fears of job cuts: 1 Feb 2011) and *31 jobs go in new Northcliffe West Country cull* (regional titles merging their subbing operations: 9 March 2010) to *Trinity Mirror centralises sub-editing on 26 London titles* (16 editorial jobs cut after centralising production on 26 local papers in London and the South East: 7 January 2009).

Newsquest, Johnston, Northcliffe (since November 2012 part of the Local World group), Trinity Mirror – that's all the big regional newspaper groups.

On the face of it this is not encouraging for a subeditor – although as Chapter 1 showed, the position subediting and production actually occupy in newspapers and magazines is evolving in a way that allows considerable optimism. Yet despite all the changes and their accompanying headlines there still seems to be a core of agreement on what it means to be a subeditor even if new technology and cost-cutting have had far-reaching effects on the way journalists are expected to do their jobs.

Reorganisation of print media work processes began when the development of increasingly powerful and sophisticated computer layout packages allowed production journalists to take over typesetting and layout. This could not have happened without a massive diminution in the powers and influence of graphical and print unions, a process that was accelerated by the industrial relations policies of Conservative governments in the 1980s, most notably the miners' strike. After NGA and SOGAT[9] lost their stranglehold on typesetting and graphical processes, former typesetters and compositors retrained as layout artists, but their new jobs with scalpel and steel rule lasted only as long as it took early desktop applications such as Ventura Publisher, Adobe Pagemaker and QuarkXPress, along with the first systems for larger users such as ATEX, to conquer the publishing world.

But even the adoption of computerised production systems was not sufficient in itself, the whole process had to be adapted – or completely reshaped – to match the new reality. One newspaper executive who has consistently tried to envision how things should be in the modern age of production is David Montgomery, a controversial figure whose CV includes stints as chief executive of the Mirror Group, as chief executive of Mecom, a pan-European newspaper group he founded, and (at the time of writing) as chief executive of Local World, which has the former Northcliffe newspapers at its centre. In a 1997 speech to the World Newspaper Congress and World Editors Forum he said:

> [M]any of the structures that were created in the hot-metal
> days of the 1930s still survive. The technology of the 1980s,
> as it became widespread, was simply imposed on top of those
> old structures . . . When the screens arrived not a lot changed.

Montgomery's idea, part of a broader scheme for what used to be the
Daily Mirror Academy of Excellence training centre, was that all journalists would be trained in a number of skills and would take up roles as
either writers or page editors. Of subeditors he said:

> The modern sub-editorial function was conceived in the
> 1930s. Sixty years later it is no longer appropriate to employ
> single-skilled text editors, or people who have little function
> but to cut copy to length.

> The technology and screen skills of the journalist should
> enable the modern subeditor to be, in fact, a fully fledged
> editor. This modern-style journalist can select stories, put
> them in order of prominence, design the page, write the head-
> lines, put in and manipulate the pictures, edit the text, review
> the work in total and send the page to the printer. This effec-
> tively eliminates four or five departments. . . [and] inevitably
> means the death of the sub-editor and the birth of the page
> editor.

Unlike many managers with radical ideas, Montgomery was speaking
from experience of the job – he had been a subeditor on the *Sun* in the
1980s. Furthermore, his remarks only articulated what had already, or
was about to, become standard practice at a number of local and regional
newspapers, as subsequent correspondence in *Press Gazette* showed.

'If he wants to see his vision of the future in action, he is welcome to
visit us', said the editor of the *Ealing Gazette and Leader*; and in the
following weeks first the *Hull Daily Mail*, then the Midland Independent
Newspapers (MIN) group revealed new production structures that were
more or less identical to Montgomery's outline. A little delving in the
archive allowed *Press Gazette*'s Jean Morgan to remind readers that the
first newspaper to plan a sub-less system was *The Independent*, back in
1986. However, according to Michael Pilgrim, who was involved with
the launch, 'the computers weren't really up to it at the time and you
still needed a lot of sub-editors' (*Press Gazette* 1/8/97: 11).

Since then computers have become more than up to it and David Montgomery's vision of how a modern newspaper should organise its production systems found favour elsewhere even if others explained it differently. When *Daily Express* editor Richard Addis found it necessary to cut 19 production jobs after the introduction of Quark Publishing System (QPS), he tried to present it as a return to tradition:

> I am increasing the power of sub-editors . . . they have grad-ually had parts of their skill removed and given to other people – design, pictures, imaging departments, the back bench. With the right subs . . . it will be a good thing to have them doing design, headlines, captions and full pages.
>
> (PG 9/1/98, p. 3)

Even when newspapers decided not to go down the route outlined above, the combined effect of communications technology and cost-cutting led to subs working at a distance from the newsroom. In 1996 United Provincial Newspapers (UPN) developed a central subbing unit that served eleven titles across the north-east. Commenting on the develop-ment, Peter Sands of the Editorial Centre consultancy said, 'In most regional newspapers the days of having banks of sub-editors and armies of reporters have long gone' (PG 13/9/96, p. 14).

Such changes are never made without teething troubles or without leaving some workers uncomfortable with the new situation. According to former UPN editor Danny Lockwood, centralised production systems had a number of drawbacks: a combination of cost cutting, confused lines of responsibility and human nature almost guaranteed that, 'corners are cut, editions and change pages are sacrificed, cock-ups proliferate, legal bills mount and the editor is left doing an impression of General Custer with a pop gun' (PG 16/7/99, p. 15).

Yet despite many similar examples of rearguard criticism – and indeed many problems of exactly the kind outlined by Lockwood – the Montgomery version, as we might call it, has become the norm. As Montgomery told the *Telegraph*'s Amanda Andrews in May 2009, 'You are never finished cost-cutting. We have to produce more out of a much smaller cost base. The industry has to understand that cost-cutting is here to stay. The old model will bankrupt publishing businesses if it isn't changed' (http://tgr.ph/costcutting).

Developments in magazines

Magazines and periodicals have not escaped the winds of change that have swept through newspapers. Electronic production (desktop publishing, content management systems) and digital distribution (online magazines) are widespread, bringing with them exactly the same opportunities, threats – and not always successful experiments with production systems over the years.

In February 1996 the editor of women's weekly *Bella*, Jackie Highe, announced that the magazine would use 'copy fitters' to match words to layouts, with writers subbing their own work. Her memo to staff included the line, 'This involves removing the subs department' and an insider reported that 'subbing duties are being imposed on department heads' (PG 12/2/96: 1).

One reason this failed was because those heads had no experience of working with page layout software (QuarkXPress in this instance). Before the end of the year, *Bella*'s editor had changed her mind about the value and cost of subs. *Press Gazette* reported that Highe had offered an experienced sub-editor a job as 'chief text editor' but had then withdrawn the offer in favour of 'plan A . . . the continental system of having a dedicated sub-editor in each department'. A rival editor was quoted as saying, 'No one I know thought she could manage to run the magazine without a proper subs team' (PG 15/11/99: 10).

There will always be rival editors to offer criticism but in the years since that quote a great many magazines have begun to operate with either partially or fully centralised subbing and production teams. For example, one magazine might have its own dedicated sub but send other production work such as layout to a centralised studio; another might produce editorial content in its own office then send that material to a production studio for all further processing. Yet others may have their own production team but draw on a centralised hub in busy spells.

Sometimes the person doing the production may be a lone freelance operating from a remote office or their home; sometimes that work might have been outsourced to a large agency such as the PA. We have seen above that Newsquest centralised magazine production at an in-house facility – Johnston press went even further in May 2009 when it outsourced not only the design, subbing and pre-print processes for 15 of its local magazines to PA but also 'additional content covering topics such as fashion, beauty, health, interiors, food, gardening, motoring and travel' (http://bit.ly/Johnstonmags).[10]

However, it is still common for magazines to have their own art editor, or someone with a similar title, responsible for the layout. Not even Jackie Highe wanted to make *Bella*'s 'copyfitters' or writers do the layouts. The highly stylised nature of magazines means it is still common for titles to have dedicated designers or art editors, although smaller operations and more news-oriented weeklies may rely on subeditors or production editors to lay out some sections. (The very smallest magazines will probably rely on everyone doing everything, and 'everyone' may well mean 'one'.)

Since appearance and projection are such important elements in a magazine's relationship with its readers, this is something that has to be preserved, at least for features pages and at least for design-led magazines. News or other regular pages that can be laid out according to a standard template are a different matter and subs may well find themselves tackling this; likewise uploading material to a content management system that will automatically format the appearance of web pages. If that material includes pictures, as is very likely, they will have to be formatted correctly (size, shape, density, file type). Even with automated formatting, a sub who has a smattering of hyper text mark-up language (HTML) to draw on will be at an advantage when it comes to tweaking content for best appearance on screen.

Headlines such as the examples from *Press Gazette* that opened this section will doubtless continue to appear until the final newspaper has had its production system centralised, and then the complaints will continue in memoirs and autobiographies of old school journalists, as they have down the decades: there's always something to resent or regret. The only certainty is production processes will continue to be affected by technological advances that will lead to different working practices, skill requirements and job descriptions.

Towards the end of the last millennium Ric Papineau, then director of the Mirror Academy of Excellence, told *Press Gazette*'s Jean Morgan, 'Newspapers were once a heavy industry and the way they were run tended to reflect a heavy industry, and not a heavy industry of the 1990s, but probably more one of the 1920s' (PG 1/8/97: 11). Twelve years later this thought was reproduced by communications guru and futurologist Clay Shirky in *Newspapers and Thinking the Unthinkable*, an essay that achieved widespread notoriety. Echoing Papineau – and Montgomery before him – Shirky wrote, 'With the old economics destroyed, organizational forms perfected for industrial production have to be replaced with structures optimized for digital data' (http://bit.ly/shirky2009).

One newspaper executive who has continued to think about a new political and organisational economy for the changing industry has been David Montgomery. Or rather, he has continued to develop the ideas we have seen above. In January 2011 he stepped down from his role in Mecom and by January 2013 he had put together Local World, a business that had the old Northcliffe and Iliffe local groups at its centre – 16 dailies, 36 paid-for weeklies and 40 free weeklies. At the heart of the new company's mission was the intention to 'harness its proven publishing capabilities with new technologies to provide audiences – both print-readers and online consumers – with high quality, reliable and useful content in whatever format they choose' (http://bit.ly/lwmission).

Before the first year of operation was out, Montgomery had composed a 2,000 word essay (acquired and published by *Press Gazette* on 21 November 2013) setting out his vision of how things would be in future. It starts in his usual uncompromising way:

> Apart from the elite and usually elitist newspaper writers the role of the journalist remains entrenched in the industrial age as a medium grade craft. Usually it is a role involving a single skill organised in hierarchies invented to ease production and work flows when typewriters, fixed line phones and pencil wielding sub-editors all inhabited long benches shrouded in cigarette smoke.
>
> The school leaver culture of learning a trade dominated or media school graduates poured into newspapers with unquestioning academic thinking that perpetuated this industrial past.
>
> (http://bit.ly/montysubs)

According to Montgomery, the hierarchies will be dismantled and, eventually:

> The journalist will embody all the traditional skills of reporter, sub-editor, editor-in-chief, as well as online agility and basic

design ability, acquired partly in training but in the case of on-screen capability this is expected as a basic entry qualification as it is now generally present in most 12-year-olds.

(op. cit.)

In other words – the subeditor is dead; long live the subeditor.

Notes

1   Leslie Sellers (1968), *The Simple Subs Book*. Oxford: Pergamon Press: 1.
2   F. J. Mansfield (1931), *Sub-editing: A Book Mainly for Young Journalists*. London: Isaac Pitman & Sons, 1–2.
3   Despite the best intentions of a union-friendly manual for journalists published by the National Council for the Training of Journalists in the 1960s which stated that "a journalist must never, never carry his co-operation to the point of handling type. One good craft deserves another", the modern subeditor will routinely be expected to set, manipulate and correct type (L. J. Dicker in Dodge and Viner 1963, p. 182).
4   The original Latin, should you wish to adopt this motto as your personal crest, is: Qui librum mendis undique scatentem habet, certe non habet librum sed molestiam.
5   deWorde also helped to establish Fleet Street as the centre of English printing when he moved his prolific press there in 1500. By the time of his death in 1535 he had published almost 800 books (Inwood, 1998, 137).
6   http://bit.ly/grubst.
7   Grant's study has been digitised by Lee Jackson at www.victorianlondon.org and it is worth reading the whole of this section to get a proper understanding of the freelance scene in Victorian London. George Gissing's *New Grub Street*, published in 1891, provides a fictional take on a similar theme.
8   "For instance, W. T. Stead's famous articles on 'The Maiden Tribute of Modern Babylon,' . . . had no bold headlines; the first of a series which caused a great sensation in the country began a few lines from the foot of a column!" – Mansfield 1931: 133.
9   National Graphical Association and the Society of Graphical and Allied Trades, respectively.
10   Men's magazine *Palladium* went one step further in June 2009, outsourcing *all* editorial content to Parsleymedia (http://bit.ly/palladiummag). By November 2011 it had given up the print version and moved online (http://palladiummagazine.com). By January 2013 that link led to an architecture website.

3
Professional subediting practice

With Glyn Mottershead

Let's start with a joke.

A man in a hot air balloon realised he was lost. He reduced altitude and spotted a woman below. He descended a bit more and shouted, 'Excuse me, can you help me? I promised a friend I would meet him an hour ago, but I don't know where I am.'

The woman below replied, 'You are in a hot air balloon hovering approximately 30 feet above the ground. You are between 40 and 41 degrees north latitude and between 59 and 60 degrees west longitude.'

'You must be a chief subeditor,' said the balloonist.

'I am,' replied the woman, 'how did you know?'

'Well,' answered the balloonist, 'everything you told me is technically correct, but I have no idea what to make of your information, and the fact is I'm still lost. Frankly, you've not been much help so far.'

The woman below responded, 'You must be a writer.'

'I am,' replied the balloonist, 'but how did you know?'

'Well,' said the woman, 'you don't know where you are or where you are going. You have risen to where you are thanks to a large quantity of hot air. You made a promise which you have no idea how to keep, and you expect me to solve your problem. The fact is, you are in exactly the same position you were in before, but now, somehow, it's my fault.'

Like most jokes, there are elements of truth in this one and if some of them can be teased out it might help to explain what is involved in a subeditor's work.

First of all, you need to be aware of the most mundane, banal facts ('You are in a hot air balloon'). It is easy to overlook the obvious, especially when you're in a hurry and there's a deadline approaching. Make sure of the ground beneath your feet before rushing to complete a job.

Then you need to apply more detailed knowledge ('latitude and longitude'); this might require you to check facts, names or figures in the copy. It is important for a subeditor to have a wide range of information to hand, but it is also important to admit when you don't know something. Then you can turn to reference books, reliable sources on the internet or phone a person to check.

Finally, you must be prepared to accept the blame if something goes wrong and to be completely overlooked if it all goes right.

Analysing a joke and drawing metaphorical lessons is all very well, but what does all this mean in practice? Here are some general rules to follow when setting about your work as a subeditor.

Know what you have to do

Subediting was always about more than just correcting spelling but the job now entails a host of other responsibilities. In addition to shaping and presenting stories, you may find yourself responsible for sourcing multimedia content, including images, video and audio; you may have to create hyperlinks that take readers to material on your own site or external sites; you may have to promote published stories via social media updates. The following responsibilities all appeared in subediting job ads placed on Gorkana.com:

- ensuring articles meet our audience's high standards;
- writing headlines for a video interview;
- creating captions for a digital magazine;
- spotting a typo on an e-commerce campaign;
- coming up with a killer subject line for a customer email;
- fitting pages quickly and accurately;
- being a bone fide grammar geek with a relentless ability to check facts;
- maintaining the magazine's snappy, upbeat tone across a range of content;

- ensuring consistency of style, grammar and taxonomy;
- helping others articulate their ideas;
- managing and uploading both long-form and short-form articles using a CMS;
- formatting all text and written sources;
- resizing and uploading images;
- publishing all content;
- creating and managing flatplans;
- overseeing the workflow;
- managing deadlines;
- being both meticulous and creative.

Know how to get at the copy

In days gone by this might have meant shouting for the copy boy, locating your in-tray or opening an envelope. For most subeditors, however, it is likely to mean something digital. Copy comes in many forms, ranging from the traditional marks on paper through a variety of computer storage devices to a series of ones and zeros encoded by software. Dealing with copy from in-house journalists should be straightforward if everyone is using an integrated system or network of computers. Copy from external sources can sometimes present more of a challenge.

If it is on paper, it must eventually be transferred to screen which may mean typing it in yourself. However, there is one advantage to this format; most people still find it easier and more accurate to sub on hard copy than on screen, so if you have time to get to grips with the raw text before transferring it, so much the better.

Copy on a USB stick (or possibly still a disk of some kind) should present no problems, provided that a) the file has not been corrupted, b) you have access to a machine that will read that kind of device and c) the writer has used a form of software compatible with yours. Both of the latter should have been clearly specified before the writer submitted anything.

Material may also come as email attachments, which may not survive digital transportation in exactly the same format in which they were sent, or shared via a service such as Dropbox or Google Drive. The sub's first job must be to locate, download and file the copy, then start work on it.

Any rational organisation will take responsibility for ensuring that you are familiar with or trained up in whatever system is in use, but it is also up to you to become better acquainted with it. No one likes being constantly interrupted by a newcomer who can't get on with the computer, so resolve now never to be that person.

Know what to do with the copy when you've got it

When you have the copy in front of you, you can start to work on it. The likelihood is that this will be an entirely digital process, so take full advantage of spelling and grammar checkers, either the built-in version or a plug-in such as Ginger (from gingersoftware.com). Don't forget you can magnify the text by zooming in and out, and to speed up the editing process learn keyboard shortcuts for whatever programme you are using. If your standard word processor is Word, make friends with the find and replace option and learn how to set up macros – a macro is a single instruction that expands automatically into a set of instructions to perform a particular task – which can automate a lot of house style operations. You can find information about how to do this in the Help section of the programme, there's plenty of free instruction online, or you could do a paid-for course.

When thinking about working at a computer, it's also worth remembering that an employer has certain duties under health and safety legislation to anyone working with display screen equipment: you can check these on the Health and Safety Executive's website: www.hse.gov.uk/pubns/indg36.pdf.

There is a significant reason, apart from health and safety, why many people prefer to read a piece from paper rather than from a screen; the human eye and brain still find it easier to scan a solid processed tree than a flickering collection of points of light. So whenever possible, get a printout and clear enough space on your desk to spread out with it. Read line by line, avoid skipping over sections, mark the corrections or facts to check. You will, of course, still have to transfer the corrections to the digital version. You might also consider wearing earplugs if your office is noisy – anything to aid concentration because that's what you will need from now on.

Your tasks will be these. To make sure that:

- the piece deals with what the writer was asked to deal with;
- it will make sense to the reader of your publication;
- it is in keeping with your publication's overall style;
- it is wholly accurate in every respect;
- it is legally safe to publish;
- it is as easy and pleasant to read as possible.

Know how to knock it into shape

There will be some kind of shape already if the writer is competent, but the first thing to do is make sure that they have dealt with the correct subject in the manner asked for (this is the equivalent, to refer back to our opening joke, of knowing that you are in a balloon). It helps to have a good idea of what the commission was and how this piece is planned to fit into the issue as a whole. This will give you a firm basis on which to start making judgements about quality and appropriateness. You must also know the length that was commissioned because it is your job to make sure the piece has the required number of words and will fit the space available for it – which may change if a page layout or overall pagination is altered to accommodate a more important story or more advertising.

Know your medium

It is very likely that the curatum for which you work will take more than one form; it could be printed, it could be uploaded onto a website, it could be delivered to smartphones and it could also appear on an electronic programme guide or even television. Although there is still no fully standardised extended-publishing model, most newspapers and magazines have associated websites and apps. Reading habits differ across them, so you need to know whether to make copy short and punchy or whether you can let it stretch out. If there is a layout element to the job, you must be aware that what works beautifully across the double page spread of an A4 glossy will not work in the same way on a computer screen and differently again on a smartphone. (See Multiple Versioning, below.)

Know your readers

This is a key rule for all journalists, including production journalists and subeditors. You need a very clear understanding of the readership of your curatum, and most importantly of how much they are likely to know about a subject. Only then can you make sensible decisions about clarifying or condensing copy. How much specialised jargon will they understand? Are the basic principles of a complex technical process clear enough for a general readership? Conversely, has the writer taken a *Janet And John* approach when Stephen Hawking would have been a better model? The editor and the publisher should have the idealised reader engraved on their hearts, so ask them.

Know your house style

As the first edition of this book noted:

> House style is the way a publication chooses to publish in matter of detail – single quotes or double, use of capitals and lower case, when to use italics, and so on. Putting a piece of copy into house style is the straightforward process of making it fit in with the rest of the publication. The main purpose is consistency rather than correctness ... House style, then is for the benefit of the reader – and the writer – whereas style books, which codify house style, are primarily for the benefit of the sub. They exist to save time and trouble: to make it possible to apply a consistent style without wasting time checking in back issues or discussing all over again what was settled last week.
>
> (p. 19)

Having a firm grasp of your publication's preferences in matters of alternate spellings (capitalize or capitalise; spelled or spelt; ukulele or ukelele), usage, whether numbers are written or set in figures, the way that dates are shown and points of punctuation is essential for fast and accurate subediting.

Although there are still printed style books, it is far more common to find them online now – which also means that curata looking for an established style to follow, or adapt, can easily locate one. Two excellent examples are those from *The Economist* (http://bit.ly/econstyle – and see the section on italics to discover why the *The* is capitalised and italicised) and the *Guardian* (http://bit.ly/guardstyle). The *Guardian*'s style section also has a Twitter account (@guardianstyle), on which people can raise and discuss questions about usage, spelling and other points.

There will also be house rules on how page furniture should be used with which production journalists with responsibility for layouts must be familiar.

Know your spelling and grammar

It is a sad truth that many people will not have been taught how to spell accurately, how to construct a sentence and may not even be aware of the importance of these elements in written communication. If this sounds like you, do something about it. At the very least you need a big dictionary and a copy of a book such as *English For Journalists* – and you need to use them both. There are also some very useful free online resources to help with grammar:

- the BBC College of Journalism (http://bit.ly/beebwriting);
- the British Council's English language course (http://bit.ly/Brit english) – which has some excellent self-assessed tests.

People who have been through the traditional mill of parsing sentences and spelling bees may still have blind spots when it comes to certain words. Acknowledge these entirely human weaknesses and use a dictionary whenever you are unsure of either the spelling or the meaning; the *New Oxford Spelling Dictionary* is one printed reference book still worth buying – 110,000 words at your fingertips and quicker to access than a website.

Know what you don't know

Even if you are a champion Trivial Pursuit player there will be times when you are unsure of a fact. Do not assume that the writer is correct, do not assume that your 95 per cent certainty will suffice, look it up on the internet – but not before you have read the Fact Checking section below.

Know why you are changing something

Despite what writers (including Giles Coren of the *Times*)[1] sometimes pretend to believe, a good sub will not change copy for no reason. Elementary corrections of spelling, grammar or factual error are easy to justify but it may be more difficult to explain why you altered the structure of a feature or rewrote a news story. If you find yourself thinking, 'Why not change this?', turn the question around and ask 'Why change this?'. It might save both time and an ear bashing. As former copy editor Steve Buttry observes, 'Your newsroom doesn't have time today for you to rewrite stories that another editor has already edited. Don't rewrite a clear sentence just because it wasn't written the way you would have written it.'[2]

On the other hand, if you do change something for reasons that you believe to be sound and necessary, don't back down if the writer challenges you. The same applies to production journalists with layout responsibilities; a writer might not like the headline you put on their piece but if you did it in good faith and it helped to project or liven up their copy don't let even tears, whether of rage or sorrow, persuade you to change it.

Note where the copy needs to be tweaked up or rewritten but bear in mind that guideline about having a good reason to change something. A sub working on a customer magazine for a major retail store came up with the following advice:

> Keep the original tone and voice of the writer; they have been asked to write that piece for a reason. Return to the author for advice if a piece has to be slashed to bits; sometimes asking them what has to stay in can speed everything up and keep everyone happy (well, happier, depending on the writer).

GETTING DOWN TO WORK

Everyone knows the old saying: if you can't get their attention in the first sentence (or the first eight seconds) they won't bother with the rest.[3]

(Nicholas Bagnall, Newspaper Language)

The guidelines above offer general advice on how to regulate your job but they don't tell you how to get started. In fact, it's obvious – the first thing to do is read the copy. Look at it from the point of view of your readers, and trust your instincts: you're being paid to read it but if you find it boring or difficult to get into, so will the reader. The copy should, ideally, have been written by someone else, as subediting is essentially a matter of checking other people's work. However, in the real world of small staffs and editorial cutbacks, it is increasingly common for writers to sub their own work and on many websites it is standard practice. Subbing your own work is much more difficult than working on someone else's, making adherence to the following guidelines even more important.

Principles of copy editing

The quote by Bagnall that opens this section is often used to remind writers to be precise in their communication and hook in the reader with the intro – research shows the average person would take that long to read the first paragraph. This is where the basic principles of reporting come in and it is, in some circumstances, translated into a specific format – a single sentence of around 25 words that encapsulates the idea of a story and allows the reader to be well informed.

But, what if your writer isn't able to nail this formula of loading key information into the start of a story? This is where the copy editor – or downtable sub as they were traditionally known in twentieth century journalism – comes in. The role of this type of subeditor was to deal with text rather than design or layout.

Copy editing has always been a key part of the production process (see Chapter 2), and a vital part of the quality control within the production of a print or digital product. The copy editor's task is to add clarity to confusion, safety to that which is legally or ethically dangerous or even just tidy up the spelling, punctuation and grammar of a writer who isn't very strong. In other words, to ensure the information being given to the reader is clear, concise and accurate.

When the cost of printing materials added up to a significant proportion of the production budget this was a vital role that helped save ink and paper (the biggest cost of all). In the digital age, clarity and concision help with *search engine optimisation* (SEO – a way of ensuring that you are being found quickly by web searchers by helping search engines deliver a useful result to their customers) and *usability*; according to usability guru Jakob Nielsen, 'Usability is a quality attribute that assesses how easy user interfaces are to use. The word "usability" also refers to methods for improving ease-of-use during the design process.'[4] It is easy to understand why those two characteristics are important to a digital publication – if readers can't find your material they can't read it and if they do find it but it's too hard to use (i.e. read and comprehend), they will click away, probably in less than the eight seconds a print publication might enjoy.

As we have seen already, the skill set required by a subeditor has changed over the years, from grappling with the mysteries of *casting off* (being able to calculate how many words would fit in a given amount of print space at a given type size) to being able to use computer software that will allow you to easily change the look and feel of copy. But what has stayed the same is the importance of ensuring the text is clear, precise and accurate. The subeditors who used scalpels, pasteboards and glue to do their job still have a lot in common with their newer colleagues who use a web content management system.

Whatever the technology you work with or tools you use, if you expect anyone to read the text on your page, it has to be clear, simple and make sense. If it doesn't you can introduce confusion or even worse annoy your reader so much that they will just leave, affecting the reputation of your product. This quality control, including the standardisation of words and phrases with a house style book, is central to a subeditor's job. In computing terms it is part of the usability of the package you are offering – how easy is it to use, does it confuse people, make them think too hard or unable to use it? Usability and related disciplines such as human computer interaction (HCI) are heavily rooted in the psychology of how people interact with the things they engage with. This is not the twentieth century approach to subediting – which was more about seeing the printed page in terms of interface design and information architecture – but it is a good way to approach your editing and you can bet the web developers and designers who worked on your website or app will have thought about their work in this way.

The job of a subeditor – be it the design editor, copy editor or web editor – is to ensure that what could be termed as reader-text interaction is efficient or, put simply, to ensure the copy is usable. There's an excellent article on Nielsen's website (www.nngroup.com/articles/) looking at writing for the web and getting the best out of it that concludes readers find it easiest if the copy is short, snappy and in a good looking layout. In print terms all of these targets are achieved from the subs desk.

Starting to edit

The basic principles of copy editing are very similar to those that the writer used in the first place – an understanding of what is important for the target community. This will have a significant impact on the kind of language used – the tone, feel and choice of words will be different according to who is being served. An interesting example to look at here is science journalism. Scientists root their work in complex language to allow for ease of communication between the initiated, but that causes problems for the rest of us – scientific terminology, methodologies and ways of working can seem opaque and secretive. Science reporting then has to walk a thin line between keeping that transmission of complicated ideas while using clear communication and language appropriate to the audience being aimed at.

The variable ability of non-specialist journalists to walk that line successfully has led to some very serious issues, for example with the reporting of the Measles, Mumps and Rubella (MMR) vaccination scares. In 1988 *The Lancet*, a highly respected medical journal, published research by Dr Andrew Wakefield that appeared to show there was a link between the vaccine and the development of colitis and autism spectrum disorders in the children who had been vaccinated. The story was not taken up immediately by the media but when Wakefield published further papers in 2001 and 2002 there was a slew of vaccination scare stories in newspapers that led to many parents not getting their children vaccinated; this in turn was followed by outbreaks of measles and mumps that, it is claimed, led to some deaths. Media commentator Roy Greenslade has alleged a further complication to this issue – in his opinion, the problem was not just that non-specialist journalists were not fully able to understand the science, but also that the right wing press, led by the *Daily Mail*, fomented the MMR scare as a means of attacking the then Labour government.[5] Perhaps as a form or redemption, the truth behind Dr Wakefield's claims was uncovered by journalist Brian Deer[6] of the *Sunday Times*; *Guardian* science commentator Ben Goldacre[7] has also analysed the MMR episode in detail.

The politico-editorial stance of a curatum is well beyond the province of a production journalist but the way that MMR was reported demonstrates the ethical issues that are faced by anyone who works in the media – and the moral imperative to ensure that all stories are as factually accurate and clearly told as possible.

Fact checking

Checking that the facts of a story are correct should be an important part of a subeditor's job. In the UK it has never been given as much emphasis as it was in twentieth century American journalism, although media commitment to the practice has begun to waver as budgets are cut.[8] Nevertheless, at its peak, fact checking was something like a science or religion; to get a proper flavour of how far a painstaking fact checker can go – and how long the process might take for a long, complex story – it is well worth reading John McPhee's *New Yorker* (9 Feb 2009) article *Checkpoints*.[9]

The twenty-first century subeditor is better advised to follow a simpler routine though, and realistically the pressure to publish immediately means even this may be abbreviated or dispensed with. Whenever possible, go through the copy and mark up or make a note of the things you need to check – dates, names, prices (especially if it's a consumer piece or you work on a contract or customer magazine), quotations,[10] song titles. The latter can be surprisingly important for your self-esteem, as a sub working on *The Stage* weekly newspaper once noted: 'Be mentally prepared to get zero credit for making absolute tripe copy come up smelling sweet, but much credit for knowing where the exclamation marks go in titles of Shania Twain songs.'

Where do you check? At this point it would be traditional to cite the canon of subeditors' favourite reference books – *Crockford's Clerical Dictionary*, *Who's Who*, the *Army List* – but the truth is subeditors check where everyone else checks – on the internet. Not only are all those publications online, the internet is both quicker and more far reaching *for those who know how to search it properly*. The ability to search for information is a key skill that all professional journalists should possess.

It starts with choosing the right words or phrases to search on. Murray Dick, in his very useful book *Search: Theory And Practice In Journalism Online*,[11] offers many useful suggestions:

- find keywords by visualising the information you want in the words you would expect to see it;
- envision the background and education of the possible source and use the appropriate linguistic register;
- incorporate informal names for the search subject – Becks for David Beckham; Posh for Victoria Beckham;
- use a thesaurus (available in print or online) to find variants of search words;
- avoid using homonyms – two or more words having the same spelling or pronunciation but different meanings and origins. For example, *cleave* can mean either to stick tight to something or to split or sever something; both forms are derived from Old English but are related to different words in Dutch and German.

Finding the right search term, however, is just the start. You can put it into the ordinary search bar of your favourite search engine . . . or you can key in Google Advanced Search and start from there. The home screen offers many more choices that allow you to narrow, or expand, your search. Twitter also offers an advanced search facility and Facebook's search box can be persuaded to offer up more options if you click on the 'See more results for . . .' link and filter by the 'result type'.

Knowing about search engines other than vanilla flavour Google and Bing is also useful. Google Scholar searches academic work. Wolfram|Alpha describes itself as a computational knowledge engine with a mission 'to make all systematic knowledge immediately computable and accessible to everyone', which it does by 'doing dynamic computations based on a vast collection of built-in data, algorithms, and methods'.[12] Clusty is a meta-search engine that clusters results. Of course, search engines come and go like any other kind of website; keep up to date with developments in this sector at searchenginewatch.com.

Editing longer pieces and features in print

Paul Dring, who is now managing editor of Jamie Oliver's *jamie magazine*, started out as a subeditor on monthly print magazine *Waitrose Food Illustrated* and embodies the career trajectory open to production journalists. His remit as a sub working on features was to take care of headlines, standfirsts, captions and blown quotes; to make sure copy fitted the space available; to fact check names, spellings, titles, as well as assertions of fact themselves; and to ensure the piece was well written – concise, to a good style, well-structured and with a good narrative flow.

The raw material would be presented in one of two ways – as an article already laid out by a designer, or as raw copy from the contributor, not yet laid out.

To begin subbing, he would take a print-out of the piece and read it through from start to finish, trying to maintain the same pace of reading as any first-time reader. After getting an overall picture, he would make another print-out on which he underlined names and facts to be checked – his 'facts copy'.

Before getting down to words and grammar, he would assure himself that the piece was correctly structured: did all the paragraphs follow points set up in the previous paragraph; were the linking sentences between paragraphs strong enough; was there a clear narrative thread throughout the piece that addressed its central arguments?

Once the structure had been established, he turned to the fine detail. His approach might be directed by how much overmatter [extra copy that would not fit into the layout] there was and how much space he had to reclaim. To cut to fit, he started by removing excess verbiage and paying particular attention to paragraphs that had, or nearly had, orphans [a single word as the final line of the paragraph].

Paul recalls:

> I could usually cut a piece by a third in length before I had to start thinking about making a direct cut, and removing any of the sentences. Obviously though, if a sentence didn't work, or was too much off at a tangent to the rest of the piece, I would cut it regardless of the length of the piece. If I did have to cut any sentences, I kept in mind which pictures we were using, as the cut could then become a caption. Fiddling with the tracking [using software commands to change the spacing between letters and words] was my last option, for single lines, and never to more than minus 10, or minus 15 at a push.
>
> These days, my job takes in many aspects of magazine publishing – from circulation and distribution to licensing, syndication and subscriptions marketing – but I haven't left

subbing behind. I still read final proofs for every story we publish and act as the last line of defence against mistakes, which also allows me the opportunity to pass on the subbing experience and knowhow I've picked up over the years to a new generation of subeditors.

Subbing longer pieces for newspapers involves very similar principles. William Ham-Bevan honed his skills as a subeditor working for the *Daily Express* features section before moving on to the *Daily Mail*, *Sunday Times Travel Magazine* and the *Daily Telegraph*, where he became deputy editor of the editorial projects unit. He is now a busy freelance writer and editor.

'When I first received a story,' he remembers:

> I would go through it and take out any extraneous returns – these often creep in when importing raw text. This gave me a rough idea of how long the copy was, and how much I needed to cut. On the rare occasions when the copy was short, I would alert the chief sub to this, so that he could alter the geometry of the page or, if all else failed, chase up the writer for more copy.

> I would then edit the copy for grammar and house style, and make any obvious cuts. It was rare for me to have to make drastic alteration to the structure of the article, but I would occasionally re-jig an intro to make it stronger, or shuffle a few pars around to make the train of thought clearer. Nuts-and-bolts operations such as turning hyphens into dashes and single into double quotation marks are always best tackled at this stage. Styling up the text came next – putting in drop caps, cross-heads, bullet-points and the like. That done, I would prune the copy to fit. Because page geometry can change very quickly on a newspaper (for instance, depending on advertisements) it's not unusual to have to take out a quarter to a third of all the words. Another consideration is the look of the copy across columns: the *Express* was fairly liberal about this, but widows and orphans needed to be taken out.

> Once the text fitted, I would go into the publishing system and check out the headline, standfirst and captions. There

were strict rules about writing display copy; nothing could be repeated in the furniture of the same page (such as a word appearing in both a headline and in a caption). I then spell-checked everything, and checked the page components back in to the publishing system database. One of the senior subs would then give the piece a second reading, often making small alterations to a headline or caption. It would then be passed up to the chief sub and assistant night editor for final approval, and they'd lock and pass the page when they were satisfied with it.

Editing features demands a different approach from handling news copy, he says.

Of course, accuracy and clarity are still paramount, but you can't just cut from the bottom. You have to be sensitive to the writer's style and ensure you don't stop their voice coming through. It's what they're employed for, after all – particularly in the case of columnists and other star writers, who will often have been given an undertaking that their copy won't be heavily edited.

The golden rule is to read the piece several times before begin-ning your edit, to get a feel for it. If you really do think it needs major surgery, it's best to alert the chief sub or someone else in the editorial hierarchy straight away rather than plunge in with the editing shears. Hell hath no fury like a feature writer whose copy has been insensitively pruned.

Details for print

Paul and Will refer to a couple of technical details that subeditors working in print need to be aware of and know how to fix.

Widows and orphans: in traditional typesetting terms a widow is the final line of a paragraph that is taken over onto the top of a new column of text, and sits there all on its own; an orphan occurs when the final line of a typeset paragraph consists of a single word. Both are considered poor practice but generally speaking more attention tends to be paid to orphans, which can be fixed in three ways – you can shorten the paragraph by cutting or changing words; you can lengthen the paragraph by adding or changing words; or you can do what Paul mentioned and manipulate the tracking of the paragraph by making it tighter – adjusting it in the publishing software so there is less space between letters and words. The danger with the third method is that if you tighten the tracking too much it becomes very obvious asthewordsallruntogether.

Widows and orphans also occur on screen-published pages and can be fixed by subbing the copy if time allows. Try at least to get rid of them in the headlines and sells.

Dashes and hyphens: there is a difference between a hyphen (-), an en-dash (–) and an em-dash (—). Hyphens are used to join words into short phrases but as the *Guardian*'s style guru David Marsh notes in *For Who The Bell Tolls*,[13] 'hyphens in compound words are certainly in decline … Many people, including me, think they clutter up text (particularly when your computer breaks already hyphenated words at the end of a line) and look old-fashioned' (p. 125). There is no universal law about this and use of hyphens will vary according to each publication's house style. However, hyphens should not be used to separate or bracket clauses in a sentence – that is a job for the en-dash – or possibly the em-dash, depending on house style. The en- and em- prefixes denote the length, which is roughly equivalent to a lower case n or upper case M respectively. On an Apple Mac, en-dashes are created by using *alt+hyphen* and em-dashes by using *alt+shift+hyphen*.

Alignment across the page: look at any well produced piece of print and you will see that the lines of text in each column align across the page. Where other elements such as illustrations and pull quotes intrude on the text area, this finish is much easier to achieve if the page has been made using separate text boxes that can be manipulated individually. You can check the alignment by using pull-down rulers; if you use InDesign, the help section is highly recommended.[14]

Drop caps: these are the enlarged letters at the beginning of a paragraph, often used to denote the starting point of a story, or the restart after a break. They are part of the Paragraph sub-menu[15] in InDesign. Make sure all paragraphs that start with a drop cap are flush against the left hand margin of the text column, with no indentation (*full out*). The drop cap itself may be set in a typeface that is different to the body copy (Figure 3.1).

rop caps are the enlarged letters at the beginning of a paragraph, often used to denote the starting point of a story, or the restart after a break. They are part of InDesign's Paragraph sub-menu (under Type). Make sure paragraphs that start with a drop cap are flush against the left hand margin of the text column, with no indentation (full out).

Figure 3.1 Drop cap illustration.

Source: Courtesy of the author.

Details for digital

Someone who knows more than most about the importance of subbing in a digital context is Ed Vanstone, Digital Editor of *Men's Health* and recipient of the Outstanding Digital Talent award at the PPA's 2014 Digital Awards.

'In their bid to produce exponentially more articles – more stories means more traffic; more traffic means more money; or so the thinking runs – many online publications have let their subbing standards slip,' he comments.

> The need to be first, fastest and most frequent often trumps a commitment to pristine copy. In fact, employing brilliant sub-editors is perhaps even more important in online journalism. While being able to sniff out errant punctuation and spot a typo at 50 yards isn't quite so crucial – after all, an army of finicky readers are on hand to kindly inform you of errors through social media – refining headlines, sells, and opening paragraphs (albeit as much for search engine optimisation as fluency), picking the right pictures (often the online sub's responsibility) and, of course, adding sparkle to rapidly dashed off sentences is often the difference between a piece racking up a million views and sinking without a trace.

> More than ever before, speed is of the essence, and curbing perfectionist instincts is (sadly) critical, but the the age-old task of refining copy into sentences that sing remains unchanged. Just grit your teeth and learn to leave a little clunky repetition in the first few paragraphs. Google is great, and all, no matter how prestigious, must genuflect to its algorithms.[16]

Multiple versioning

In the 2002 edition of this book, the introduction included a quote from Danny Meadows-Klue of the *Electronic Telegraph* who in an interview with *Press Gazette* said:

> Subbing will become the battleground for new media . . . The art of the sub is to take copy and decide what they can do to

make it relevant to the medium. They will decide where copy will go and what it will become.

And he wasn't wrong. Since then subs have not just had to deal with changes to paper sizes and the web but with social media, search engines, RSS readers, tablets and smartphones.

This has led to the requirement for multiple versioning of content, which is essentially where one story is translated into a number of different formats – print, web, mobile, social media or app. Although the basic requirements for good spelling, grammar, punctuation and accuracy remain the same there are other elements that will need to be changed, and technical skills to be grasped, to get the best out of the particular platform. Some of this may be automated, inasmuch as the systems reporters write into are already set up to allow them to provide separate headlines for web and print, but it goes further, as two quotes from the *Guardian* show. Writing on this very subject, Barbara Harper explained that a subeditor preparing an article for the website would be expected to write headlines optimised for search engines so the article could be easily seen online:

> add keywords to make sure it appears in the right places on the website, create packages to direct readers to related arti-cles, embed links, attach pictures, add videos and think about how the article will look when it is accessed on mobile phones and other digital platforms.[17]

Charlotte Baxter added: 'Working online, we choose and upload pictures and add keywords – to index a piece within the guardian.co.uk site – and links, trying to use primary sources where possible.'[18]

Marshall McLuhan, the Canadian cultural theorist who coined the term 'global village', famously said the medium was the message[19] and as with many of his apophthegms, he was right. For a sub the medium will change the message in a number of subtle but important ways and one of the key ones to think about is how it will be consumed.

People don't go to the shop to buy your product

Once, people used to walk to the local newsagent or corner shop to buy your content in an attractive printed package or a teenager was employed to put a copy through your front door if you subscribed. On the news stand a key element is what is sometimes known as shelf appeal – is your cover or front page enough to make you stand out among all the other products on the shelf? The combination of headlines, coverlines, mastheads and images used by magazines and newspapers are done to catch the eye and entice people to buy a copy.

But what if your product can't do that, because it isn't a physical thing at all? On the web, one of the most crucial elements is to ensure copy is optimised for both search and for social sharing as these are your virtual shop front.

Search engine optimisation

Google's advice on search engine optimisation is similar to the points outlined in this chapter, keep it simple and accurate if you want your copy to be found by both the web crawlers and the searchers.

There is an issue here though. Google, and the other search engines, change their algorithms from time to time, partly to increase their usefulness and partly to foil marketers who have discovered how to game the existing algorithm and boost their websites up the list of search results. Any change will have a significant impact on how you can optimise your pages effectively and Google is often guarded in giving specific advice.

But sticking to some basic principles means it's not so difficult to get results, says web specialist Robert Niles:

> Most SEO techniques reduce to providing clear, concise writing that stays on topic – that frequently references the key words and phrases that an article's supposed to be about . . . Unfortunately, in print journalism . . . too many reporters and headline writers became more focused on being clever than clear.[20]

People don't read on the web . . .

Research into how people read on the web offers a real insight into some of the differences between print and web design. Nielsen's research[21] from

1994–7 shows that people actually scan rather than sit back and read. Nielsen conducted eyetracking studies that showed people looking at a web page tended to scan it in a rough approximation of an F-shape.[22] However, this finding has been challenged, or at least refined, by Miratech[23], who claim that the F-pattern only applies when a piece of text has distinct paragraphs; other types of layout, particularly those with multimedia elements, result in different patterns of eye movement.

The Poynter Institute of Florida has also undertaken a series of EyeTrack studies of newspapers and their websites. A summary of the studies, and links to the full documents, can be found on the Poynter website,[24] but these are the main points they discovered about reading news online:

- Readers start in the upper left of a page, hover in that area then go left to right.
- Navigation elements at the top of a home page attract a lot of attention.
- Dominant headlines draw the eye when first entering a page – especially when they are in the upper left. Larger headlines draw more attention than small.
- Underlined headlines and visual breaks – such as a line or rule – discourage people from looking at items beyond the breaks. *Ditch underlines and breaks in online text.*
- Text is the entry point into home pages, not images.
- Short paragraphs receive twice as much attention as long.
- Lower parts of the screen – especially areas one would have to scroll to see – are not much looked at.
- The standard one-column story format works better than multiple column formats.
- Summary descriptions (extended deck headlines, paragraph length) leading into articles are popular.

. . . but people want to read more on the web

The world wide web is a series of interlinked pages and they can be accessed from one another by the use of hyperlinks. Online readers expect to see links – they add value to a web page – and subeditors are now expected to add them. However, rather than scattering links willy-nilly, they should be deployed in certain contexts:

- when explanation or definition are required;
- to give context or background;
- for attribution of source content;
- when required to link back by a copyright or Creative Commons licence;
- for navigation to related material;
- if an email link is required.

The normal form of a link is a word, phrase or piece of text highlighted in blue and underlined; it doesn't have to have either of these attributes, but it has become the convention and is what readers not only expect to see but also what they actively look for on a page. Words *within a sentence* can be used as a link, but according to Nielsen links need to have "good information scent" and one of the worst types of link is a description of the content of what is being linked to followed by the word *here*. Nielsen's advice is:

- start with keywords; readers focus on the first two words;
- be concise but use as many words as necessary for an accurate description;
- do not use the same description for links that go to different places;
- avoid generic links (click here; read more).

Finally, although you are adding value for readers by suggesting additional sources of information, make sure links do not send readers away from your site completely by specifying that they open in a new window. This should be a formatting option within the content management system, but you can also use HTML code to ensure the same result by including a target='_blank' command: <a href='http://www.jomec.co.uk/' target='_blank>Learn to sub at Cardiff School of Journalism </a>.

People want to look at pictures

Adding images has become an important part of digital production work; when there is no specially commissioned photograph or artwork, subs may also be expected to source photographs and illustrations. Your curatum may have its own archive of images to draw on or may have a contract with an image bank or photo agency. If not, where should you look? The internet, of course – but remember that images on the internet are subject to copyright restrictions in the same way as images published anywhere else. The photo-sharing site Flickr.com hosts millions of pictures, many of great technical and creative quality; they are published under terms that range from no restrictions to all rights reserved; many will have a no-commercial-use restriction and all will require attribution and a link to the photographer's Flickrstream. The site has a lot of useful help and advice about licensing images for use – check it for current terms and conditions.

Creative Bloq, a magazine website (www.creativebloq.com) for graphic designers and other creatives, published a useful list of photo libraries in February 2014.[25]

Tagging the work

If you search any of the photo libraries mentioned above, you may well find yourself blessing photographers for giving their images useful *tags* – or cursing them for not. A tag is simply a keyword attached to a piece of content, be it image or text, that helps to classify and identify it – this is what Charlotte Baxter of the *Guardian*, quoted above, means by indexing a piece within the paper's website. Tags allow readers to search for or identify content, but they also have a commercial value to the publication or organisation, because they allow better management of digital assets. This could be finding material to license to others, selling advertising around particular types of content, finding already published material to link back to. In technical jargon, tags are an example of *metadata* (data that describes data [content]) and idio Ltd, a company that specialises in content marketing strategy, cites seven main purposes for tagging:

- Future-proof existing archive of content and future authoring
- Frees content from technological and organisational restraints
- Monetise archive content through better advertising rates and recommendations
- Increased syndication for marketing services
- Increase licensing potential

- Generate tag-clouds of reader preferences and interests for insight
- Improved content search capability
  (http://bit.ly/idiotags)

Needless to say, tag words must be chosen carefully; they should be relevant and specific rather than bland and generic. It is an excellent idea for everyone to have a systematic approach to tagging that avoids near-duplication and excessive choice. Simon Williams, a digital communications consultant from communicatingcauses.co.uk, explains that tags are there to improve content search; on a website there is no point in using a tag word that is the same as, say, one of the section headings, since that does not add any useful information. However, tagging a type or genre of music (folk, heavy metal, dance) would add to the granularity of search results, as would tagging a particular venue.

Tags must also be accurate. An incorrectly tagged photograph can lead to all sorts of trouble, as both the *Daily Express* and the *Daily Mirror* discovered when they used pictures of the Dutch dressage team to illustrate stories about the British dressage team's Olympic gold medal (8 August 2012) – though you might have thought the bronze colour of the medals and the orange collars to the team's jackets would have been warning signs.

Think simple, tell it short – getting social with your news

In addition to all the above, subs may also have to incorporate promoting the story via social media into their schedule. One simple way of thinking about this is the use of newspaper bills – the poster that you will see outside the newsagent used to sell what is in that particular edition of the paper. It's a simple idea, an A-board poster that will stop people in their tracks. It is usually done on a sheet of A2 paper in a font and size that can easily be seen by passers-by.

Before publication, one or more subs will be expected to write these posters picking up on key stories for an area. Given the size of a poster these are much more condensed than a headline and it requires some real thought to encapsulate a story in just a few words.

This isn't that far removed from the idea of creating an update for social media to sell a story to an online audience. As with a bill, Twitter is limited in terms of the message you can get across, on the face of it to 140 characters (any spaces or punctuation that are used count as a character). So the trick here is to use concise language that is in keeping with the platform – Twitter updates can be short and punchy but a professional account shouldn't be using *txtspk* (text speak) as this wouldn't be in keeping with the requirements of the organisation.

However, it isn't quite that straightforward for media organisations. First you'll want to include a link to a story, so people can read it and it will take a large amount of space before you start to think about the message. For example, 'http://www.mymediaorganisation.co.uk/newsstory.html' is already 52 characters and doesn't leave much room to play with the rest of the Tweet. This is why you'll see companies using URL shorteners, tools that literally cut down the number of characters used, such as Twitter's t.co, ow.ly or bit.ly which facilitate a more succinct link.

Thus, the link to a blog post on the *Guardian* may be 117 characters 'http://www.guardian.co.uk/media/greenslade/2011/aug/03/internet-journalismeducation?commentpage=last#end-of-comments' but by using bit.ly we can cut it to 20 'http://bit.ly/oRf5Bc' – remember that bitlinks can be customised and apply the advice given above about finding appropriate words. Like other companies, the *Telegraph* uses its own shortener, so all its own links will allow http://tgr.ph as the starting point while the *Guardian* actually uses http://gu.com.

Given the importance of sharing content over social media, another thing to work on is how much space to leave for retweeting – forwarding on a message. There are two ways of doing this, a simple forwarding, which just reposts the message, or an edit that incorporates an observation from the reader. So, to allow someone to comment you'll need to think about leaving space for the RT characters and then space for a message. Reducing your message to as short a count as possible, while still leaving it effective, will allow your readers to engage with you.

Checklist 1: copy editing

A lot of the advice in this chapter is quite simple and can be boiled down into a simple checklist to be used when editing or preparing copy.

- Have you checked for errors in style and grammar?
- Tailor your content to fit.
- Remember who you are writing for.
- Think about your language and phrasing.
- Remember how people read.
- Is this a long, lean back read for print or a tablet or is it a short snappy piece for the web or a smartphone?
- Remember where they are reading it.
- Think about your intro.
- Think about links.
- Think about SEO.
- Know how to source and licence images.
- Have a clear social media policy.

Checklist 2: Accuracy and resources for production journalists (also works for reporters and feature writers)

In an ideal world, where the aim of journalism was to be 100 per cent accurate rather than 100 per cent first, this checklist would be mandatory for everyone involved in the process. However, items are listed in order of likely completion – production journalists are unlikely, for example, to have either the time or the resources to check quotes with sources.

- spelling and grammar

    Resources: a printed spelling dictionary; BBC Academy or British Council grammar pages; www.oxforddictionaries.com; dictionary.cambridge.org;

- spellcheck errors

    Make sure the software preferences are set to the correct vernacular (e.g. UK English in the UK)

    Resources: computer spellcheck; www.gingersoftware.com;

- titles of books, television programmes, films, albums, bands (be very careful about the use of definitive articles and unusual punctuation marks – Grateful Dead, Blue Öyster Cult, Motörhead); don't forget to put titles in *italics*, 'quote marks' or nothing, depending on your house style

Resources: official band websites; publisher, record company, production company, television channel official websites; house style guide;

- titles of people

  Formal titles are still used for royalty, aristocrats, the armed services

  Resources: Debretts Handbook; Burke's Peerage; National Archives and British Library for Army, Navy and Air Force lists

  Honorific titles are used for religious leaders (the Reverend John Smith; Rabbi Julia Neuberger; Imam Amjal Masroor)

  Resources: Crockford's Clerical Directory (for Anglicans); Catholic Directory; The Buddhist Society; Hindu Council UK; Muslim Council of Britain; Wikipedia (usual warnings apply) has a useful page on honorifics http://bit.ly/honorifics;

- trade names

  PowerPoint not powerpoint, Land Rover not Land-Rover; get the initialisation and punctuation correct; be wary of trade names that may have become part of the vernacular ('genericized trademarks' in legal lingo) such as hoover – even though the word itself is a registered trademark the Hoover company (now part of Candy) cannot enforce it in the UK; Wikipedia (usual warnings apply) has a useful page listing generic trademarks http://bit.ly/generictrademarks

  Resources: manufacturers' official websites; Intellectual Property Office register http://bit.ly/tradenamesearch;

- locations and place names

  Whatever country you work in there will be place names you need to check – Sauðárkrókur in Iceland or Greenland's Uummannaq come to mind. In the UK this might be Scottish, Irish and Welsh locations, especially if there are different spellings per language – is the river that flows through Cardiff (Caerdydd) the Taff or the Taf?

  Resources: Gazeteer of British Place Names; Google Maps (but remember the Apple maps fiasco http://bit.ly/appmaps);

- numbers and maths

Journalists are often accused of being innumerate, so double check figures, percentages and statistics; whenever possible get someone who is good with figures to check the maths. If you are a maths graduate you can probably do it yourself;

- online attributions

  If there is a quote from an online or social media source, check that it is a) still accessible and b) correct; insert links back to sources for full transparency, remembering Jeff Jarvis's commandment to 'Cover what you do best. Link to the rest' http://bit.ly/jarvislink

  Resources: the web; social media platforms; your browser;

- verify URLs

  If the piece cites URLs, check to confirm they are still live and the content is still available

  Resources: the web; your browser;

- verify phone numbers

  Nothing more annoying for both parties than trying to call the wrong number

  Resource: telephone;

- verify prices

  If a consumer-oriented piece gives a price, do your best to make sure it's accurate

  Resource: check with the retailer or supplier;

- verify names

  This should be much higher in the list – top of the list for reporters and writers – but it is relatively unlikely that a production journalist will have access to a full set of notes and no guarantee that the author will have spelled the name correctly. If the person concerned is well known or has a website or blog it should be possible to run checks. Who is that bouffant-haired, Taylor-Swift-ex guy in One Direction anyway – Hari Styalls, Harrie Stiles or Harry Styles? And the Clinton who used to be Secretary of State for the USA? That would be Hillary, not Hilary (tut-tut *Doctor Who Magazine*, Winter 2014/15, p. 16).

Resources: original author; *Who's Who* for prominent people; possibly websites and blogs;

- verify definitions

I say a tomato is a red vegetable that grows on long stalky plants, you say it is the fruit of the *Lycopersicon esculentum* and comes in many shades; be especially careful around definitions that 'everybody knows' because it often happens that what 'everybody knows' is wrong; as William Goldman wrote in his book about the Hollywood movie industry *Adventures in the Screen Trade* (1983): 'Nobody knows anything' (p. 39).

Resources: encyclopaedias; expert websites; expert humans;

- check for assumptions

Has the writer made a 'commonsense assumption'? Or even a nonsensical one? You have three choices – verify it, fudge it or remove it

If you are not sure about an assumption or anything else, read the final copy to someone who does understand

Resources: authoritative publications or websites; annoyingly well-read colleagues.

Acknowledgements to Steve Buttry[26] (that's B-U-T-T-R-Y) and Craig Silverman.[27]

Notes

1 http://bit.ly/corenrant, accessed 7/11/14.
2 http://bit.ly/buttrycopy, accessed 11/11/14.
3 W. Hicks *et al.* (2008), *Writing For Journalists*. London; New York: Routledge, p. 17.
4 http://bit.ly/usabilitydef, accessed 6/11/14.
5 http://bit.ly/mmrmail, accessed 7/11/14. There is also a good analysis of the MMR scares on Wikipedia (all usual warnings about Wikipedia apply) http://bit.ly/mmrwiki, accessed 7/11/14.
6 http://bit.ly/mmrdeer, accessed 7/11/14.
7 http://bit.ly/mmrgoldacre, accessed 7/11/14.
8 http://bit.ly/factcheck01, accessed 7/11/14.
9 http://bit.ly/NYcheckpoints, accessed 7/11/14.
10 Of course this could be difficult if you are working on a newspaper such as the *Sun*, which, evidence to the Leveson Inquiry attested, makes up quotes (section 4.1) http://bit.ly/Sunquotes, accessed 7/11/14.

11 Murray Dick (2013), *Search: Theory and Practice in Journalism Online*. London: Palgrave Macmillan.
12 http://bit.ly/aboutwa, accessed 7/11/14.
13 David Marsh (2013), *For Who The Bell Tolls*. London: Guardian and Faber & Faber.
14 http://bit.ly/pagerulers, accessed 14/11/14.
15 http://bit.ly/droppedcaps, accessed 14/11/14.
16 Personal communication, 24/11/14.
17 http://bit.ly/harpersub, accessed 14/11/14.
18 http://bit.ly/baxtersub, accessed 14/11/14.
19 Marshall McLuhan (1964), *Understanding Media: The Extensions of Man*. New York: McGraw-Hill.
20 http://bit.ly/seoniles, accessed 14/11/14.
21 http://bit.ly/write_web, accessed 14/11/14.
22 http://bit.ly/nielsenF, accessed 16/11/14.
23 http://bit.ly/miratechF, accessed 16/11/14.
24 http://bit.ly/poyntertrack, accessed 14/11/14.
25 http://bit.ly/photolibraries, accessed 17/11/14.
26 http://bit.ly/buttrylist, accessed 14/11/14.
27 http://bit.ly/silvermanlist, accessed 14/11/14.

4
How to create great news headlines

What is page furniture?

Every magazine, newspaper, website and blogpost published uses page furniture. It is used in primary school essays and academic journals, comics and encyclopedias, newsletters and tweets.

What is page furniture? It's the collective way of referring to headlines, standfirsts, captions, pull quotes, straplines, logos, repeating graphics – in fact all the elements that:

- help readers navigate through a collection of curated material[1] (a *curatum*);
- help readers navigate around a page;
- help readers navigate around a story;
- direct readers to particular stories;
- provide extra information about content;
- reinforce the curatum's[2] identity.

This chapter and those that follow will look at the most effective ways to create page furniture for news, features and different kinds of content in magazines, newspapers, websites and other publishing platforms. It will give hands-on advice to guide you through all the stages of preparation and research needed to bring online readers to your pages and to direct print readers to your story. Whether the members of your interest-community are searching for something in Google or flicking through a magazine in WH Smith, the secrets of attracting them are shared in the following pages.

However, before looking at the mechanics of creativity, it is worth considering the last of the bullet points above. Page furniture might seem insignificant in the greater scheme of things but its importance in setting the right tone has long been recognised. Writing an instruction manual for subeditors in 1932, F. J. Mansfield noted, 'The character and class of a newspaper are plainly shown by its headlines, ranging "from grave to gay, from lively to severe" . . . The sub-editor has to produce headings of the nature and quality demanded . . .' (1931: 119). Several decades later, Harold Evans wrote: 'any newspaper which is careless with its headline writing is careless with its own purpose and vitality . . . Where every headline goes unerringly to the point with precision or wit, the whole newspaper comes alive' (Evans, 1974: 13).[3]

In addition to reinforcing character, class, vitality and wit, headlines – particularly news headlines – can be used to both reflect the concerns and interests of the reader community, and indicate in a subtle or not-so-subtle manner the political affiliations of the publication. This contribution to identity applies to every other element of page furniture too – dull captions give a dull overall tone, just as much as captions straining to be funny give a tone of desperation. Page furniture is an integral part of the package and must be given the attention it demands.

Headlines – the oldest and most obvious form of page furniture

> Headline: 'line at the top of a page containing title, folio, etc
> . . .title in newspaper . . . a news item given very briefly [. . .]'
> (Chambers Twentieth Century Dictionary)

In any discussion of news headlines two examples are always cited, so let's get them out of the way immediately:

Super Caley Go Ballistic, Celtic Are Atrocious (the *Sun*, 8 February 2000)[4]

Gotcha (the *Sun*, 4 May 1982)[5]

The first is notable because it is a clever play on words, or rather on a single made-up word used in the 1964 Disney film *Mary Poppins*: supercalifragilisticexpialidocious.[6] The story beneath the headline was about a David vs Goliath victory in Scottish football when Inverness Caledonian Thistle beat Celtic.

However, Scott Murray claimed in the *Guardian* (12 December 2008[7]) that the *Sun* was following in the footsteps of the *Liverpool Echo* by drawing on this reference. Apparently, **Super Cally Goes Ballistic, QPR Atrocious** had been used to record the prowess of Anfield central midfielder Ian 'Cally' Callaghan against Queens Park Rangers in the 1970s.

The second has become notorious rather than notable as it was a celebratory reaction to the sinking of an Argentinian cruiser (a large warship), the General Belgrano, during the Falklands War. According to Roy Greenslade, writing in the *Guardian* on 25 February 2002,[8] the *Sun*'s features editor Wendy Henry shouted the word when she heard the news and editor Kelvin MacKenzie adopted it for the front page. When it became obvious that large numbers of Argentinian sailors had lost their lives, he changed the splash (the main headline) to **Did 1,200 Argies Drown?**.

Why do those headlines work or not work?

Super Caley only works if:

- you know the song (quite likely for people who were growing up in the 1960s or had children then);
- you know the Scottish football teams (quite likely for football aficionados).

So within those categories there is likely to be a fairly large element of recognisability.

In print it certainly attracts attention on the page, if only because of its length. Those who do recognise the original reference and the extended pun are also likely to appreciate the clever manipulation of words: the fact it has passed into the mythology of journalism argues for a continued recognition of the skilled wordplay. It is representative of a particular kind of British genius in production journalism.

The subeditor (or team) who came up with it hardly had to consider the way it would work online – even though longsighted newspapers such as the *Guardian* had embraced the world wide web as an important mode of distribution as early as 1995, the *Sun* in 2000 was not, in any consistent manner, acting as if the web existed. The clause would not have scored highly for searchability,[9] although the words 'ballistic', Celtic' and 'atrocious' might have found more-or-less relevant matches. (It is search-able now, of course, because its mythological status has ensured widespread reproduction.)

Gotcha works brilliantly as a device guaranteed to capture attention in print, especially when used in large, bold type across the top of a tabloid front page, in combination with 'our lads sink gunboat and hole cruiser' as a sub-head[10] and photographs of the ships in question. Its purpose is to arrest the eyes, to pique curiosity and stir the emotions, perhaps even to the point of shock; on this level there can be no doubt it succeeded.

The world wide web had not even been invented in 1982 (although Tim Berners Lee had written the programme that laid the groundwork: http://bit.ly/tblenquire), so searchability didn't come into Kelvin MacKenzie's considerations. The word still doesn't work as a searchable term, although Googling it brings up a very informative Wikipedia page: http://bit.ly/gotchawiki. (The usual caveats attached to using Wikipedia as a reliable source apply.)

One problem with headlines such as these, and the tradition from which they come, is that they encourage the perception that all headlines have to be funny or contain a pun or some other wordplay. Inexperienced headline writers often fall into this trap and end up creating work that is inappropriate or weak. Headlines that use shocking, funny or clever wordplay certainly have a place in media, and the best can indeed be described as 'genius' but the reality is that the main function of a head-line is not to make the reader smile or invoke a 'That's clever' reaction but something altogether different. Like it or not, the headline is a form of marketing for the journalism that follows.

When and why did British publications start to use headlines?

In April 1642 a prototype newspaper with the snappy title *A Continuation of certaine Speciall and Remarkable Passages from both Houses of Parliament and other parts of the Kingdom* used three italicised headlines to draw atten-tion to articles in its pages. Its publishers, Walter Cook and Robert Wood, also included a contents page to help guide readers to the things they were most interested in and historians of the British press (Herd 1952, Lee 1976, Lake 1984, Harris and Lee 1986) consider this to be the first use of these components. A month later, in May 1642, another early newspaper called *Mercurius Civicus* started to make regular use of head-lines and also of illustrations, so between them these two publications recognised the need to provide readers with:

- navigational aids (headlines, contents page);
- points of visual interest (headlines, illustrations); and
- effective ways of dividing up content (headlines).

In other words, the publishers realised that content would not sell itself to readers (or potential readers) and instituted these devices to attract attention, pique interest and encourage engagement. Looked at in one way, it could have been the start of a long-drawn-out process of dumbing down – but only if the idea of causing someone to read something they might otherwise have overlooked is regarded as an unenlightened act.

Nevertheless, the headline was slow to develop as an important element of journalism, restricted by a mix of technology, tradition and the unin-tended consequences of legislation. Allen Hutt's scholarly work *The Changing Newspaper* (1973) documents progress in great detail, noting that the *Perfect Occurences of Parliament* of 1644

> ran a whole series of summary points, in italic, immediately under its title. Separated by full points, these amounted to headlines strung together in summary form, enabling the reader to see at a glance the pieces of news contained in the issue . . . The same summary technique was used in the *London Post*, *True Informer* and *Weekly Intelligencer*.
>
> (op. cit.: 14–15)

By the start of the nineteenth century important events reported in the *Times* 'called forth headlines of a certain size, such as this four-liner, in 12pt and 18pt full-face capitals, of 16 September 1807:

SURRENDER OF

COPENHAGEN

AND THE

DANISH FLEET.'

However, ever since the first Stamp Duty act of 1712 newspapers had been taxed on the amount of paper they used and the Newspaper Stamp Duties Act of 1819 increased the tax to such an extent that publishers had to squeeze as much news as possible into as few pages as possible. Among the first things to go were these prototype headlines: 'Now there were to be no more than one-line labels in italic capitals of the body of the paper', observes Hutt (op. cit.: 37).

Even after Stamp Duty was reduced and then abolished, the introduction of heavily mechanised printing presses also had unintended consequences, in this instance technological limitations that restricted the width of columns, and thus headlines, that could be printed. Small, unobtrusive headlines became part of the culture of newspapers, to the point where Hutt comments:

> The essential point to grasp about the evolution of the mid-nineteenth-century minimal-size, single-column, news titling headline is that, far from being confined to the *Times*, it became the universal morning paper style ... Indeed, this mid-nineteenth-century determination of news headline style was to become the overall British newspaper style and to last right through the following period ... and even beyond.
>
> (op. cit.: 50)

American newspapers were less bound by tradition and although many of the technical restrictions were the same, papers such as the *Sun* and James Gordon Bennett's *New York Herald* began to use single column but multi-decked headlines, particularly to announce wars and disasters.

In 1861, the *Sun* announced the start of the Civil War with seven decks plus labels, in a mix of typographic styles and punctuation:

THE LATEST NEWS.

BY TELEGRAPH TO THE N.Y. SUN.

Civil War Begun!

THE MADNESS OF TREASON.

FORT SUMTER

ATTACKED!

FURIOUS BOMBARDMENT.

GALLANT DEFENCE OF THE FORT.

'Our Flag is Still There'

Arrival of the Relief Fleet!

PRELIMINARY OFFICIAL CORRESPONDENCE.

However, all of these headlines ran across single columns, technical restrictions and tradition combining to create this straightjacket. When newspapers wanted to create more impact they could only do so vertically, leading to a situation where the *Chicago Tribune*'s multi-decked headline for the great fire of Chicago in 1871 took up almost the whole of the first column of the front page, although crossheads, subheads and French rules[11] were used to break up the mass of text that followed. Harold Evans calls this system an 'absurdity' but also notes 'the Americans had introduced the important concept that display should be proportionate to the worth of the story' (Evans, 1974: 1).

In the UK tradition began to change with the innovations of the 'New Journalism'[12] of the *Pall Mall Gazette* and the *Star*, both London evening papers. The *Star* particularly adopted many conventions of American journalism, including the 'descriptive headline' (Hutt, op. cit.: 67). Henry Massingham, a British journalist and editor, 'noted that the multi-decker American heading amounted to a 'shorthand description' of the following text, thus conveniently allowing the reader to get the gist of the news by glancing at the headlines [. . .]' (Hutt: loc. cit.).

The *Star* adopted multi-deck headlines soon after its launch in 1888, but the really revolutionary aspect of this innovation was the use of upper and lower case for secondary decks and shorter stories. The practical point was to allow more room for effective descriptions but British newspapers had always used capitals for headlines – even the *Daily Mail*, which broke with so many newspaper conventions when it launched in 1896, stuck to single column, all capitals headlines, although they were multi-deck.

The *Star* had also experimented with double column headlines but it was not until 15 January 1895, however, that a headline spread itself across most of the front page of the *Evening News*. This did not immediately break the mould and although newspapers generally adopted decks, they were limited to single columns with rare exceptions. The British newspaper that really pioneered new techniques in headlines and page furniture was the *Daily Express*, launched in September 1900 by Arthur Pearson.

During the First World War newspapers generally began to use more dramatic and larger headlines but it was the *Daily Express* that led the way, so that what Hutt calls the 'streamer-and-double-column' style became normal (op. cit.: 95)

The next major change came in the 1930s, at a time when newspapers realised that they had lost the monopoly of news production to radio. The treatment of stories, including headlines, became more graphic and there was an increased emphasis on readability – getting the gist of a story across quickly – that required a knowledge of typography. Rather than leaving the choice of headline fonts and treatments to the printing staff, journalists themselves began to see the advantages in getting their work promoted effectively:

> Typography . . . was more and more seen as a central ingredient of headlines and text alike. Journalists started to get the upper hand in the choice, and use, of type; the old 'leave it to the printer' attitude died a deserved death; the ranks of the sub-editors (copy readers) gave birth to a new breed, the production journalist – the editorial man concerned with the typographic design of his paper.
>
> (Hutt, op. cit.: 107)

With the essential elements brought into the twenty-first century, we can turn to the next phase.

How to write great headlines

The main print section of my preferred newspaper has 36 pages today.[13] That section contains 77 news items (not counting letters or reviews), some of which will be of more interest to me than others. To save my time and direct my attention I need a guide and the most obvious and effective guide is the headline. Good headlines make a significant positive contribution to the experience of consuming a print publication, but it is an individual experience. Print newspapers are usually read by one person at a time, and the competition is restricted to different items (stories) on the page. Uncommitted consumers who just want to know the news might be swayed one way or the other by a front page splash headline, or may be persuaded to buy a second paper in addition to their primary one, but the reality is that most people who set out to buy a newspaper will know exactly which title they want and will only reluctantly accept a substitute. The headlines in print newspapers are therefore 'internal' aids to navigation.

For newspapers, magazines and other curata published digitally the situation is different. Specific newspaper sites will attract a core readership – and a newspaper's tablet app will attract subscribers – but the overwhelming majority of online readers come to specific stories via a search engine, not because they have set out to find *that* iteration of the story. Shareaholic, a company that analyses online traffic sources to 200,000 publishers, found 48.8 per cent of traffic in February 2012 came from Google search, with a further 1.6 per cent and 1.2 per cent from Yahoo and Bing respectively. Facebook links provided 6.38 per cent, Twitter .82 per cent and then-newcomer Pinterest 1.05 per cent. Thus search provided 51.6 per cent of traffic and social media 8.25 per cent compared with 18.2 per cent from direct diallers.[14]

The inference from this data is that headlines in a digital publication play a vitally important 'external' role in making stories visible in the digital smog; they make this significant contribution by using searchable words and phrases or tapping into topics that are trending online, techniques that are highly compatible with print-based skills. Although this book is written 'as if the web exists',[15] these technical and cultural differences mean we still have to distinguish between headlines written for print and those for digital distribution but in fact the greatest difference is not between writing headlines for print or digital but between writing headlines for news and features. 'The distinction of the hard news headline,' Harold Evans tells us, 'is that it always gives information' whereas the aim of a feature headline is 'to explore, discuss or relate a rich narrative whose ideas are too complex and diffuse to be done justice by a hard news headline focused on a single key point' (Evans 1974: 25).

Creating great news headlines

Whatever the distribution channel, a news headline has some specific, enduring characteristics:

- It condenses complicated facts into a few words.
- It represents accurately a situation that is probably confused and still evolving.
- It piques curiosity.
- It requires every word to be carefully chosen . . .
- . . . and each cluster of words to be carefully assembled.
- Time spent crafting a headline is never wasted.

Sir Harold Evans, former editor of the *Sunday Times* and author of a canonical series of books about the practice of journalism, wrote: 'The art of the headline lies in imagination and vocabulary; the craft lies in accuracy of content, attractiveness of appearance and practicality' (Evans, 1974: 13). His advice is still widely applicable but headline writing, and the use of page furniture in general, has developed since his heyday in the 1960s with most of the changes being driven by a combination of changed usage, completely different print production methods and the needs of digital publishing. Not only that, but by using online metrics (methods of measurement) the *effectiveness* of a headline can be judged almost instantly, taking assessment of its value out of the hands of the producer and giving it to the consumer.

The main role of a news headline is to sell-and-tell the news story. That is, to attract a reader's attention by explaining the content of what follows. Like a super-condensed intro, the headline must let the time-poor reader know what the story is about, and at the same time have something about it that converts the casual browser into a reader. Conversely, headlines also signal to readers what *not* to bother with: as Andrew Marr notes 'for every headline that says "read this", there are several more which say "it's fine to ignore this bit"' (Marr 2005: 249[16]).

A good way to start the headline creation process is by finding the key actions in the story – shave it down to the one or two elements that define this piece of news. Harold Evans advises the subeditor to 'read the copy carefully and decide on the basic news point' (Evans, 1974: 16). If the story is about a situation that has been current for some time, look for the newest developments then isolate the key phrase or words that encapsulate what has happened. That should give you the heart of the headline, the fundamental news elements, and from there you can construct a functional, useful and, where appropriate, pleasing structure. It could be the plainly informative **Jealous woman hit partner in the face with rolling pin** (*South Wales Evening Post* 8/8/12: 16) or the more playful and allusive **Don't blame recipes for sinking feeling, Berry tells home bakers** (*Daily Telegraph* 7/8/12: 11) – a headline that requires the reader not only to make a connection between 'sinking' and 'bakers' but also to recognise from the context that the Berry in question is Mary Berry, a judge on TV programme *The Great British Bake Off* (and a very well known cookery writer in her own right). Incidentally, both of those examples demonstrate that it is acceptable, indeed common practice, to omit words that would normally be called for in a grammatically constructed sentence. The **jealous woman**, should properly hit **her** partner (**the** could also have been omitted before **face**); omissions in the *Telegraph*'s headline are less straightforward to analyse but there is no doubt it is an abbreviated form of syntax.

Hot and Cold headlines

When media theorist Marshall McLuhan published his ideas of Hot and Cold media he almost certainly did not have British newspaper headlines in mind but it is possible to apply the theory in this context. In *Understanding Media* (1964), McLuhan explained that a Hot medium is 'well filled with data' whereas a Cold medium is 'high in participation or completion by the audience'; a photograph is Hot, while a cartoon is Cold; radio is Hot, a telephone Cold (Moos 1997: 162). By extension, therefore, a Hot headline is one that leaves very little work for the reader to do – the **Jealous woman** example above is Hot – whereas headlines that call for participatory input from the consumer such as **Don't blame recipes** can be categorised as Cold. Provided the input expected is appropriate and worthwhile – even on this small scale – it may add to the reader's satisfaction in understanding and interpreting the medium.

Ten steps to success with news headlines

By now it should be clear that creating news headlines is not a straightforward matter of contriving a pun or following a set routine. Nevertheless, there are certain helpful guidelines that will assist in the process. Here are ten tips to bear in mind:

1   Sell the story and tell the story
2   Use active verb forms

3   Use the present or future verb tense
4   Be objective
5   Phrase each line carefully
6   Keep punctuation to a minimum
7   Avoid jargon
8   Make sense
9   Make it fit
10   Make it legal

1 Sell the story and tell the story

A headline has about one second in which to catch the reader's attention and in that time it has to do two jobs:

i)   make it clear what the story is about;
ii)   make the reader want to read the story.

In short, the headline must tell the essential point of the story in a supercondensed form and at the same time make that story seem vitally interesting.

Venezuelan diplomat charged with murder
(Guardian 7/8/12: 16)

A classic news headline that conveys the main elements of the story clearly and unambiguously. The details of which diplomat, where it happened and who was murdered are given in the first paragraph.

Hooligan hit by judo medallist sitting next to him
(Daily Telegraph 7/8/12: 8)

This example works on its own – there is no doubt about what happened – but it is actually part of a continuing story. Just before the 2012 Olympic men's 100 metre final started a bottle was thrown onto the track (watch it at *http://bit.ly/100mbottle*) – the man alleged to have thrown it ('hooligan' Ashley Gill-Webb) happened to be close to judoka Edith Bosch (bronze medal in the 70kg category), who knocked him to the floor before he was removed by security guards. The use of the word 'hooligan' is the *Telegraph*'s way of commenting on the man's behaviour and while it is not directly an ideological choice of word it indicates the paper's social stance. The construction is passive, but the phrasing contains a lot of action (see 2 below).

Gold-plated pension schemes threatened by EU bureaucrats
(Daily Mail 7/8/12: 2)

This is a far from straightforward headline because it seems to be operating on several different levels. The phrase 'gold-plated' when applied to pension schemes could be interpreted as a criticism (imagine it applied in the context of a merchant banker's bonus payments) but the story is more concerned about proposals that could 'rob millions of workers of their chance of a lucrative pension pot', so in this instance 'gold-plated' is a term of praise. The most important phrase in the headline is, in fact, 'EU bureaucrats' as these semi-mythical beings are regularly demonised by the *Daily Mail*. Using these two words is an immediate signal to the *Mail* community that something egregious is afoot and they should continue to read the story to enjoy their daily dose of outrage, making this an example of an 'ideological' headline. The construction is also passive (see 2 below).

2 Use active verb forms

An active headline tells of people doing things or saying things, rather than having things done to them or told to them.

G4S using untrained staff to screen visitors *(Guardian 7/8/12: 9)*

This could easily be **Untrained staff used by G4S to screen visitors** but the active version conveys much more by making it clear that G4S is following a deliberate policy. The construction also puts the news-trigger term 'G4S' first as this was a time when the company was coming in for widespread criticism.

Spyker launches $3bn lawsuit against GM *(Guardian 7/8/12: 17)*

A clear and dynamic sequence of action heading a business story. The *Daily Telegraph* went with the passive **General Motors being sued for**

$3bn by Spyker for 'blocking' Saab rescue (7/8/12: 21) though why it was thought to be better than **Spyker sues General Motors for $3bn after 'blocking' Saab rescue** is not clear. Perhaps General Motors was thought to be more recognisable than Spyker, or perhaps it is intended to show the giant American car maker as a victim of the small Dutch manufacturer of specialist vehicles.

An active headline must contain a verb or the verb must be strongly implied, although this works best when the verb is a form of 'to be' (is/are) or 'to have' (has/have). The following example illustrates both an implied verb and an active construction in a two-part headline – the splash (main headline) and an accompanying deck (see separate section).

BRITISH BANK'S LINKS TO GLOBAL TERROR

US accuses Standard Chartered of laundering billions for Iran and Hezbollah

(*Daily Mail* 7/8/12: 1)

The splash (main headline) implies that the British bank concerned *has* links to terrorist organisations and the deck is so much stronger than the alternative possibility **Standard Chartered accused of . . .** which would be passive.

The *Mail Online* had a far more elaborate set of page furniture heading this story on the afternoon of 7/8/12, comprising a splash and four decks. One reason for this is that the story had moved on, so information has been added, another is that the extra page furniture gives the story more visual weight; finally, the searchable keyword count is raised and there's room to include some swearing:

> **Standard Chartered share price falls a quarter, wiping £10BILLION from its value, after claims the UK bank laundered billions for Iran and Hezbollah**
>
> • **Standard Chartered is accused of conspiring with Iran for a decade**
> • **New York State Department of Financial Services called the bank a 'rogue institution' and said the bank's Iran affairs had been a threat to global peace**
> • **Sixty thousand financial transactions were cited as suspicious**

- Investigation quoted London-based executive saying: 'You f***ing Americans. Who are you to tell us, the rest of the world, that we're not going to deal with Iranians?'
(http://bit.ly/mailbank: accessed 17.30, 7/8/12)

Although passive headlines can work too.

Hooligan hit by judo medallist sitting next to him
(*Daily Telegraph* 7/8/12: 8)

As noted above, this is a passive construction but still contains a lot of action. Use of the passive is approved by Harold Evans when 'the injunction to bring in the news point early overrides the injunction to use the active voice ... when what has been done to the individual or nation or company is more important than who has been doing it' (1974: 28).

Using the passive voice works if the agent (usually a person) performing the action is unknown, unimportant, or clear from the context. It can also be an effective way for a writer to delay mentioning the agent until the end of the sentence or even to avoid mentioning the agent completely. It is widely agreed that the passive voice can provide increased emphasis and sometimes using a passive construction is the only way to craft a sentence that does not sound unnaturally forced, for example when the receiver of the action is more important than the actor.

In the example above it is possible to argue that the story derives its news value from the fact it was an Olympic medallist who meted out instant justice and therefore it might seem perverse to disguise her agency by using the passive voice. On the other hand, making her the active agent could over-emphasise the aggressive nature of her deed.

Overall, however, the rule still stands – active verb forms are the preference.

Headlines without verbs usually become labels

The print version of the *Mail* headline quoted above has an implied verb but it is very easy to turn a properly constructed sentence, which traditionally takes the grammatical form of subject + verb + object, into a label – a construction that describes something but includes no action.

The following headline, originally from the *Guardian* (21/10/02) provides an example of what the three different forms – active, passive and label – look like:

Active (as used): **Britons on trial in Egypt tell of torture**

Passive: **Torture suffered by Britons in Egypt**

Label: **Britons' Egypt Torture**

3 Use the present or future verb tense

This helps to keep headlines active – we are dealing with news, not history.

Assad's premier defects as crisis escalates
(Guardian 7/8/12: 1)

Strictly speaking this should have been **Assad's premier has defected** . . . as it is referring to something that has already happened but using the present tense gives it far more immediacy.

Car industry is buoyed by a £2bn buying spree
(Daily Mail 7/8/12: 20)

Again, strictly speaking the car industry **has already been** buoyed by the spending spree since it happened in July 2012 but this wording is so much more vibrant.

4 Be objective

There is a long cherished belief that news reporting should be done in as impartial and objective a manner as possible. This is, of course, bunkum because not only are news reporters human and subject to the same kinds of prejudice and selection as every other human, they are also working within highly politicised organisations. This should be plainly obvious to anyone with an ounce of intelligence but the pretence that it is not so was largely demolished by evidence to the Leveson Inquiry throughout the spring and summer of 2012.

Nevertheless, lip service is still paid to the convention of objectivity, as much in headlines as anywhere. Every time you see quote marks in a headline it indicates the publication is either:

i)   attributing authority to a third party;
ii)   formally distancing itself from a statement or an opinion made by a third party;
iii) indicating that an assertion of fact has not yet been confirmed;
iv)   marking a departure from the direct quotes in the story.

Closing hospital stroke units has 'saved lives and money' – study

(*Guardian* 3/8/13: 13)

The authority for this apparently paradoxical statement comes from a study published in a journal (*PLoS One*).

Pussy Riot trial 'worse than Soviet era'

(*Guardian* 4/8/12: 20)

The headline is making a very clear point – justice in Russia is partial and opaque – but by putting the key phrase inside quote marks the appearance of objectivity is maintained. Around two-thirds of the way through the story the words are attributed to Pussy Riot's defence lawyer Nikolai Polozov.

State schools 'letting down' Olympians of the future

(*Daily Telegraph* 7/8/12: 8)

Of the three Tory figures quoted in the story below this headline (Lord Coe, Lord Moynihan and Jeremy Hunt) none actually uses these words but all of them suggest state schools could provide better sports teaching. The *Telegraph* puts the words in quote marks not just to indicate someone else has said them but, in this instance, to indicate it has made them up itself as some kind of paraphrase. Andrew Marr is of the opinion that 'headline quotation marks are mostly a warning sign, meaning "tendentious, overblown story follows [. . .]"' (Marr 2005: 253).

'Traitor' Clegg sparks civil war in Coalition

(*Daily Mail* 7/8/12: 12)

As with the *Telegraph* example above, the word traitor is not used by anyone quoted in the story – unidentified 'senior Tories' and a 'Cabinet minister' refer to 'treachery' and 'betrayal' – so the quote marks are used to indicate a paraphrase. Six pages later Max Hastings's column is headed **Spineless Mr Clegg**. Clearly it would be impossible to divine the paper's political ideology from any of this evidence.

5 Phrase each line carefully on the page

When a headline is split over several lines it can potentially lead to unintended double meanings. In *Essential English for Journalists, Editors and Writers* (2000: 211) Harold Evans cites the example of **Judge gets drunk driving case** – on a single line it's unproblematic but if it is split to read

> **Judge gets drunk**
> **driving case**

the words can be interpreted differently.

To avoid this problem make sure that each line of a multi-line headline is a complete thought unit; an adjective and its noun (*white van*), a verb and its auxiliary (*was driving*), should be on the same line.

> **Last laugh for the star**
> **who split from model wife**
>
> (*Daily Telegraph* 7/8/12: 5)

has clearly been split to ensure the first line is a complete clause; this appears to have been done deliberately as on the page there is room to fit 'who' after 'star'. (There may also be a play on the possible meanings of 'model' when used to describe 'wife'.)

> **Facebook gambles on hitting the jackpot**
> **with bingo app and virtual slot machines**
>
> (*Times* 8/8/12: 14)

is an excellent example of careful phrasing; the first line is a dramatic clause that will attract attention given that a) Facebook is such a well known brand and b) the Facebook stock market launch turned out to be something of a flop.

**Hopes for Alzheimer's treatment
dashed after a decade of trials fail**

(*Times* 8/8/12: 33)

by contrast, appears to promise something optimistic in the first line only
to become pessimistic in the second.

6 Keep punctuation to a minimum

Punctuation in headlines should be used sparingly and for a well justified reason. Quote marks are employed for the reasons given in Be
Objective (4 above) but they are sometimes used to distance the publication from the word being used for reasons that are nothing to do with
attributing authority. This usually comes down to a matter of aesthetics
or snobbery, neither of which is a convincing argument.

Michael accused of using the show to 'plug' his new song (*Daily
Telegraph* 14/8/12: 5) is a perfectly good headline (although the verb
mode is passive – who is doing the accusing?) so why does the *Telegraph*
feel the need to distance itself from the word *plug*? Even though the print
version of the *Telegraph* attracts an older community (the biggest group
is aged 65+ http://bit.ly/teledemog), *plug* is not an unfamiliar word in this
context: the 1972 edition of *Chambers Twentieth Century Dictionary* lists
exactly this definition ('a piece of favourable publicity, esp. one incorporated in other material', p. 1029) so all the *Telegraph*'s readers have
had 40 years to become accustomed to the meaning and as those now
aged 65 would have been 25 in 1972 this use of plug should not be too
shocking or risqué. Encasing it in quote marks is clearly intended to put
it in quarantine but all it does is make the paper look out of touch in
the same way that Judge James Pickles did when he asked, 'Who are
The Beatles?' (http://bit.ly/whoarethebeatles).

On the other hand, strategic use of certain punctuation marks can work
very effectively, as in this example from the same edition of the *Daily
Telegraph* – **Tablets, apps and red buttons: the other success stories of
Games** (p. 2). The colon is used correctly to separate the list from the
explanatory clause and allows a neat conjunction of the related elements.

The colon is also commonly used to contract the structure of a sentence
and separate two related but not contiguous clauses –

River tragedy: help police to identify victim
(South Wales Evening Post, 8/8/2012: 11)

From soggy to sizzling: Get set for a heatwave
(*Daily Mail* 7/8/2012: 20 – note that using a capital letter after a colon is not generally recommended usage)

Bruises and lies: tell-tale clues to a family secret long denied
(*Guardian* 4/8/2012: 15)

Note, however, this is the full colon; semi-colons are very useful in narrative writing but are very rarely used in British newspaper headlines.

What of the comma? Its use is relatively widespread. The *Times* favours attributing opinionated headlines with a 'says' phrase that requires a preceding comma:

Park could play host to national arts festival, says opera chief
(14/8/2012: 7)

Team GB is way to go, says GB
(14/8/2012: 11)

The *Guardian* also uses the comma to separate clauses or descriptors:

From Russia, without much love from USA
(7/8/2012: 9)

Teenage criminals make for a shocking, compelling drama
(7/8/2012: 23)

As does the *Daily Mail*:

Hoarding disorder, or why refusing to throw anything away is all in the brain
(7/8/2012: 21)

We've landed, said the tweet from Mars
(7/8/2012: 31)

Despite the general observance of this rule about minimising the use of punctuation in headlines, it is not hard to find more unusual forms or combinations, as these two examples from the *Guardian* show:

'So painful': Adlington third behind American who got faster and faster
(4/8/2012: 3, a double whammy of quote
marks and colon)

Curiosity lands on Mars. No sign of life . . . yet
(*Guardian* 7/8/2012: 1, full stop plus ellipsis)

Of all points of punctuation the exclamation mark – also known as a screamer – is the one that should be used most sparingly of all and yet exercises a fascination for amateur, inexperienced or over-enthusiastic writers and subeditors. Harold Evans puts it well when he notes that subs 'sometimes make the mistake of giving themselves a medal with the exclamation mark – using it after a clever heading so that buffoons shall not miss their wit' (1974: 93). On the other hand, F. J. Mansfield cites **LOOK, THERE'S A HORSE!**, over a story about the paucity of horses in Yeovil, as an example of a headline with 'challenge and novelty' (1931: 123).

It is possible to find question marks in news headlines but they are rare and, as Evans and others observe, more generally used over features or columns – **Tell me, exactly when did idealism become a criminal offence?** or **Am I a philistine for being happy to see the Inverkip power plant chimney go?** which respectively head Deborah Orr's and Ian Jack's contributions to the *Guardian* Saturday section – two question-marked headlines in the same location on successive right hand pages (3/8/13: 35, 37). Andrew Marr believes that a headline with a question mark at the end is 'often a scare story, or an attempt to elevate some run-of-the-mill piece of reporting into a national controversy and, preferably, a national panic.' (Marr 2005: 253). His advice to readers is – 'If the headline asks a question, try answering "no"' (loc. cit.). This motto has since been parlayed into a 'law' – Betteridge's Law, named for Ian Betteridge after he wrote a piece for *Technovia* questioning the validity of a news item published under a headline that ended in a question mark (http://bit.ly/betteridge[17]).

Sometimes, however, a question mark can make a huge contribution. This often happens when the newspaper wishes to make a definitive statement without putting itself directly into the line of legal fire. The *Independent* used this technique on 28 January 2004 when it gave its verdict on the Hutton Inquiry into the death of Dr David Kelly. The report, which in essence cleared the government of all wrongdoing in the matter and put the blame firmly on the BBC, was greeted with widespread scepticism by public and media alike. The *Independent* expressed this very effectively by starting a special report on its front page with the following words set in a sea of white space (Figure 4.1):

WHITEWASH?

THE HUTTON
REPORT
A SPECIAL ISSUE

Without the question mark this could easily have been interpreted as an assault on the integrity of Lord Hutton and his procedures and might have laid the newspaper open to a legal action (defamation, libel, malice aforethought, contempt ... a half decent lawyer would have many options). *With* the question mark it becomes a debate or discussion around a subject that has caused widespread concern.

7 Avoid jargon

The standard advice for most forms of journalism is to use short words that readers will understand immediately and that may have a striking effect on them. Winston Churchill is reputed to have said, 'Short words are best and old words when short are best of all' and the *Economist* is just one of many places to quote him, in this paean (to use the short word that comes from Latin via Greek, or *hymn*, in Old English) to Anglo-Saxon: 'Tough as boots or soft as silk, sharp as steel or blunt as toast, there are old, short words to fit each need' (http://bit.ly/shortwinston). F. J. Mansfield in his 1931 book *Sub-Editing* agrees: 'Short striking words are essential in bold headings, and the Anglo-Saxon language has a great fund of these' (127).

Churchill, the *Economist* and Mr Mansfield are all correct but there is another angle to the argument – journalists have developed a lexicon of short, sharp words that are used almost nowhere else but headlines and bad tabloid writing: bid, tot, probe, slash, rap, romp, dash, quiz, axe, mar, and the like. Hutt attributes this characteristic vocabulary to the historic

THE INDEPENDENT

No 5,392   www.independent.co.uk   THURSDAY 29 JANUARY 2004   60p

WHITEWASH?
THE HUTTON
REPORT
A SPECIAL ISSUE

Eight months ago, BBC reporter Andrew Gilligan broadcast his now infamous report casting doubt on the Government's dossier on Iraq's weapons capability, a vital plank in its case for war. In the ensuing furore between No 10 and the BBC, Government scientist David Kelly, who was revealed to be Gilligan's source, was found dead in the woods. Tony Blair appointed Lord Hutton, a former Lord Chief Justice of Northern Ireland, to hold an inquiry into the circumstances surrounding Dr Kelly's death. He listened to 74 witnesses over 25 days, and yesterday published his 740-page report. In it, he said Gilligan's assertions were unfounded and criticised the BBC, whose chairman has now resigned. He said that Dr Kelly had broken the rules governing civil servants in talking to journalists. He exonerated Tony Blair, cleared Alastair Campbell and attached no blame to the government for the naming of Dr Kelly. So was this all an establishment whitewash? And what of the central issue which Lord Hutton felt he could not address? If the September 2002 dossier which helped persuade the nation of the urgent need for war (and triggered this tragic chain of events) was indeed reliable, where, exactly, are Iraq's weapons of mass destruction?

Figure 4.1 Front page of *The Independent*, Thursday 29 January 2004.

Source: Courtesy of The Independent. © The Independent.

limitations imposed by single column, multi-decked headlines detailed earlier, restrictions that 'engendered a special jargon or headlinese language of three- and four-letter words' (1973: 79). Evans observes that these words can often be used as nouns, adjectives or verbs and in highly contracted structures such as headlines 'the key word can become ambiguous' and such ambiguity can lead to a confused reading (1974: 99).

You do not have to look far to find examples of headlinese, even today:

> **Speaker told, axe pension**
>
> (*Sun* 13/9/2012: 6)

> **Anger at MoD air deal axe**
>
> (op. cit.: 8)

> **A hot romp foils Chez**
>
> (*Daily Star* 13/9/2012: 11; extra points for knowing Chez means Cheryl Cole)

> **Rob packs it in for tot**
>
> (op. cit.: 13; Rob, of course, is Robbie Williams)

The *Sun* even used 'probe' on the front page, as a shorthand description of the Hillsborough Independent Panel and its report on the Hillsborough football ground disaster of 1989: **41 lives could have been saved, says new probe** (13/9/2012: 1) although 'says report' would have been more dignified and appropriate.

These words form a kind of jargon – a set of special words or expressions used by a particular group of people or profession – that is easy to use in a lazy or hackneyed way. Just as some headline writers think they *have* to create puns, others clearly believe that they *must* use this jargon. However, the following example from the *Daily Mirror* seems to indicate that whoever composed the headline for this story about a nurse harassing a patient knew they were making ridiculous use of tabloid language – otherwise why use quote marks?

> **'Romp nurse stalker hell'** (13/9/2012: 33)

Chief among the critics of this over-used vocabulary was Keith Waterhouse, whose book *Waterhouse on Newspaper Style* has become canonical since he first wrote it as a style guide for (irony alert) the *Daily Mirror*. Although he accepted that short, sharp words could – if not over done – be very useful for headlines and that most readers were likely to know what they meant, he rejected their wider use:

> Why, if these words are now so common, are they not in common use? Why do we not hear housewives at bus-stops saying, 'Our Marlene used to be a till girl at that blaze super-store' or 'Did I tell you about young Fred being rapped after he slammed his boss? He thinks he's going to be axed.' Words that have never managed to get into the mainstream of the language are suspect as a means of popular communication.
>
> (Waterhouse 1989: 229–30)

Waterhouse was also opposed to the idea that journalists should use the jargon of the industry or profession they were writing about, not just in headlines but anywhere:

> to use outsiders' jargon is to take their own evaluation of themselves on trust – or anyway to give the impression of doing so. This is one good reason why journalists should never resort to the jargon of the field they cover.
>
> (Waterhouse 1989: 141)

He had a good point – journalists who get too close to their sources, who want to be taken as an insider by the outsider group, run the risk of, at best, developing Stockholm Syndrome[18] and, at worst, going native and thus becoming uncritical of the group and accepting of their social and moral outlook. Many commentators thought financial journalists had become too close to their sources to analyse clearly the circumstances that led to the global financial crisis of 2008 (the Frontline club hosted an informative debate[19] about this); Raymond Boyle discusses a similar situation that affects sports journalists, particularly football writers, in *Sports Journalism: Context and Issues* (2006).

8 Make sense

It sounds like a statement of the obvious but a headline must make sense on its own. One of a headline's main functions is to attract readers to the story not leave them scratching their heads, so

'Drunk star attacked air crew with yoghurt'
(*Independent* 13/11/2001)

makes perfect sense and contains more than enough teasers to tempt most readers into discovering that Peter Buck, lead guitarist of REM, became over-refreshed on a transatlantic flight and thought it would be amusing to redistribute some fermented dairy product among the cabin crew.

On the other hand:

Angels rally strongly thanks to Spiezio and more monkey business
(*Independent* 28 October 2002)

might just cause some people to want to find out what the heck the story is about (basketball, as it happens) but seems likely to cause more to skip it.

The need to make sense is another reason to avoid jargon, which is, after all, a specialised vocabulary intended to exclude outsiders.

9 It must fit

Another very obvious point but one that has to be made because it is possible to believe that one's words are the most important thing. In journalism, and particularly news journalism, that's not true – the space is most important, every time. Bernard Levin[20] may, or may not, have written 'The best headlines never fi' but all the effort put into devising a great headline will be wasted if it's too long or too short for the space available. 'A headline set up but rejected because it will not fit the column is a serious production delay', says the *Kemsley Manual* (115). In order to avoid just this situation, Harold Evans gives a detailed explanation of how to count the 'units' that make up the words (and spaces) in a line of type. One major difference between now and then is the advent of on-screen electronic page make-up, which not only allows production journalists to know immediately whether something fits or not, and thus to change it straight away, but also permits a degree of manipulation of the spacing, tracking and compression of the type.

Ways to change a headline to make it fit

i)   change one word for another, find a shorter/longer alternative;
ii) increase or decrease the tracking, the space between letters – but not to the extent to which it becomes obvious;
iii) compress or expand the type.

Be very careful with the latter two options – it's very tempting just to change the settings in InDesign or Quark but it's also very easy to overdo it and spoil the look of the type. Even an amateur can see the difference between

EXAMPLE OF NORMALLY TRACKED LINE
EXAMPLEOFTIGHTLYTRACKEDLINE
EXAMPLE OF LOOSELY TRACKED LINE

EXAMPLE OF 100% COMPRESSION
EXAMPLE OF 80% COMPRESSION
EXAMPLE OF 120% COMPRESSION

10 Be legal

Headlines can bring legal troubles just as much as the copy of a story. Watch out for double meanings, implied meanings, possible libels, and unfortunate positioning or juxtaposition – although this may not be obvious until the page has been put together (Figure 4.2). A headline such as 'Mad axeman rapped by judge' appearing next to a picture illustrating a story about how cheerful the mayor looks in his new ceremonial gear is at best unfortunate and at worst defamatory.

A good example of unfortunate juxtaposition was published in the *South Wales Evening Post* of 3 August 2013 (page 14). The lead story on the right side of the page is a court report headed **Man is facing accusations of sex offences**. Immediately underneath that story, and separated only by a thin rule, is a photograph of ex-Swansea City footballer and club ambassador Lee Trundle posing with a group of Korean girls he was showing around the Liberty Stadium. Clearly there is no connection between the stories but on a first, quick glance at the page the dominant elements are the headline and the photograph. The smaller headline at

The Daily Telegraph

Friday, March 2, 2012   FINAL   telegraph.co.uk   No 48,757 £1.20

NICE ENOUGH TO WEAR   The Queen, the Duchess of Cornwall and the Duchess of Cambridge admire a coronation cake on a visit to Fortnum & Mason in London's Piccadilly yesterday. Performing their first royal duty as a trio, they were at the store, known as the Queen's favourite grocer, to mark a Diamond Jubilee gift of a United Services Tin to all members of the Armed Forces serving abroad   Report and picture: Page 3

Witchcraft threat to children

Police warn of growing danger as couple are convicted of murdering boy they believed cast a spell on another child

By Nick Britten and Victoria Ward

CHILDREN in Britain are being abused and murdered in increasing numbers because its belief in witchcraft is rife in some African communities, police said yesterday.

The warning was issued as a couple from the Democratic Republic of Congo were found guilty of murdering the woman's 15-year-old brother during an "exorcism ceremony".

The Metropolitan Police yesterday said it had investigated 83 "faith-based" child abuse cases involving witchcraft in the past 10 years but believed it was still an "under-reported, hidden crime".

Children's charities and campaigners urged communities to report abuse and said social workers must be braver in investigating abuse in immigrant groups.

Kristy Bamu, 15, was relentlessly tortured and eventually drowned in a bath on Christmas Day 2010 by his sister, Magalie, and her partner, Eric Bikubi. The killers are facing life sentences.

They believed he had cast spells on another child and punished him with increasing viciousness. The teenager "begged to die" because he was in such pain after three days of being attacked with knives, sticks, metal bars and a hammer and chisel, suffering 130 separate injuries.

Among the cases that have come to light are four murders, including that of Victoria Climbié in 2000, the case that first raised awareness of the problem in Britain.

Detectives warned that while they were investigating around eight cases a year, they believed many more incidents went unreported.

Det Supt Terry Sharpe, the Metropolitan Police's lead on Project Violet, a team set up to tackle religious-based child abuse, said: "The

intelligence from the community is that it's far more prevalent than the reports we are getting."

The NSPCC said: "We must not be afraid to challenge these communities to cut the wrongdoers within them. Sadly, this deeply disturbing case is not a one-off incident."

The Victoria Climbié Trust, which was set up after the death of the eight-year-old, said that, while the number of children affected was relatively low, the impact was significant. "The reality is that no one really knows the full extent across the many communities for whom traditional belief systems are the norm," said director Mor Dioum.

The charity Trust for London said some officials may be unaware how to deal with abuse cases linked to witchcraft and spirit possession.

"Those working with children need to remember that no faith or religion promotes cruelty to children

and not be afraid to intervene if someone is wrongly using belief as an excuse to harm children."

Many cases involve immigrants from African countries such as the DRC, where witchcraft is widely practised, and are nurtured by an increasing number of African churches.

Kristy had come to London with five half-brothers and two sisters from Paris to stay with their sister and her boyfriend for Christmas, but within hours Bikubi, 28, had accused them of bringing kimbioti - a form of witchcraft - into his home.

Two sisters, aged 18 and 11, were beaten but escaped further attacks after "confessing" to being witches.

Kristy was singled out because, to show terror, he wet himself. He was struck in the mouth with a hammer, had battles and tiles smashed over his head and his ear twisted with pliers.

In what prosecutors called "a staggering act of depravity and cruelty",

the siblings, who included a 13-year-old boy and an autistic brother aged 22, were made to join in the torture.

At one point, Bikubi, 28, a football coach from Newham, east London, told the youngsters to jump out of the window to see if they could fly.

One of the victims, Kelly Bamu, said: "They started talking about kimbioti, witchcraft and this and that. It was as if they were obsessed by witchcraft."

The Old Bailey heard that sovereignty service were greeted with a horrific scene when they were called to the eighth-floor flat following Kristy's death. In the blood-spattered flat, police found his brothers and sisters "hysterical, terrified and making wet," the court heard.

Bikubi and Bamu, 29, who had denied murder, will be sentenced on Monday.   Reports: Page 6

Yes, I probably did ride Brooks police horse, admits Cameron

By Christopher Hope
Senior Political Correspondent

DAVID CAMERON is "likely" to have ridden a retired police horse lent to the former News International chief executive, Rebekah Brooks, Downing Street admitted yesterday.

Aides confirmed that the Prime Minister had ridden horses with Mrs Brooks's husband, Charlie, on several occasions and that he "probably" rode the horse lent to Scotland Yard.

The disclosure raises questions about the close friendship between the Prime Minister and Mrs Brooks, the former Sun and News of the

World editor who quit as chief executive of News International at the height of the phone hacking scandal last summer.

Mrs Brooks was lent the horse in 2008, the year after Clive Goodman, who worked for her as royal editor of the News of the World, was jailed for phone-hacking with the private investigator Glenn Mulcaire.

The horse, called Raisa, was stabled at Mrs Brooks's farm in the Cotswolds from 2008 to 2010 before it was handed back to Scotland Yard.

After three days of failing to say whether Mr Cameron had ridden the horse, aides last night disclosed that in all probability he did, although he could not be sure as he rode several of Mr Brooks's horses.

One of the Prime Minister's aides said: "It is highly possible that he was on that horse. It is likely that he rode that horse. He used a number of

Charlie's horses." She also confirmed that it was possible Mr Cameron had also gone riding with Mrs Brooks, because the Prime Minister could not be "100 per cent sure".

Reports: Page 4

"Yes, sugar lumps did change hands . . ."

Patients given kidneys from cancer victim

THE NHS has admitted negligence after two transplant patients received kidneys from a donor with an aggressive form of cancer.

Just days after their operations, Robert Law, 60, and Gillian Smart, 45, were informed that they required lengthy chemotherapy.

Yesterday Lynda Hardyn, chief executive of NHS Blood and Transplant, offered "sincere and unreserved apologies" for the error at the Royal Liverpool University hospital in November 2010.

She disclosed that the incident included human error by a specialist nurse who had not completed her training and was receiving support from a colleague.

Compensation is yet to be agreed in both cases.

Mrs Smart, a mother of two from St Helens, Merseyside, said the events had been "psychologically and physically draining".

Navy carrier plans hit by further delays

By Tim Ross
Political Correspondent

BRITAIN could be left without an aircraft carrier equipped with fighter jets for the next decade after scrapping costs throws Ministry of Defence plans into doubt.

Philip Hammond, the Defence Secretary, is to reconsider plans for up to 50 new fighter jets, which have been billed as the world's most advanced warplanes, after the Government admitted it had no idea what the programme would cost.

The rethink also comes amid fears that a design flaw in the new Joint Strike Fighter makes it unable to land on aircraft carriers.

Leaked Pentagon documents found the plane had failed eight simulated landings.

A redesign is likely to prove costly and delay the project, meaning that when Britain's only aircraft carrier comes into

service in 2020 it may have no jets. Mr Hammond may be forced to choose an alternative model of the Joint Strike Fighter, which would throw into doubt an agreement between France and Britain to share weapons and equipment, including aircraft carriers.

Ministers are currently reviewing the "risks" and expect to make an announcement in late 2012 on the future of the programme before Easter.

The decision to scrap the Harrier fleet means that British still have no carrier aircraft capability until 2020. The next aircraft carrier, the Queen Elizabeth, will not be operational for another eight years.

Fears have been raised that there could be further delays. Jim Murphy, Labour's shadow defence secretary, wrote to Mr Hammond last night demanding urgent assurances on the future of the Joint Strike Fighter programme.

Figure 4.2   Front page of the *Daily Telegraph*, Friday 2 March 2012.

the bottom of the page – **Liberty stop on Koreans' tour of Wales** – is easily overlooked.

There is a highly educational selection of *17 incredibly unfortunate headline and photo juxtapositions* collected at www.happyplace.com (see http://bit.ly/headlinefails).

Final caution: do not over-egg the pudding

On the morning of 18 July 2013 readers of the *Times* woke up to find the front page of their newspaper of record proclaiming **Hundreds perish as heatwave takes hold.** This sounded like a very serious situation . . . until you read the accompanying story which made it clear the figure was a projection based on an academic study of probabilities. Clearly the decision to run this somewhat sketchy report as the splash story on the front page cannot be blamed on a production journalist but it provides a useful lesson for subeditors, a lesson that George Bernard Shaw pithily encapsulated in the Preface to his play *Too Good To Be True* as the inability of newspapers to 'discriminate between the news value of a bicycle accident in Clapham and that of a capsize of civilization'.[21]

Sadly *BBC News* online followed the *Times*'s lead on its Wales page with **Heatwave: 100 people in Wales could have died so far, according to study** although at least they included the modifier 'could' (http://bit.ly/beebheatwave) (Figure 4.3).

Notes

1   This rather clumsy phrase is used in an attempt to find a neutral collective description of newspapers, magazines, webpages, especially one that carries no connotations of print on paper.
2   The vocative case of the neuter gender of the Latin word meaning 'arranged'. Cognate with curate and curation. Taken to mean any collection of content that has been put together intentionally and that appears on any publishing platform or substrate. The plural is curata.
3   Harold Evans (1974), *Editing and Design: A Five-volume Manual of English, Typography and Layout.* Book Three: *News Headlines.* London: Heinemann.
4   http://bit.ly/supercaley.
5   http://bit.ly/sungotcha.
6   http://bit.ly/supercalifrag.
7   http://bit.ly/supercally. This would be nice if true but it is difficult to track down a match in the 1970s where Ian Callaghan went 'ballistic'. I have seen 1976 given as a date for this headline but when Liverpool beat QPR 3–1 on 11 December 1976, Callaghan did not score, although he took a free kick that led to a goal.

Figure 4.3 Front page of the *Times*, Thursday 18 July 2013.

Source: Courtesy of the Times/News UK.

8   www.guardian.co.uk/media/2002/feb/25/pressandpublishing.falklands.

9   Searchability: creating a website or elements of a web page such as a headline in a way that allows search engines to find the pages easily, index them and rank them as high on the results list as possible.

10 i) A subordinate heading that serves to expand or explain the main headline; ii) the heading of a subdivision of the text.

11 The French rule, or dash, is a line with a diamond at its centre. Much used in Victorian times, it is still employed by modern newspapers. Will Ham Bevan recalls that during his time as a production journalist at the *Daily Mail* in the early 2000s:

> when the op-ed page was judged to be too serious for the usual single-word crossheads ('Betrayal', 'Filth', etc) the command would go out to replace them with diamond spacers to break up text columns. Likewise if it was a 'full page leader' day when some outrage meant the leading article was expanded from a column to a whole page. So only the rantiest of rants were blessed with French dashes.

> (Personal correspondence)

12 We have had opportunities of observing a new journalism which a clever and energetic man has lately invented. It has much to recommend it; it is full of ability, novelty, variety, sensation, sympathy, generous instincts; its one great fault is that it is feather-brained.

> (Matthew Arnold, *The Nineteenth Century*
> No. CXXIII (May, 1887) pp. 629–43)

13 Tuesday, 7 August 2012

14 Shareaholic report for February 2012: http://bit.ly/sharefeb accessed 8/8/12 The figures do not add up to 100 per cent in the Shareaholic report.

15 Something Clay Shirky took to saying in 2012. 6.14 and 8.26 in this video: http://bit.ly/shirkyasif.

16 Andrew Marr (2005), *My Trade: A Short History of British Journalism*. Basingstoke: Pan Books.

17 Other relevant 'laws' include Murphy's Law (if you write anything criticising editing or proofreading there will be some kind of fault in what you have written) as set out by John Bangsund of the Australian Society of Editors http://bit.ly/murphylaw and the Law of Exclamation (a statement's validity is called into question by the number of exclamation marks used).

18 Wikipedia has a good explanation of the phenomenon: http://bit.ly/stocksynd. For those who do not trust Wikipedia as a primary source there are citations to follow.

19 http://bit.ly/financemedia.

20 Bernard Levin, journalist and pundit, 1928–2004 (http://bit.ly/levinobit). Like many literary witticisms, this is neither as clever nor as profound as it appears.

21 If you don't happen to have a copy of this 1931 play you can read the Project Gutenberg version here http://bit.ly/shawtoogood.

5
Headline systems and searchability

A news headline usually sits on its own at the top of a story, but it is possible to create a headline 'system' by augmenting the main heading with one or more subsidiary headings. These may be above or below the headline and are known as overlines and decks respectively. Although this terminology is usually associated with print it can also be applied online; in fact it is arguably more important to create a headline system for digital publication because the increased repetition of key words makes it easier for potential readers to find the story via search engines.

Decks

Subsidiary headings that run below the headline are traditionally known as decks. In fact, as the *Kemsley Manual* makes clear (along with Hutt and Evans, as seen previously), this practice dates back to at least the 1850s, and reached a zenith at the beginning of the twentieth century; in 1900 the *Daily Graphic*, for example, headed a story about the Boer War with a very bland main head followed by eight decks that added a great deal more information:

THE WAR.

THE AMBUSH NEAR BLOEMFONTEIN

DESPATCH FROM LORD ROBERTS

FRENCH ON THE SCENE

BOERS IN GREAT FORCE

SEVEN GUNS LOST

HEAVY CASUALTIES

FIGHTING IN PROGRESS

PLUMER NEAR MAFEKING

Although it was a mix of tradition and technology that meant only a single column was given over to that headline system, the use of decked headlines is making a comeback in the print versions of some newspapers. In fact it is possible to argue that the decked system gives readers in a hurry a much clearer précis of events than a single banner headline would. As Harold Evans (1974: 19) says, 'The purpose of a deck is to cope with a more complicated or important story where several news points have to be made'. The top line must be a self-contained headline, then each deck must present another aspect of the story, still in a proper headline format but taking the overall context as given. The production journalist writing a decked headline should establish the main news points, give them a hierarchy, lead with the most important and then follow on. The example above does all of this, and also illustrates the 'rule' that words should not be repeated.

Somewhat surprisingly, given its rapid and determined expansion into digital news provision, it is the *Guardian* that makes the most extensive use of decks in its news pages, perhaps because they help to explain complex stories by delivering the key information quickly, as these examples demonstrate:

Beijing warns US to stay out of South China Sea dispute
Tensions rise in six-party rift over shipping waters
US diplomat called in after 'provocative' comments
(7/08/2102: 14)

Pussy Riot trial 'worse than Soviet era'
Judge refuses to allow 10 defence witnesses
Lawyers: women tortured with lack of food and sleep[1]
(4/08/2012: 20)

Although it has not revived the practice to anything like the same extent, the *Times* uses a single deck below some of its headlines in a way that combines subhead and standfirst (see below for more on standfirsts):

Home Office chief joins Whitehall exodus

Rift with Theresa May blamed for early departure
(14/08/2012: 11)

Tia's body lay in bag in the attic as police team hunted below

Grandmother's boyfriend charged with murder
(14/08/2012: 13)

Overlines

Another way to augment a headline is with an overline – literally a line of type that runs on top of the main heading (they are also known as kickers, particularly in the USA). If there is no picture accompanying the story, the overline should be treated like a deck line; however, if there is a picture the overline can be used to draw attention to something in the image. *Metro* uses this device regularly, sometimes to augment a set of photographs showing something unusual, perhaps a pigeon that chose to perch on the bars of a lion's cage but managed to fly off with only the loss of some tail feathers:

> **Daredevil pigeon defies the odds and dodges death at the big cats' enclosure**
>
> ## On a wing and a prayer [. . .]
> (*Metro* 25/10/13: 3)

On other occasions the paper will use an overline on the front page splash headline, even if there is no related image:

> **Hacked domestic appliances send a torrent of junk email**
>
> ## A fridge full of spam
> (21/1/14: 1)

was positioned to the right of a large picture of a small woman (Keira Knightly) and beneath a small picture of a large man (John Goodman).

Searchable headline system

Writing eye-catching headlines for stories in print is one skill; writing searchable headlines for online stories is another. With newspapers and magazines moving into digital publishing the range of skills required to write, test and spread headlines will only grow in importance for production journalists and publishers. At the most fundamental level, however, headline writing has one intention and one intention only – to attract a reader's attention – so all of the information on preceding pages remains relevant but is no longer sufficient on its own, meaning the subeditor or production journalist has to acquire and practise new skills. But they are new skills to perform an old job – modes of delivery may be different (flicking through pages as opposed to entering words in a search engine) but the optimal result is the same: someone finds the story, stops awhile and reads it.

Headline writing is vitally important to digital circulation (we can adopt the term from print and broaden it to include concepts of literal circulation, given that readers share content with their personal and professional networks) as a 2012 article in *Monday Note*, the media blog run by Frédéric Filoux and Jean-Louis Gassée, makes clear. Entitled *Transfer Of Value*, the piece looks at how *Huffington Post* adds value to the content it aggregates from other sources. Filoux gives a couple of examples but the most striking concerns the *Wall Street Journal*, which headed an opinion piece about presidential hopeful Mitt Romney's response to Barack Obama's plans for healthcare, **Romney's Tax Confusion**. This was good enough to attract nearly 1,000 comments – perhaps because it contained Romney's name, the election was coming up and healthcare was a highly controversial issue. A thousand responses seems like a reasonable outcome until you compare it with the 7,000+ comments and 600 Facebook shares that *Huffington Post* inspired for what was a very similar piece. Filoux explains that rather than running a single 1,000 word article, *HuffPo* published a 500 word treatment that included a 300 word article and a 200 word excerpt of the WSJ opinion. But more importantly, the headline was **Wall Street Journal: Mitt Romney Is 'Squandering' Candidacy With Health Care Tax Snafu** – it had the important name 'Romney' but also the key words 'health care', 'candidacy', 'tax' and, unlikely as it seems, 'snafu'.[2] Filoux's conclusion is:

> what we're seeing here is a transfer of value. Original stories are getting very little traffic due to the poor marketing tactics

of old-fashion publishers. But once they are swallowed by the *HuffPo*'s clever traffic-generation machine, the same journalistic item will make tens or hundred times better traffic-wise.
(http://bit.ly/filoux01)

Five steps to success with searchable headlines

You don't have to have access to '*HuffPo*'s clever traffic-generation machine' (which includes software custom-built for this purpose) to improve the chances of digital headlines being found by search engines, commented on and shared. Here are some simple and obvious strategies for better marketing tactics that everyone can adopt.

1 Adopt the searcher's mindset

Think about the kind of tag you would apply to the story – what are its main points? Put yourself in the position of someone looking for information of the kind you are offering and think about the words they would use in their search. If you are used to working on a print title it is important to think outside the customary practices of the publication and think globally. Literally sketch out the potential search terms and then construct a headline, teaser and intro (see *Develop a system* below) that incorporates as many of those words or phrases as possible. It cannot just be a list; you must use your word-crafting skills to make it a literate clause or sentence that is relevant to the story that follows.

2 Use Twitter to check what's trending

Twitter is accepted as a tool for reporters seeking eyewitness information and feature writers seeking particular types of people, but it can also be a useful friend to the online headline writer. Since September 2008, it has been possible for every Twitter user to see what is 'trending' – that is, to see the most popular topics people are tweeting about. This information can be used to tailor headlines. At the time I checked (7pm, Monday 5/8/13), the top two non-promoted topics were Peter Capaldi (the actor who had recently been announced as *Dr Who*'s next regeneration) and Tina Brown (the *Daily Beast* editor who had just 'twitterbombed' a former employee who had written an unflattering account of her management style). Getting these names into headlines – assuming you were working on appropriate stories – could help surf the waves of popular interest and lead to people picking up on your content. Frédéric Filoux reports of *HuffPo*, 'I was told that every headline is matched in realtime against Google most searched items right before being posted' (http://bit.ly/filoux01).

Huffington Post has also used crowdsourcing to help tweak its headlines, as Arriana Huffington herself explained in September 2009:

> We tried an experiment . . . to see if we could . . . crowdsource headline suggestions. [We] sent out a tweet with a link to our story on Obama heckler Rep. Joe Wilson, asking followers to reply back with their headline suggestions.
>
> We got a lot of smart, sharp, creative responses [. . .]
> (http://bit.ly/crowdheads)

3 A/B Testing

Print is permanent – once a headline has been typeset and processed through the printing press, the ink on paper can remain extant for decades or even centuries. On-screen headlines are transient; they can be changed in an instant, so if a better idea comes along it can be substituted without much trouble. Furthermore, it is increasingly common practice to create two headlines for a story and test which one works best by publishing them both for a short period of time and counting the number of clicks each attracts. This is a version of A/B Testing, a marketing technique that allows business to refine their products and services. *Huffington Post* uses it on a regular basis, as senior news editor Whitney Snyder explained in a Q&A session on Quora (10/2/2102). Answering the question 'How does the Huffington Post A/B test its headlines?' Snyder replied:

> The A/B testing was custom built. We do not, however, A/B test every headline. We often use it to see if our readers are familiar with a person's name . . . or to play up two different aspects of a story and see which one interests readers more.
> (http://bit.ly/snyderqa)

Further information in an October 2009 post by Zachary M. Seward for Nieman Journalism Lab makes it clear that the A/B testing is only done for about five minutes, at the end of which there will be enough data to show which headline has attracted more clicks, and that will be the one selected. However, there are other tweaks that can add traffic:

> Paul Berry, chief technology officer at *The Huffington Post*, spoke briefly about their real-time headline testing [to] the Online News Association conference … but he wouldn't disclose much about how or how often it's done … placing the author's name above a headline almost always leads to more clicks.
>
> (http://bit.ly/niemanhead)

American business magazine *Fast Company* added a little more detail:

> At HuffPo editors put together two versions of the headline text: "For five minutes, visitors to the site get to see either one or the other version of the headline at random … then the final headline is fixed … Sometimes [a headline] taps into a public mojo the writer wasn't expecting."
>
> (http://bit.ly/fastcohead)

Inspired by the *HuffPo*'s system, Brent Halliburton and Peter Bessman developed a free version of A/B headline testing software for Wordpress installations at the 2010 Baltimore Hackathon. Halliburton explained how it worked:

> When you set the alternate headline, we will A/B test your original headline and your alternate headline until one is deemed the winner (most clicks out of total impressions shown). Then we show that headline going forward. It could not be easier for you to split test headlines in WordPress.
>
> (http://bit.ly/wordpressab)

Their efforts won them the prize for best software development and it is still available as a plug-in – but has not been updated since version 0.1.

Wales Online ran an interesting, but perhaps accidental, form of A/B testing on the evening of 15 January 2014. Welsh singing icon Sir Tom Jones had been spotted on a night out in Los Angeles – but he had shaved off his goatee beard! The headline above the photostory was **Sir Tom**

Jones shows of his news smooth look on night out in LA. If this was a test it was quite successful as the headline was extensively tweeted and Facebooked; however, it must have lost out in the A/B stakes as by the following morning **Sir Tom Jones shows off his new smooth look on night out in LA** had taken its place.

4 Change the headline to suit the territory

In the Nieman Lab piece cited above, Zachary Seward also wrote that *Huffington Post* was considering separate East and West coast editions to take account of the time difference, meaning that different stories with different headlines would be served to New York and LA.

But the *Guardian* has gone a step further with its international editions for the US and Australia. So, for example, anyone in the UK logging on to the homepage of the US edition on the morning of Thursday 8 August 2013 would have found a story headlined **Obama cancels summit with Putin over Snowden asylum** at the top of the left-hand column of major news items. In the UK edition, the same story was positioned much further down the column and headlined **Obama cancels meeting with Putin** (the same headline was used for the Australian edition). However, by the afternoon that story no longer appeared in the UK edition's major news column at all; select the World news: United States splash page, however, and the story popped up in the list of Top Stories, with the headline **Obama cancels meeting with Putin over Snowden asylum tensions** (again this was the same in the Australian edition).

On the same day (in the afternoon), the US edition ran a piece about Iranian political prisoners asking President Obama to end sanctions that was headlined **Iranian prisoners appeal to Obama**, whereas the same piece in the Australian edition was headed **Iran prisoners' sanctions plea to US**.

These differences might seem slight or subtle but looking at the way key words will play in different countries reveals important changes in emphasis – the American version of the headline is almost personalised (a direct plea to president **Obama**), whereas the Australian version is both more informative (**sanctions**) and more distant (**US**). This way of thinking will apply everywhere, not just across continents. The polities of the UK may be closely associated but a story will have different connotations in Cardiff, Edinburgh and London, and different key words will elicit different responses. Just one example from 8/8/13 will make the point: the *Telegraph* headlined a story about UK population growth **UK has fastest growing population in EU with 48 more every hour** whereas *Wales Online* went with **UK population soars – but Wales still home to regions of emptiness**: similar starting points but very different developments, one pointing outwards to Germany and France, the other pointing inwards to Powys and other sparsely populated counties.

The *Guardian*'s decision to launch separate editions for the UK, US and Australia and to make all of them available from their homepage has resulted in a very useful continuing case study in tweaking headlines for different locations. In the US, *Huffington Post* is so widely acknowledged as a centre of expertise in creating (or engineering) strong online headlines that it is definitely worth observing and *analysing* what they do – there is no point in simply copying; try to understand the underlying principles. And in the UK the *Mail Online* has achieved such a level of success that, like or loathe what either print or digital editions do, it cannot be ignored. Again, there is no value in simply copying – especially when you observe the number of times phrases such as '**bikini body**', '**pert derriere**' and '**TINY . . .**' (capitalised and in association with various body parts, usually female) are repeated – but analyse and arrogate.

5 Develop a system

Just as we saw with headlines, decks and overlines in print, so headlines on webpages can form part of a more complex system. The extra elements of the online system are generally a 'teaser' (a short paragraph that performs a similar role to the 'standfirst' of a feature, summarising additional information) and the first paragraph of the story (the intro).

Let's take those population growth headlines again and look at how they are deployed within a Headline + Teaser + Intro system. On its homepage the *Telegraph* combines the headline with a teaser – a brief paragraph that adds more information:

> **UK population jumps 0.7pc to 63.7m between 2011 and 2012, boosted by immigration and accelerating baby boom.**

On the story page the headline and teaser change to:

UK has fastest growing population in Europe

Britain has the fastest growing population in Europe, boosted by immigration and an accelerating baby boom, according to official figures.

The intro (first paragraph) is:

The total population of the UK jumped by 0.7 per cent to 63.7 million between the middle of 2011 and 2012, according to the Office for National Statistics.

The words **population** and **UK** are repeated multiple times in the *Telegraph*'s system, with **EU/Europe** also featuring prominently. The story page teaser adds more trigger words – **immigration** and **baby boom**.

Wales Online uses a similar system but considerably less effectively. The homepage headline is followed by this (which includes an acronym that will mean nothing to readers who do not know that ONS is the Office for National Statistics):

ONS stats reveal baby boom across Britain, raising population at a faster rate than our main EU competitors

On the story page the headline and teaser are the same as the homepage. The intro runs:

The UK population is soaring as London expands and a baby booms roars but Wales remains home to many of the most empty areas of the country, according to new findings.

Thus **population** still features prominently and **baby boom** makes an appearance but the opportunity to ring subtle changes and reinforce the number and context of key words is lost.

Some publications make a conscious effort to run these three elements together into a continuous narrative online, whereas they would usually be treated as separate but related components in print. So, for example, the *Mail Online* of 8/8/13 ran the following on its homepage:

Huge data blunder by the Serious Fraud Office sees 32,000 pages of evidence in BAE Systems bribery case released by mistake

The blunder is major embarrassment for SFO director David Green (pictured) and relates to the huge investigation into BAE contracts in Saudi Arabia, Czech Republic, Romania and South Africa.

The first clause is the headline, the second the teaser but there is no clear narrative separation. On the story page, the same headline is used, followed by online bullet-point equivalent of decks:

- **Documents, tapes and data files from 58 sources sent to wrong owner**
- **Serious Fraud Office insists national security was not threatened**
- **Labour condemn 'government incompetence of the first magnitude'**

And a first paragraph that reads:

> The Serious Fraud Office has lost thousands of pages of confidential evidence obtained during its high profile probe into defence giant BAE Systems.

All the elements of a system such as this give the subeditor or production journalist more opportunities to include searchable words or terms, and although there will be a template for every page, there are not the same pressures on space as those imposed by the spatially finite paper of a printed publication. Finally, let's have a look at the *BBC News* online system. The *BBC* was a pioneer of online news and has put a lot of effort into developing its delivery system; for many people it became the leading example of how to do online well. We will use the population story as an example and start with the homepage headline + teaser + decks:

Most UK births since 1972, says ONS

More babies were born in the UK in 2011–12 than in any year since 1972, contributing to the highest population growth in the EU, official figures show.

One and a half born every minute
Scottish population at record high
ONS: No internet in 17% of homes
Net migration 'down by a third'

And on the story page, headline + teaser + intro:

More UK births than any year since 1972, says ONS

More babies were born in the UK in 2011–12 than any year since 1972, the Office for National Statistics says.

In all, 813,200 UK births were recorded in the year, said the ONS, contributing to population growth that was, in absolute terms, the highest in the EU.

As with the *Guardian*, *HuffPo* and *Mail Online*, the *BBC News* online site repays careful study; even when stories retain the same headlines and other page furniture on different pages (for example, on Home and World), there are changes to the placement on the page and in the amount of page furniture on display. For example, on 9/8/13 it was possible to see a story about Oprah Winfrey on several pages:

- a homepage video clip labelled **Oprah tells of 'racism' in Zurich** led to a page headlined **Oprah Winfrey 'was victim of racism' in Switzerland**;
- a homepage single line heading **Oprah shop snub a 'misunderstanding'** led to the same video-enhanced page, the teaser for which ran **The owner of a shop in Zurich where US talk show host Oprah Winfrey says she encountered racism has called the incident a 'misunderstanding'**;
- the World page used the 'misunderstanding' headline as above, along with the same teaser, then used the line **Oprah 'suffers racism' in Zurich** (perhaps best described as a link-deck) to link to the same story;
- under that was another link (**Oprah tells of 'racism' in Zurich**), leading to the same page.

One way or another, that's a lot of opportunities to find **Oprah, racism** and **Zurich.**

6 Try more directive language

If all else fails you could follow the example of Dustin Curtis, who experimented with sign-off lines for his Twitter account and found that giving people a forceful instruction rather than a polite suggestion achieved better results, in the sense of gaining more followers. Moving from **I'm on Twitter** to **You should follow me on Twitter here** (with the final word being a link, which runs against the usual advice about usability) increased the click through rate from 4.7 per cent to 12.81 per cent. You should read about his work *here*: http://bit.ly/dustincurtis.

Two final cautions

1 Be extra careful about word/phrase choice online

Chris Elliott, the *Guardian* readers' editor, wrote a very thoughtful piece about how much easier it is to misunderstand headlines online, when they are not seen in the context of a complete page that may include pictures, captions and extra explanatory page furniture. The headline that inspired his thoughts related to *Channel Four* cancelling a documentary about the origins of Islam and the ill-informed comments that followed (from people who had clearly not even read the article). Part of Elliott's piece reads, 'on the web, the headline is often all people see, for example on a search engine or on Twitter. In a world of increasing aggregation, it is disaggregation that often threatens meaning.'

You should read the rest of it *here*: (http://bit.ly/elliottheads)

2 Do not over-egg the online pudding

We saw earlier with *BBC News* online's **Heatwave: 100 people in Wales could have died so far, according to study** the danger of exaggerating. Some scholars of the media would classify this kind of headline as 'clickbait' (a temptingly worded link that does not deliver on its promise); Finn Bruton of New York University might go as far as to call it spam, judging by the definitions in his book *Spam: A Shadow History of the Internet*.[3] So if you don't want to be categorised as a spammer, make sure that your headlines always fall on the right side of the line between enticement and empty promises.

News headline exercises

1   Cut the headlines out of the news pages of a newspaper and write new ones. This only works if you don't cheat, so it might be better to get someone else to do the cutting. Using the advice in this chapter, read the stories, decide the main news points and create your own headlines. Compare your results with the originals and analyse the differences.

2   Refine the first exercise by adding a given number of decks for your headlines, remembering that each must add something new.

3   If the story has a significant picture attached to it, also add an over-line.

4   Refine the exercise further by getting the person who cut the headlines out to note the number of characters on each line of the headline, so you might end up with something such as 'Three lines, a maximum of 20 characters on each line'. Then you have to tailor your headline to fit.

5   Now do the same using words of no more than four (or five, or three – you could decide or throw dice) letters.

6   Rewrite the *Guardian*'s online UK edition headlines for readers in the USA – don't cheat by looking at this edition. When you have finished, compare your results with what appears in the overseas edition.

7   Repeat the exercise for Australia. (And if the *Guardian* develops new overseas editions, perhaps for India, or other newspapers follow suit you can expand this exercise accordingly.)

8   Find a news story that has repercussions for England, Wales and Scotland. Write headlines for each polity and compare with newspapers from those countries – e.g. *Telegraph, Wales Online, Scotsman*.

9   Find a current heavyweight news story, and write a linkbait headline for it. Compare your work with what is trending on Twitter, then put your headline into a search engine and see what comes up.

10   Now do the opposite – check what is trending on Twitter, find a current news story that has some relevance to a highly ranked term and write a linkbait headline for it. Try the search engine test again.

NB: Exercises 9 and 10 are intended to help find the line between what is an acceptable build-up of interest and what is exploitative spam.

Notes

1   The use of quote marks in this headline has already been discussed; also note also the use of the colon.
2   Military slang that stands for Situation Normal: All Fucked Up. Its origins are not clear but the word is generally held to be from WW2. It has since been given a more general meaning of running into a big and unforeseen problem or mistake – as Romney did.
3   Finn Bruton (2013), *Spam: A Shadow History of the Internet*. Boston, MA: MIT Press.

6

How to write great feature headlines

Sometimes a headline is so *right* it makes you want to hug yourself. This may sound odd but anyone who has spent any part of their working life attempting to craft the right words at the top of a feature will recognise the feeling. Thus it was on Friday 25 October 2013 when *Metro* ran a picture feature on pages 20 and 21. The photographs showed a bald eagle with a fish in its talons flying over a lake; so far, so unexceptional. But perched on the eagle's head was a much smaller kingbird, pecking away at the big bird's bonce, protecting its nesting area. The headline was **How to mock a killing bird**.

Explaining why that works so well will destroy the enjoyment, but here goes. First, it's apposite – the small bird looks as though it is mocking the eagle, which is undoubtedly a killing bird. Second it was clearly and obviously inspired by a twentieth-century classic of American literature, Harper Lee's *To Kill a Mockingbird*. Using cultural references in feature headlines is a common device, as we shall see, but it is less usual to achieve this depth of connotation, for not only is the title of the book an excellent starting point for the words used, the theme of the book – the importance of justice for all – could be applied to the situation captured in the photographs: the small guy asserting his right to protect his brood against a much larger potential aggressor.

Finally, the word **How** that introduces the headline serves a triple purpose. It makes the headline 1) fit the overall space available, 2) yoke the two pages together so that the layout becomes a true double page spread rather than two single pages and 3) situates the feature in a well-known type of feature, the *how-to* – a guide to improving performance.

The paragraphs above may seem an overly complex analysis of six words that someone put together, probably in a hurry, to head up a photo-feature but the feature headline does a very different job to the news headline. The job of a news headline, as we have seen in Chapter 4, is simple – it must give key information that markets the story.[1] Like all simple actions it is difficult to achieve without practised effort and like all restricted tasks it requires regulated creativity to maximise its potential. News headlines are likely to be given a standardised typographical treatment – a considerable amount of Harold Evans's 1974 book on the subject is given over to the best type to use for impact and clarity – within a predictable layout: everyone knows what typical news pages look like and they look like that because they have been found to work well. But even Evans, a news man through and through, recognises that the feature headline performs a different role. He explains it thus: 'the aim is not to give immediate information but to explore, discuss or relate a rich narrative whose ideas are too complex and diffuse to be done justice by a hard news headline focused on a single key point' (1974: 25).

This is a useful starting point that takes us some way towards a definition, but it overlooks several key elements. The feature headline works as part of a *system* of page furniture intended to guide the reader around the publication and the production journalist can draw on a navigational repertoire that includes:

- the headline itself
- a sell or standfirst
- pull quotes (also known as blown quotes and call outs)
- captions
- subheads
- crossheads
- box-outs.

In addition, feature headlines, particularly outside the confines of a newspaper's pages, are open to all sorts of visual and typographic treatments. This is truer for magazines, and particularly print magazines, but as newspapers become ever closer to the condition of a magazine (Brett and Holmes, 2008: 199[2]; Holmes and Nice, 2012: 2[3]; Leslie, 2013: 8[4]) and as the typefaces available to digital magazine apps become richer so treatments change across all platforms, making a broad knowledge of the possibilities necessary.

The system of page furniture consists of those interlocking, complementary but separate elements suggested above. However, the system is not merely a set of textual compositions, it is a set of signifiers that provides a combination of immediate practical guidance – telling readers what the content is about – and implied cultural reference – providing reassurance that the reader is in the right place and among friends or like-minded companions. Thus the page furniture will contribute to:

- navigation around the curatum;
- creation of identity (for the curatum);
- reflection of identity (of the individual reader);
- community consciousness.

This seems like a heavy burden for such slight components but words are powerful agents for both information and culture and it is our privilege as journalists to work with them.

Now, before we can proceed to look at how to create great feature headlines there is a fundamental question to be answered: what is a feature? It is important that we find, or at least move towards, an answer because unless we understand what it is we are trying to serve, we will not be able to serve it properly.

The traditional newspaper definition of a feature is, basically, anything that is not a hard news report: crosswords, competitions, columns and cartoons are all feature material to a newspaper – as well as those longer pieces of writing that do more than give an account of the latest happening by explaining background, context and consequences. Features of the latter sort have long been a staple for magazines, usually illustrated with specially commissioned photographs or artwork. This description also holds true for many features published online.

A feature is very often a long and detailed piece of writing that aims to explore, amplify and explain a particular issue, opinion, experience or idea; digging deeper to explore the why and the how of an event or trend while adding human interest elements to a story. Features are intended to entertain and inform the reader; they may employ some techniques of the short story or use a conversational tone to present the reader with information to evoke an emotional response. Typically, they are extensively researched, descriptive, colourful, thoughtful and reflective writing about original ideas and, unlike news stories that simply provide the facts, features are intended to serve readers with the writer's interpretation of a story.

Descriptions similar to the above, attempting to define what distinguishes a feature from news, can be found everywhere. They are standard tropes of the how-to-write-a-feature guides aimed at would-be journalists and they are, within their self-limited boundaries, quite right. Tony Rogers, journalist and educator, is a little bit less prescriptive in his online guide: 'Feature stories aren't defined so much by subject matter as they are by the style in which they are written. In other words, anything written in a feature-oriented way is a feature story' (http://bit.ly/featurestyle)

The thing is, he is closer than most because a feature does not have to be a long series of words comprising a traditional narrative, nor a series of short narratives linked by a common theme, nor even a narrative at all in the conventional sense. There may be very few words and a lot of images; there may be a single image that is capable of complex interpretation. In short, the feature is not a thing that can be given a straightforward definition. I have discussed what constitutes a feature in chapter 4 of *The 21st Century Journalism Handbook* (Holmes *et al.* 2013) and there is no need to do more than recap here – 'a feature is whatever a creative mind, or set of minds, decides it is' (op. cit.: 88). There are, however, practical limitations on how far this idea can be taken in the context of any given curatum, limitations derived from a matrix of consumption that includes the expectations of the audience, technical boundaries to presentation and budgetary considerations. The point is that subeditors and production journalists have to be nimble enough to cope with and cater for this variety of forms and formats. Features are written and published for a variety of purposes, everything from straightahead guidance to writing bug free computer code through retrospective analysis of punk albums to thoughts on upcycling vintage fabric, and there is no one-size-fits-all solution to creating great headlines for them.

However, we can establish three basic principles to act as initial guidelines. A feature headline should:

- inform the reader of the likely subject – information that can be provided in an oblique or straightforward way;
- intrigue as to what the angle is – which is where an oblique approach might be advantageous;
- invest the subject with as much interest as possible – drawing on appropriate cultural archetypes for the audience and purpose.

The principles above may be basic but they are not necessarily simple. Information about the subject matter may be imparted in a very elliptical or cryptic manner, the angle may be disguised rather than exposed and the interesting elements could be hinted at rather than shouted about . . . or not, depending on what the readers of that particular curatum prefer – the *Economist*, the *People's Friend* and *Fantastic Man* will all use different vocabularies, tones of voice and writing styles because they have very different readerships with very different expectations, as do the *Daily Mail* and *Guardian*. Although our major concern in this chapter is features rather than magazines per se, the immense variety of verbal dexterity required by magazines is both a challenge to and a reward for the production journalist. Therefore, as well as the realisation that a feature is a polyvalent artefact, it is vital to have a clear understanding of the hopes and fears, aspirations and inclinations of the reader community you are serving.

The platform of dissemination may also affect the choice and format of words – print and digital publications (or those versions of a publication) operate within different matrices of consumption. They are generally discovered in different ways and consumed in different circumstances. Print magazines and newspapers still rely mainly on newsstand sales, so the front covers and splash headlines play a vitally important role in attracting initial interest; newspaper readers generally know the paper they want and stick with it and although magazines have many loyal readers, they also rely on attracting passing trade. Potential readers of a magazine will often pick an issue up to flick through and this is when headlines (as part of the whole feature treatment) can become make-or-break elements in the decision to purchase.

Systematising headlines

Creative writing in all its forms, including production journalism, is somehow supposed to come naturally, a flash of genius from the muse of subeditors – but as the saying credited to Thomas Edison has it, 'Genius is one per cent inspiration, ninety-nine per cent perspiration'. One way to reduce the undesirable side effects of perspiration (in this case, staring at a blank screen or reorganising your pencils to match the colours of the rainbow) is to have a system that can help guide the creative Paracelete to descend in flames of celestial fire.

Note: the headlines quoted below are taken from a wide range of magazines but have been selected as typical of their type and not been saved over the years as outstanding examples in their category. This is a deliberate policy as all page furniture has to be representative of the curatum all the time; there will be issues that seem particularly good or leave the production journalist particularly satisfied but the effort has to be made for each headline, for all captions, in every issue. The use of upper and lower case in headlines has also been reproduced from the originals to demonstrate the variety of usage. *The sampling is not scientific but aims to reproduce the chance factor of buying and reading a magazine.*

1 Types of feature headline

Feature headlines can be divided into several general types:

- Straightforward
- Guiding
- Numerate
- Questioning
- Aspirational
- Quote
- Culturally referential.

Picking which is (or are) most appropriate will depend on the subject matter and angle of the content, along with the general tone of the curatum. The taxonomy is explained below, along with examples from a variety of titles.

Straightforward

The Straightforward headline is, depending on your mood, (i) the most obvious label possible, (ii) what you come up with when imagination (and perhaps time) has expired or (iii) a cleverly themed element of the content. Its main advantages are universal applicability – there is practically no curatum for which it will not be appropriate – and online searchability. Its main drawback can be obvious dullness, but depending on the subject matter it can also be very intriguing: **the pope's astronomer** (*oh comely*, Sept/Oct 2013: 58) is as bald a description as you could wish for, but who wouldn't want to read the feature? On the other hand, **SURFBOARD DESIGN** (*Get Into Surfing*, June 2013: 64) is functional but appropriate for the target audience of beginners, while **Some Cornish**

Heroes (*The People's Friend*, 31 August 2013: 7) is positively take-it-or-leave-it.

Straightforward-thematic

The September 2013 issue of *Esquire* (UK) featured an unmissable picture of Kate Moss on the cover, with a big, fluorescent coverline **KATE MOSS ROCKS** just in case the point had not been made clear enough. A much smaller, spindlier type, however, declared this to be a **Special Issue: Made in Britain**. The bulk of feature material was just that, a celebration of the very best the UK had to offer: Kate Moss, it seems, was part of that – **THE GIRL Kate Moss/Made in Croydon**. She was, though, given a bit of a headline (**IN THE FLESH**) unlike most of the other British-made items which were introduced in the most straightforward way possible: **THE CUSTOM KITCHEN KNIFE; THE TIMEKEEPER; THE NATIONAL DISH; THE RAINCOAT** and so on.

Straightforward name-you-should-know

Sometimes a Straightforward headline need be nothing more than a name – especially if it's in a hipster magazine that assumes its readers (i) will recognise the name or (ii) will not be so gauche or unhipsterish as to admit not knowing the name (and anyway, once they have read the piece they will be better informed). Thus *Dazed & Confused*'s September 2013 issue contains multiple names-as-headlines, from **EIJIRO MIYAMA** (p. 78) through **CLAIRE STOREY** (102) to **FRED HERZOG** (224).

Guiding

You could argue that the sub-category immediately above is also a Guiding headline (directing readers to people they should recognise) but a more common type would be something like this example from *Elle Decoration* (September 2013: 106) – **THE TEN KEY TRENDS**. It offers readers a simplified route through the multiplicity of design modes, the selected styles being approved by 'The world's leading homes magazine'. Magazines offer a lot of guidance to their readers, whatever the subject matter, one of their recognised functions being that of a mentor and source of expertise. This has been the case throughout the magazine's history, whether print or digital – the idea of community interaction around particular titles began well before the world wide web and social media (for more on this see Holmes and Nice 2012, especially chapters 1 and 7). It stands to reason, therefore, that a lot of headlines (and cover-lines) will be of this type.

The Guiding category can also be applied to regular features such as *Uncut*'s **ALBUM BY ALBUM** series, each of which is a review/appreciation/analysis of a particular band or artist's recorded output (e.g. **Smashing Pumpkins**, October 2013: 52–4). Of course headlining a series of this kind is also Straightforward but there is a large element of guidance in the content inasmuch as the magazine, and its extremely knowledgeable staff, are making their expertise and access available to the averagely knowledgeable reader (in the same magazine see also **THE MAKING OF . . . I Feel Like I'm Fixin'-To-Die Rag**: 42–4).

What could be more guiding than an actual guide – **MAZDA RX-8 BUYING GUIDE**, for example? (*Japanese Performance*, November 2013: 86). Specialist hobby, craft or making-and-doing magazines contain numerous 'how-to' features that take readers through a process stage by stage and step by step. Sometimes they are very clearly labelled as a how-to by including those words in the headline – **HOW TO BUY . . . BRITISH INSTRUMENTAL GUITAR RECORDS**, *Uncut* October 2013: 87; **How to make a messenger bag out of trash** (*Cooler* April/May 2009: 54; **HOW TO BUY A BIG NAKED** (*Ride* August 2013: 60).

This category of headline may also be 'disguised' with a more thoughtful composition that can overlap with other categories: **3 STAGES OF Papermaking** (*Pretty Nostalgic* Jan/Feb 2013: 26) contains a number but it is very definitely a guide. Similarly, **VERSATILITY keeps fish coming** (*Angler's Mail* 17 September 2013: 30) is a four page 'master class in *how to* change your tactics to keep bites coming all day long' (loc. cit.; added emphasis). A great example of the disguised how-to was used in the second issue of *Urban Cyclist* (Winter 2012), where a beautifully photographed piece about wheel building was given the headline **FEELING THE TENSION** (76). This is particularly appropriate as one of the key skills of wheel building is being able to judge the tension of individual spokes, plus it can be a nerve-racking exercise for amateurs. The feature itself could be described as an 'augmented how-to' as it is also a profile of how Matt Gibbons, an 'artisan wheel builder', works.

From time to time magazines will run complete How-to sections that allow them to cram in a mass of short-form content; this allows the publication to offer snackable items and increase reader perceptions of value.

Wired's December 2012 issue contains eight pages (119–26) of How-to tips, from solving a Rubik's Cube quickly to building a fusion reactor. As far as headlining goes, the opening page of the section is clearly labelled **how to** (echoing the contents page) and all the material that follows can be given a straightforward label (e.g. **make a kitchen garden**). *Bloomberg Businessweek* (15 April 2013) follows the same general format but expands it to 37 pages (59–95) and adds big name credits that demonstrate the title's access to powerful or expert figures. The opening page introduces the 'third How To issue', establishing How To as a standing prefix, followed on the next page by **Run Your Company Like An Improv Group** – Dick Costolo's advice about getting crazy visionaries and straight-thinking business types to work together. Costolo is CEO of Twitter and he is joined by the likes of Caterina Fake (co-founder of Flickr – **Modify Your Sleep Schedule For Maximum Efficiency**), T. Boone Pickens (CEO of BP Capital hedge fund, **Convert the Country to Natural Gas**), Paul Krugman (Nobel Prize-winning economist, **Beat a Dead Horse** – a metaphor for finding ways to deliver the same message repeatedly), Felix Baumgartner (the man who jumped out of a balloon 24 miles above the earth, **Overcome Fear**) and Hilary Mason (chief scientist at Bitly), **Make Complicated Things Simple (With Kittens)**.

Production journalists working on sections like these must remember that the How-to standing prefix removes the need to repeat those two words but it is still essential to find something appropriate, informative, amusing, creative (ideally a combination of at least two of those characteristics) to act as a standalone headline for each item.

Sometimes it is difficult to fix on an appropriate category for a headline – is **Exploring "Heartbeat" Country** (*The People's Friend*, 31 Aug 2013: 8) Straightforward or Guiding? On the one hand it's a pretty bald statement of fact – the author writes about his travels around Goathland in the North Yorkshire Moors, where popular TV series *Heartbeat* was filmed – but on the other it's a guide to the area for others who want to follow in his footsteps (quite literally as his sign off sentence is 'Just remember to bring your walking boots!'). As we shall see elsewhere, page furniture in *The People's Friend* can tend to be on the curt, not to mention blunt, side.

Numerate

Numerate headlines are, unsurprisingly, those that use numbers – but as any mathematician will tell you numbers are not neutral and can be used for many purposes. There is a massive current trend to use numerate headlines to promote listicle[5]-style features (check buzzfeed.com for any number of examples . . . or, indeed, most newspapers), in which the number appears to perform the same function as the well-established style of coverline on women's magazines: compare **15 Revolting Hangover Cures From History** (*BuzzFeed* 1/1/14; http://bit.ly/buzzcure) with **2000 WOMEN on the SEX questions we ALL want answered** (*Glamour*, September 2013: 1). In fact, although the promotional concept of using numbers as a draw is common to both, the thinking behind them is diametrically opposed – *BuzzFeed* wants to attract people by promising a manageable (i.e. short) investment of time and attention, whereas *Glamour* is emphasising the thoroughness of the research that underpins its feature (which is actually in a very easy to read photo-and-short-quote format).

There is, however, another Numerate headline in the same issue of *Glamour* that has a very different impact: **One in four WOMEN suffers from DOMESTIC ABUSE . . .** (98). This is the use of numbers as shock – there is no sensationalisation beyond the bare use of a disquieting statistic.

Numerate headlines are frequently, almost inevitably, found in curata that deal with technical subject matter such as computers, phones, motorcycles and cars – **Alfa 4C THE GOOD TIMES ARE BACK** was used in *Car* (September 13 2013: 90) to head a road test of Alfa Romeo's new sports car. A much more interesting example could be found a few pages earlier (84), where a profile of Formula 1 racing driver Mark Webber had a main headline **WASN'T BAD FOR A NO.2** preceded by a strapline that listed his achievements: **WINS 9/PODIUMS 37/ POLE POSITIONS 11/FASTEST LAPS 16**. It makes sense for readers with a passing interest in the racing scene (Webber had long been regarded as subordinate to Sebastian Vettel in the Red Bull team) but those with more knowledge will appreciate the reference to Webber's radio message to his team boss immediately after winning the Silverstone grand prix in 2010: 'Not bad for a number two driver.' (For a good background to this see http://bit.ly/webber2.)

Questioning

Will you be RICH or BROKE in 10 years? asks *Glamour* (Sept 2013: 95) in a headline that contains both a question and a number. It heads up a six question quiz about personal finance that leads into guidance about how to make sure the prognosis is rich, or at least not broke.

This category can also be used to introduce portmanteau or composite features (see Holmes *et al.* 2013: 111), as the *Economist*'s impressive lifestyle offshoot *Intelligent Life* did in its May/June 2013 issue. **What's the best philosophy?** (37) acted as an introduction to and umbrella for six short pieces about different philosophers or philosophical concepts by writers such as Colin Blakemore and Susie Orbach – snackable content that demonstrated good access to big name thinkers.

Psychologies (January 2014) worked a variation on this when it gave the regular Dossier section over to the meta-question **2013: How was it for you?**. What followed the opening spread (28–9) were six question-themed features that ranged from **WHAT CAN YOU LEARN FROM LOOKING BACK?** through **WHAT MANTRA SUSTAINED YOU THIS YEAR?** to **WHAT ARE YOU MOST PROUD OF ACHIEVING THIS YEAR?**, followed by a quiz to discover **WHAT'S YOUR REAL MOTIVATION?**. Repetition like this will only work in a planned section, but given that *Psychologies* is all about living an examined life it is apt here.

Questioning headlines often tap in to subject matter that has already engendered a degree of interest, scepticism or curiosity, so in a sense they just push an already open door slightly further ajar. *Bloomberg Businessweek* did exactly this with **Can Foursquare Check-In To Adulthood?** (15 April 2013: 31) above a feature analysing the location-based social media app's chance of ever making a profit – after a blazing introduction in 2009 that saw it compared with Twitter, Foursquare had slipped out of many people's consciousness, and certainly out of their social media habits, just four years later.

The *Economist*, which has a similar mission to *Bloomberg Businessweek*, also uses the Question to good effect in a piece considering whether Slovenia will require a Euro-Zone financial bail-out headed **The next domino?** (13 April 2013: 38).

At a different end of the magazine seriousness scale, Questions are a useful form for celebrity headlines – who does not what to know **WHAT THE HELL IS GOING ON WITH JESY & GEORGE?** (*Heat*, 31 August 2013: 21); **How old is too old, Harry?** (op. cit.: 29); **What were you thinking?** (34); **Say what?** (114). Note though that as with news headlines, the question mark can act as a distancing device – can a documentary about One Direction really be the **BEST MOVIE EVER?** (79). No, not even in *Heat* world.

Aspirational

Aspiration has a lot of different meanings. As a noun it can encompass desire and yearning, ambition and expectation. Dreams of a job that brings wealth and riches are a form of aspiration, as is a yearning to give up the rat race and live off the land. Aspiration in a feature may involve either of those extremes but will frequently:

1   offer advice on how to perform a task or undertake a role in the optimal way;
2   describe a desirable state or situation that can, in ways set out in the text, be reproduced;
3   evoke a 'golden age' from history that can be recaptured or re-enacted in the modern world, by certain actions or modes of behaviour described in the text.

As can be appreciated from the descriptions above, there can be a great deal of how-to in aspirational texts, but the trick with Aspirational headlines is to raise them above run-of-the-mill guidance. One way to do this is to use particular words that bring with them appropriate connotations – **PERFECT POP-UPS** (*Get Into Surfing* June 2013: 26), **The Women Of Extraordinary Vision** (*Riposte* Issue 1: 130), **COMFORT & JOY** (*Psychologies* January 2014: 99), **HOT THIS WEEK** (Heat 31 August 2013: 66).

Another way is to draw on cultural concepts that conjure up deeply desirable outcomes, transcendental states of being or golden age periods of history. **Space for reflection** (*easyJet Traveller*, April 2013: 84) makes the gardens of Marrakech sound like the perfect antidote to a busy working life; **Books to soothe your soul** (*Psychologies* January 2014: 57) makes reading sound an extremely cool pastime; **The OPEN Road** (*Pretty Nostalgic* July/August 2013: 64) taps into a desire for freedom, for seeing new places and, especially when the headline is used in conjunction with an evocative photograph of a horse-drawn gipsy caravan, living out *Wind In The Willows*; **THE HEROIC: CAPTURING THE GOLDEN ERA OF CYCLING** (*Urban Cyclist* Winter 2012: 61) makes a vintage cycling event in Italy sound like the opportunity to commune with the pure Corinthian spirit in which all sport should ideally be undertaken.

How many people long to **WAKE UP HAPPY** (*Psychologies* June 2013: 40)? This is just the beginning though because readers of the issue also have an opportunity to **Learn how to savour life** (42), appreciate **The**

good of small things (48, also a cultural allusion to Arundhati Roy's novel), discover **The art of contentment** (51) and take **Five steps to a joyful life**. As noted before, *Psychologies* has a particular mission to help its readers to live more fulfilled lives and Aspirational headlines are an essential element.

As with the How-to specials mentioned above, some magazines devote whole issues to aspirational excellence: *Wallpaper** is one, with its annual Design Awards. The entire magazine is given over to 'people, places and products that have lifted our spirits' (February 2012: 26). The tone is set at the start of the main editorial with a page headed **DESIGN AWARDS**, the first category being **BEST LAUNCH** (31). The 'Best + category' is followed almost without exception, but **Greenest cuisine** on page 71 makes a necessary distinction between food made specifically from sustainably sourced vegetables and food in general. There are a few more points of difference towards the back of the book when the distinguished panel of judges give their results – Jean-Paul Goude opts for a **Life-enhancer of the year** (138 – a lookout point on the Ruta del Peregrino, Mexico, by HHF Architects, since you ask).

Quote

Not everyone agrees with the idea of using a quote in a headline or to start a feature but the briefest examination of current magazines shows it to be not just commonly accepted practice but a very popular headline device, whatever the guardians of journalistic purity may say. Not only is it popular, it also comes in several variations or sub-categories.

Using a quote as a headline allows you to:

- introduce the idea of the feature very quickly;
- establish the degree of access available to the curatum (a quality that may or may not be based on truth);
- establish a timely frame of reference;
- play with the idea of using a quote;
- introduce new angles into a composite feature or section;
- start with a bang – **"I left the city to be a Maasai warrior"** certainly gets *Glamour*'s first person tale of metamorphosis from investment banker in Chicago to first female warrior inducted into the Maasai tribe off to a great start (September 2013: 85). As a quote it has the great advantage of being a self-contained statement; it does not

rely on context or background to be understood fully, which is the problem with many quotes and the reason why they are often frowned on for this kind of structural use.

Uncut uses a one–two of quote headline followed by quote intro for the long interview with the remaining members of The Clash in its October 2013 issue (30). **'THE CLASH LIVE ON!'** is the opener, followed by "'Being in The Clash," says Mick Jones, "was a defining moment in our lives, and I'd be lying if I said I'd gotten over it.'" Not a bad way to start what is essentially a puff piece for the band's recently released curated boxset, but editor Allan Jones has paid enough dues to get proper access on a personal level and the interview that follows lives up to its billing. Note the use of single quotes for the headline and double for the intro, perhaps because the headline is actually an amended version of what Mick Jones actually said, which was 'So The Clash and what we did lives on, you know?' (34).

Amending quotes in this way is quite common in page furniture – it is done frequently in call outs (see Chapter 7) – but obviously the intent and underlying meaning must be respected. It seems unlikely that Mick Jones would complain that his words had been distorted or taken out of context in the instance above, and even if Frances Phillips never uttered the actual words **I set up an erotic toy boutique** they make a great headline for her first person piece about, well, what do you think it's about? Again, there's no room for doubt about the subject matter with this *pseudo-quote* headline from *Oh Comely* (Sep/Oct 2013: 37; this piece also has a great sell, or standfirst, as we will see later).

Similar to the *pseudo-quote*, but taking fabrication one step further, is the *fake quote* which not only sets the scene but can also establish the level and quality of access claimed by the curatum. *Uncut* has great access because its writers have solid track records as music journalists; *heat* sometimes has great access (even if much of that access is restricted by prior agreements with PRs and sight-of-copy/approval-of-photos contracts) and even when it doesn't, it can imply access by using a *fake quote*. Provided the fakery can be taken as complimentary, or at least is not derogatory to the celebrity in question, and provided there is a distancing device employed, the magazine can get away with it. Thus on page 24 of the 31 August 2013 issue a paparazzo photograph of Kate Moss on holiday in Formentera, showing her taking a snap of an old geezer with nothing but a towel to protect his modesty (very badly), is headlined

Kate: "Work it, baby. Make love to the camera." The text that follows employs an obvious distancing device: 'We *imagine* that for someone who's made a living from being prodded and cajoled by photographers, it could be quite tempting to turn the tables [. . .]' (emphasis added). This headline device is repeated five pages later, where a photograph of chef Gordon Ramsay apparently plundering a rubbish bin is headed Gordon: **"Mmm, binoffee pie."** In the following text the distancing device of choice is an imagined thought: 'Mmm,' thought Gordon as he rifled through the bin [. . .].'
SERIOUS NOTE: It is important to emphasise that no journalist should ever make up a quote under any circumstances whatsoever. However, *heat* is not the only magazine to use this device and it is possible you may be put in the position of having to come up with something similar during your career. If so, be very careful about the way you approach it and always run it past someone more senior.

A genuine celebrity quote not only demonstrates access, it can also emphasise timeliness (an essential characteristic of journalism). *The Big Issue* regularly gets good access to stars who want to align themselves with its principles and mission (or want to be seen to do so) and they hit a double jackpot with Sophie Ellis-Bextor and Leona Lewis in the Christmas Edition 2013. Ellis-Bextor is a musical star in her own right, was also doing very well in the Saturday night television hit *Strictly Come Dancing* and the headline quote brings together festive season and TV exposure: **'I HAVEN'T DONE MY CHRISTMAS SHOPPING BECAUSE OF STRICTLY'** (13). A few pages later Leona Lewis (singing star and graduate of television hit *X-Factor*) is confessing **'I'M A CRAZY CHRISTMAS LADY'** (28–9).

Psychologies is another magazine that gets good access to (mainly female) celebrities and often uses quotes to headline interviews with them. The magazine also uses quote headlines in a more structural way, and the Dossier section in the August 2013 issue provides a good example (40–57). The subject is **FINDING SPACE** and the topic is illustrated with a series of features and profiles looking at the different ways in which people have found space in the ways and places they live. The overall piece works like a portmanteau or composite feature, with the separate contributions brought together under the umbrella heading. It is important that the quotes selected for headlines are accessible, comprehensible and contain words that will trigger an emotional or cultural response – see if you can get the gist of the pieces:

"It's not how I expected family life to be but we're seeing the benefits" (42: communal living)

"We wanted a deep connection with an inter-generational community" (44: private housing combined with communal facilities and offices)

"We appreciate that we help bring life back into the house" (46: homesharing with an older person)

"In Paris I am free" (48: pretty self-evident)

"They invade your space, your being, in every way" (50: a former political prisoner)

"One of the most beautiful things is how humbling it is" (51: Everest mountaineer)

Culturally referential

This is an extremely popular headline category and will often be the first thing reached for by a production editor keen to show off his or her grasp of the English language, educational background or general knowledge. It can be subdivided into several genres with references derived from high and low culture, plays, poetry, idiomatic sayings, films, music and even popular consumer products. There should be a clear connection with the subject matter and angle of the feature and the best examples will also set up connotative echoes (see below) that add richness to the text as a whole.

Take the headline **AFTER EIGHTS** from *Japanese Performance* (November 2013: 39) – it sits on a double page spread showing a silver car in a workshop with no immediate visual connection to the popular brand of wafer-thin after dinner mint chocolates (which are actually called After Eight). But to anyone familiar with the visual tropes of car racing, the look of the car (small front wheels, big rear wheels, wheelie bars, massive turbocharger cover sticking out of the bonnet) shouts drag racing. How does drag racing work? Cars launch themselves down a short track hoping to achieve the lowest possible elapsed time, which is measured in seconds. A Top Fuel drag racer, the elite of the sport, may take only four seconds to cover a quarter-mile track; a car such as the one pictured will be doing well to achieve under nine seconds – hence the team behind it are *after* (pursuing) *eights* (elapsed times less than nine seconds). In case you don't get it right away, the sell (standfirst) helpfully adds vital details: TAKE ONE 1977 TOYOTA CELICA, STICK A TUNED 100BHP SUPRA ENGINE UNDER THE BONNET AND SEND IT DOWN THE DRAG STRIP. IN UNDER 9 SECONDS IT WILL HAVE REACHED THE END OF THE RUN.

There must be something about cars and confectionery because *Fast Car* goes with **Malt Teaser** for a feature about a tuned car in Malta (January 2014: 20).

An interesting variant on the product association was used by *Cooler*, the extreme sports magazine for women, in its April/May 2009 issue. **Made in China** could hardly be simpler but it heads a feature about Dier Yin, 'the first lady of Chinese snowboarding' (78) and captures not only the kind of sticker encountered on a large proportion of consumer goods but also the fact that Yindi (as she is known) learned and developed boarding skills in her native country before moving into the European competition circuit. It may be stretching associations too far to see a certain consonance between 'made' and 'maid' (which are, of course, homophones).

Successful television programmes are a rich source of inspiration; their names are already widely embedded in popular consciousness and can often be cleverly adapted to new use. **THE ONLY WAY IS SX** (*Fast Car* December 2013: 50) is spot on in every way – SX (the car is a Nissan 180SX) sounds exactly like Essex. The only way it could be more perfect would be if the owner came from the county; sadly for the symmetry of the feature he lives in Northern Ireland. A headline with the same roots but somewhat less successful execution is **The only way is boats** (*easyJet Traveller* April 2013: 98), even if the company being profiled is based in Wallasea Island on the Essex coast. To be fair to the *easyJet Traveller* editorial team, who are usually pretty on the ball with content, these are **advertorial** pages so there may have been external influences at work.

Drama and poetry – or well known slivers of both – are another rich source for headline writers. Shakespeare is full of suitable material (he and the 47 scholars who translated the King James Version bible pretty much invented the quotable quote between them) and most people are able to tap into memories of literature from school or university – given the high proportion of arts graduates in journalism this is not surprising:

- **Green and pleasant** (*Elle Decoration* September 2013: 80) is taken from William Blake's poem *Jerusalem* and heads up a photo feature about 'six of the world's most beautiful outdoor spaces to visit';
- **Mellow fruitfulness** (*Pretty Nostalgic* July/August 2013: 30), a lift from John Keats's *To Autumn*, opens a piece about a natural holistic retreat in Wales called Mellowcroft;
- **Hope springs eternal** (*Uncut* October 2013: 24) is from Alexander Pope's *An Essay On Man* and heads a profile of Mazzy Star, whose singer is Hope Sandoval; it is a good example of a single word connection (Hope) with deeper echoes (there was a 17 year gap between albums);
- **Great Expectations** (*Classics Monthly* Summer 2013: 41) takes its headline straight from the title of Charles Dickens's thirteenth novel, although the feature avoids much of the complexity of that work, being a fairly straightforward account of one man's hopes for the restoration of his Gordon-Keeble sports car;
- **Lord Of The Rims** (*Fast Car* January 2014: 26) is a variant on the literary theme being i) modified (Ring to Rim – but the magazine is all about modifying cars and this feature is all about custom wheels), ii) both a novel by J. R. R. Tolkien and iii) a film by Peter Jackson.

Films, like television shows, also provide rich pickings for the headline magpie, either directly or in a modified form: **THE FAST & THE FRUGAL** (*Classics Monthly* Summer 2013: 9) pays obvious homage to the *Fast & Furious* series of movies starring Vin Diesel, adapting it to suit the feature about different models in the Peugeot 205 range; the same issue also uses **BRAVE HEARTS** (32) to headline an article about a difficult restoration made more difficult by illness, although it wasn't heart disease.

Car magazines seem rather fond of film as a source of headlines and *car* magazine is no exception, although the example here is i) modified to suit, ii) an idiomatic saying and iii) a novel and iv) a film. Their track test of the Lamborghini Gallardo Squadra Corse (the final version of a distinguished model; September 2013: 62) was headed **THE LAST HURRAAARGH**, a title that encapsulates the idiomatic meaning of one final effort at the end of a campaign or career, a modified word that captures the feel of driving such a fast machine and, perhaps, both Edwin O'Connor's best-selling 1956 novel and the 1958 film of it directed by

John Ford and starring Spencer Tracy – the story of an old politician trying, unsuccessfully, for one final election victory.

And, of course, music of all kinds is a well from which headline writers constantly draw, either directly or in an appropriately modified form:

> **DON'T STOP** (*Uncut* October 2013: 18) – no prizes for guessing that the feature was about Fleetwood Mac (the song is a prime cut on their classic *Rumours* album) and their comeback tour. Incidentally the title was also used by a *BBC Four* documentary shown in June 2013;

> Fleetwood Mac made another appearance in *Fast Car*, the headline for a feature about an unusual tuned Volvo being **GO YOUR OWN WAY** (January 2014: 107); this was a good issue for music lovers as *Dream Weaver* – the 1975 hit for Gary Wright (formerly of Spooky Tooth) made famous by its use in the 1992 film *Wayne's World* – was used for a piece about a custom wheel company (69);

> **Krule Summer** (*Dazed & Confused* September 2013) brings together singer/songwriter King Krule and, most obviously, the 1983 Bananarama hit *Cruel Summer*. However, as this is *Dazed & Confused* there may be other influences at work, and *Cruel Summer* could actually refer to a 1998 album by Ace Of Bass, or a 2012 compilation album of artists on the GOOD Music record label, which was founded by Kanye West, or a short film made by West and shown at the 2012 Cannes film festival. The 'summer' element is justified because the singer was interviewed on 'the hottest day of the year';

> **Hearts of Glass** (same issue of D&C: 122) is about a disco-influenced duo by the name of Glass Candy and, most obviously, references the massive 1979 Blondie hit *Heart Of Glass*, which is itself influenced by disco. However, as this is *Dazed & Confused* there may be other influences at work, such as Werner Herzog's 1976 film of the same name, although it has no obvious link to disco;

> **Slaves to the algorithm** is a lovely adaptation by *Intelligent Life* (May/June 2013: 64) of the 1985 Grace Jones album and

single *Slave to the Rhythm*. The feature examines how algorithms (which it defines as 'decision-making' processes increasingly used in digital software) are increasingly used to determine specific outcomes such as Google search results or the route an Underground train takes through the network of tunnels and, perhaps more interestingly, the companies and individuals behind the creation of algorithms.

Finally three unusual examples of cultural reference in headlines:

Rock, Paper, Scissors (*Pretty Nostalgic* Jan/Feb 2013: 83) uses the hand game to introduce a portmanteau feature about four British artists who work with paper;

Burton, tailor (*Intelligent Life* May/June 2013: 51) brings together memories of i) Richard Burton and Elizabeth Taylor, perhaps the most legendary of showbiz couples and ii) Burton Menswear, founded by Sir Montague Burton in 1903, for a profile of clothes designer Sarah Burton, who took over at fashion house Alexander McQueen after its founder committed suicide and designed the dress for Kate Middleton's wedding to Prince William;

The Alexander Technique (*Dazed & Confused* September 2013: 139) references a discipline of posture and skeleto-muscular functioning developed by actor Frederick Mathias Alexander in the 1890s to introduce an interview with Alexander Wang, creative director at fashion atelier Balenciaga.

2 Literary devices available to the headline writer

Literary devices can be defined as structures commonly used in writing. They usually take the form of recognisable constructions in a text and although they are perhaps most commonly associated with poetry or the finely wrought language of Shakespeare's plays they can be and are used in any form of writing, including headlines, standfirsts, captions and other page furniture. Within literature (as normally defined) devices such as metaphor, periphrasis or simile are used to express or heighten artistic meaning through the use of language in a particular way; within page furniture these devices are used to make them more striking or memorable. The most commonly found are:

- alliteration;
- allusion (usually to popular culture);
- assonance;
- figure of speech;
- pun;
- repetition;
- rhyme.

Some of these have been analysed above, notably allusions to cultural productions and figures of speech or idiomatic expressions; of the others the most popular device – based on the results of an unscientific survey of a range of magazines – appears to be alliteration, in which words begin with the same letter or sound group, either consonant or vowel, with the intention of creating a repetition of similar sounds. Alliteration in headlines can be short and simple or longer and more complex; the best examples include a more complex allusion to the subject matter:

Bait Bags & **Supermarket Sweep** (*Angler's Mail* September 17 2013: 40 & 43) – simple alliteration that defines the content;

Carbon Counters (*Focus* October 2008: 70) – a piece about domestic energy monitors;

Magic Mirrors (*Elle Decoration* September 2013: 86) – six pages of unusual-looking glasses;

Static Shock (*Fast Car* December 2013: 38) – a particular kind of shock absorber allows much lower wheel heights;

FastFood (*Urban Cyclist* Winter 2012: 69) – the feature is about a bicycle race that ends at a fish and chip shop;

Party Politics (*Dazed & Confused* September 2013: 154) – a profile of the mayor of Reykjavik, who has a very playful approach to his role;

My week as a STREET STYLE STAR (*Glamour* September 2013: 74) – staff scribe swathes self as seven style celebs.

All of the above examples are not just alliteration but also consonance, because the repeating sounds are derived from the initial consonant letters of the words. The opposite of consonance is assonance – also a form of repetition but applies when only vowel sounds are used:

THE MAN WITH A 20-YEAR PLAN (*Intelligent Life* May/ June 2013: 72;

All White on the Night and **Fun in Funchal** (*easyJet Traveller* September 2011: 22 and 24).

We have already looked at puns in newspaper headlines, particularly for sports stories. The pun, a form of wordplay that uses one word or phrase to suggest another and thus open up new meanings, is traditionally dismissed as the lowest form of wit, but coming up with a good one that works well as a headline is much more difficult than it looks. Shakespeare was not above punning as even the briefest skim through his plays will show; even Hamlet, the gloomy Dane, allows himself a pun or two in the graveyard scene:

Hamlet: Whose grave is this, sirrah?
Gravedigger: Mine, sir.
Hamlet: I think it be thine, indeed; for thou liest in't.
Gravedigger: You lie out on't, sir, and therefore it is not yours: for my part, I do not lie in't, and yet it is mine.
Hamlet: Thou dost lie in't, to be in't and say it is thine: 'tis for the dead, not for the quick; therefore thou liest.

Puns often rely on homophones (words that sound very similar) for their effect – John Pollack, one of president Bill Clinton's speechwriters, believes punning played a crucial role in the rise of civilisation and entitled his book defending the device *The Pun Also Rises* (http://bit.ly/ punrise). David Marsh, the *Guardian*'s style guardian quotes Jonathan Swift in defence of the pun: 'Punning is a talent which no man affects to despise, but he that is without it' (Marsh 2013: 251).

Both alliteration and assonance rely on repetition for their effects, but repetition of sounds rather than complete words. There are various forms of repetition (see http://bit.ly/litrep for definitions); a personal favourite literary example comes from the first three lines of T. S. Eliot's 1930 poem *Ash Wednesday*:

> Because I do not hope to turn again
> Because I do not hope
> Because I do not hope to turn [. . .]

However, pure repetition was the least used device in my survey of magazines to hand. In fact, I could only find one instance and that perhaps a partial repetition – **The oddest of oddballs** (*Intelligent Life* May/June 2013: 46) headlining a piece by Jonathan Meades about the Jowett Javelin car.

Rhyme was more popular, but even here a strong argument could be made that there is a great deal of overlap between rhyme and assonance in these examples:

> **Scene Queen** (*Fast Car* December 2013: 18);
>
> **Boys Toys** (*ShortList* 25 April 2013: 36).

3 Embedded connotations

Language is a system of communication that brings a great deal of baggage with it. One does not have to read the work of Ferdinand de Saussure (*Course in General Linguistics*, 1916) to appreciate the general idea that words are signs that bear a particular form (the *signifier* – orthography + sound) and bring with them associations (the *signified* – the mental image conjured up by the word), and that further associations or meanings are inevitably added to create socially constructed notions that Roland Barthes calls *myths* (*Mythologies*, 1957). This system of connotations can be called upon, consciously or not, to add levels of richness to a headline.

Let's take **Smart Alex** – a headline from an architectural magazine. The feature was about the city of Alexandria, in Egypt, and the angle was an analysis of the modern buildings to be found there. The apparently simple two-word phrase can be peeled back to reveal these layers of direct and implied meaning:

1   Smart alec (or aleck) – the headline is a simple play on the idiomatic phrase used, often in a pejorative sense, to describe a clever person (or someone who thinks he or she is clever).

2   Smart as an adjective has multiple connotations:

    a)   well presented ('You look smart');
    b)   of a person – clever or quick witted ('She's a smart girl, she'll learn it quickly');
    c)   of a person – *too* quick witted or impertinent ('Don't get smart with me, sonny');
    d)   of a machine – technologically advanced (as in smart phone);
    e)   of a place – fashionable ('A smart and sophisticated bar');
    f)   of an action – done quickly ('A smart response').

3   Smart as a verb can mean

    a)   to cause a stinging pain ('This paper cut really smarts');
    b)   to cause a feeling of annoyance or upset ('The staff are still smarting from the pay cut').

4   Smart as a noun can mean

    a)   the stinging pain itself ('The smart of a paper cut');
    b)   in the plural form it can mean intelligence or expertise ('She has the smarts for this assignment').

5   Alex is used in the headline as an abbreviation of Alexandria but film fans and readers of a certain age will associate this with the film *Ice Cold In Alex*, starring John Mills, Anthony Quayle, Silvia Syms and Harry Andrews. The story concerns a group of soldiers and nurses driving an ambulance across the desert after the fall of Tobruk in 1942. The journey is beset with difficulty and danger and Captain Anson (Mills) dreams of downing an ice cold lager at the end of it; the iconic scene in which the longed for beer is finally drunk was the best free advertisement Carlsberg ever had and Alexandria was strongly represented as an extremely desirable destination.

6   Once the association with Alexandria has been made, there are further connotations of smartness combined with architecture:

    a)   the Library of Alexandria, founded in 3BC, was one of the most significant libraries in the ancient world and its destruction (possibly by the Romans) led to such a significant loss of written material that it has become a symbol of cultural disaster and the diminishment of public knowledge;

    b)   the Lighthouse (or Pharos) of Alexandria, begun in 280BC, was one of the wonders of the ancient world and parts of it survived until 1480;

    c)   Alexander the Great (356–323BC) himself, founder of the city and conqueror of large parts of the ancient world, who is now as much legend as historical figure (despite the 2004 film starring Colin Farrell).

7   Readers of a literary bent may make further connections with

    a)   the *Alexandria Quartet*, a series of four connected novels by Lawrence Durrell said to be an early example of incorporating principles of relativity and quantum physics into literature (coincidentally in the news at the time of writing http://bit.ly/alexdurrell);

    b)   the Alexandrine, a dodecasyllabic meter frequently used by the seventeenth-century French dramatists Racine and Corneille.

Was all or any of this consciously realised by the headline writer? Certainly the play on the idiomatic phrase, that is evident, but the rest of it may have been unconscious, or perhaps only present in the mind of readers, or only a single reader. Creative headlines are as capable of being 'writerly' texts (to use the critical concept elaborated by Barthes) as the features they introduce (see Holmes *et al.* 2013: 113).

A final thought

'Be original. I tend to dismiss my first suggestion as it will normally be too predictable' – Laura Davies, subeditor, *Elle* (personal communication).

Notes

1   Sometimes apothegmised as 'Tells the story and sells the story'.
2   Nicholas Brett and Tim Holmes (2008), Supplements, in Bob Franklin (ed.), *Pulling Newspapers Apart: Analysing Print Journalism*. Abingdon: Routledge, 198–205.
3   Tim Holmes and Liz Nice (2012), *Magazine Journalism*. London: Sage.
4   Jeremy Leslie (2013), *The Modern Magazine: Visual Journalism in the Digital Age*. London: Laurence King Publishing.
5   A portmanteau word that combines *list* and *article*. Used to describe a short feature that uses a list as its structure. See http://bit.ly/listiclelist for an amusing deconstruction of the form.

7
Page furniture systems
Sells and captions

In the previous chapter we looked at how to create striking feature headlines. However, headlines rarely appear on their own – it is much more usual for them to be part of a complete system of page furniture and although the headline may be the 'glamour' element, the rest of the system is important for two significant reasons. First, there is the craft of wordsmithery involved; these elements may be quite short and in smaller type but they are nevertheless noticed by readers and absorbed even if on an unconscious level. If the production journalist has not taken care or paid attention to these words it will show and, worse, it will affect the reader's impression of the curatum – each of these elements, even those that look insignificant, contributes to the feel and vibe of the whole, to its *weltanschauung*. This is a German word that literally means 'world view' but has wide-reaching philosophical connotations. Sigmund Freud described *weltanschauung* as a specifically German notion, that is difficult to translate into a foreign language and given the continuing use of the German word, he was probably right. Nevertheless, he did attempt a definition:

> By *Weltanschauung*, then, I mean an intellectual construction which gives a unified solution of all the problems of our existence in virtue of a comprehensive hypothesis, a construction, therefore, in which no question is left open and in which everything in which we are interested finds a place.
>
> (www.marxists.org/reference/subject/
> philosophy/works/at/freud.htm)

The possession of such a *weltanschauung*, Freud thought, was one of the quintessential wishes of mankind, making the possessor feel secure in life, clear about what to strive after, and able to organise emotions and interests to the best purpose (the original can be found at http://bit.ly/weltan). Page furniture helps the curatum to establish its *weltanschauung* and to transmit that all-encompassing philosophy to the reader.

The second reason is no less significant and arises out of a simple question – how do you read any given curatum? Or, to elaborate that a little more, how do you approach reading a curatum when you are unfamiliar with it, either because you have not read it before or because it is a new issue? The answer for most people will be, 'I flick through it'. For all the thought and effort that goes into planning a magazine or newspaper, it only takes a few minutes at a news stand to understand the random nature of real-world browsing. Some will start at the back and flick forwards, some will start in the middle and go back and forth, some will actually find the contents page and locate an item of specific interest. This also works for apps, which a reader may swipe through in a similar fashion to print, stopping only when something snags. It is even more important for web publishing; if a reader arrives at a page as a result of searching, that page needs to engage her within the first two seconds or else she will click away to the next result.

In these common situations it is very important that the text is designed to offer numerous *entry points* – textual or visual elements that can attract a browser's attention and encourage deeper engagement. Nicholas Brett, publishing director of BBC Worldwide and Professor of Magazine Journalism at Cardiff University, has a vivid description for the way potential readers approach material and the importance of page furniture as entry points: 'It's like being in the crazy house at a funfair – you don't know which door people are going to come through' (Lecture at Cardiff University, 29/1/14).

If we are going to describe ourselves as professional wordsmiths, then our skills must be applied to the smaller details as well as the showy expanses so that no matter which door people come through, they find a warm welcome waiting for them.

The individual elements of the page furniture system have been called different things at different times and in different offices, so the descriptions below use the currently popular name (based on the result of a survey of former Cardiff MagLab students who now working in production roles) followed by alternatives in brackets:

Sell (standfirst) – the text that accompanies a headline. Although the old name has a more craftly ring to it, sell was the overwhelming choice of those surveyed. It does at least have the advantage of being directly descriptive of its role – if a potential reader has had her interest tickled by a headline or photograph, the sell might persuade her to dive headfirst into the limpid waters of the feature.

Caption – the text that accompanies a photograph or illustration. There is no dispute over the name but many different approaches to the form and function.

Pull quote (blown quote, display quote, call out) – short extracts from the feature displayed in large type on the page.

Subhead – a feature that deals with several disparate but associated topics may be written in chunks that cover the individual subtopics separately, rather than as a piece of continuous prose. Each chunk may be separated by a subhead set in type that is distinguished by size or emphasis (bold or italic or both).

Crosshead – a single word or short phrase used to break up long texts that might otherwise appear off-putting to readers; was commonly used in newspapers but can be found online and in the *Economist*, for example.

Page livery – repeating graphic or textual elements that identify a section within the magazine or a regular feature; the magazine identification and page number (or folio) also count as page livery.

Box-out – a piece of text, generally additional to or reinforcing of, the main text, that may be accompanied by graphics, encased in a space defined by ruled lines or by colour (a *tint panel*). The space is usually rectangular and positioned within a normal column, but it may run across two or more columns and be designed in any shape the design software can accommodate. Box-outs may have their own headlines or subheads, thus adding a system within a system.

Digital publishing has another set of furniture that must be considered, even though the results may be invisible on the page. Tags (or labels) and meta-descriptions (or meta tags) are forms of metadata analogous to keywords. A feature may be tagged or labelled with words or phrases that allow search engines to index it and people to search for it; Flickr, the photo sharing platform, allows users to tag their photographs however they choose. There are no 'wrong' ways to tag items, but they can be tagged wrongly and this, as we shall see, can have unfortunate consequences. A whole page or complete curatum may be identified with metadata that identifies it to search engines and crafting the metadata is another key skill; the consequences of not getting it right might not be so immediately obvious, but can result in a search engine excluding it from results or no one being able to find it – the same result but for different reasons.

The craft of the sell

Sells (standfirsts), as we have seen above, perform two important functions – to project the tone and *weltanschauung* of the curatum and to create reader expectations of what they are about to read.[1] As general characteristics, a good sell will:

- augment the headline;
- abstract the essence of the story;
- accentuate the positive/intriguing aspects.

A good sell will explain the story in conjunction with the headline but generate enough interest to convert the browser into a reader; be brief and well crafted (there is *always* a better standfirst to be written); often provide a space to credit the writer or photographer. These are universal traits and to see the many ways in which sells can be tailored to specific publications, we need to look at specific examples. As with the headlines, this selection is taken from a random selection of magazines on the basis that every issue must work as hard as every other issue, and the *weltanschauung* should always be evident. Some of the sells go with headlines we have already seen in the previous chapter.

A dozen common types of sell

Although individual creativity is theoretically unlimited, sells can be sorted into a taxonomy of recurrent categories.

1 Continuation . . . of headline

This type of sell can only be fully understood when read in immediate conjunction with the headline: '. . . you'll hear the distant rumble of a V8 at work. It's Ben Hamilton's Scania Topline, and when he's not fixing punctures he's hauling logs. *T&D* goes to see him hard at work' (*Truck & Driver*, February 2014: 53); this would not work without the headline IF YOU GO DOWN TO THE WOODS TODAY (ibid.).

However, use of an ellipsis in the headline does not necessarily mean that the sell will be a continuation. In the example above, the headline does not have one but the sell does, whereas in the example below, the headline and sell are separate parts of the system, even though there is an ellipsis at the end of the first element:

Once upon a time . . .

In honor of the 200th anniversary of the Grimm's fairy tales, this book inspires their timeless magic and the special illustrations they inspired.
(*Taschen*, Winter 2011/12: 98)

In this case the headline is a direct cultural reference to the way many fairy tales – such as those written by the Brothers Grimm – begin; as such it exists on its own while establishing a framework or cultural reference that the standfirst can then augment.

2 Exclusivity/Promise

Many specialist curata are predicated on the idea that they or their writers can get privileged access to special information or hard-to-reach people. This type of sell works well for interviews, profiles and 'insider' travel.

Mark Webber opens his heart to CAR (*Car*, September 2013: 84) holds a double promise – of unfettered access to the F1 driver and of exclusive and very personal revelations.

Seven astronauts are about to risk their lives to save the Hubble Space Telescope. Sanjida O'Connell gets exclusive access to NASA's most dangerous mission yet (*Focus*, October 2008: 38) does not hesitate to use the e-word (exclusive) and also contains a large element of *Jeopardy* (see below).

Wheel building, equal parts alchemy, art and instinct, is a skill which is returning to the fore. Urban Cyclist visits a top artisan wheel builder to discover what this dark art is all about (*Urban Cyclist*, Winter 2012: 76) – the key emotional words here are 'top' and 'discover', in combination with the general atmosphere of mystery. Could probably be further edited to make more impact, for example by cutting 'which is' from the first sentence.

Moroccan gardens have provided sanctuary for almost a millennium. Here, the author of Gardens of Marrakech reveals the secrets of the city's coolest places (*easyJet Traveller*, April 2013: 84) – if these words don't inspire a strong desire to access this 'secret' information you're not much of an adventurer. Note the choice of 'millennium' rather than '1,000 years' and think about the (at least) double meaning of 'coolest' in this context.

Fresh from taking the helm of Balenciaga, Alexander Wang tells Dean Mayo Davies why he's bringing the house back to its roots (*Dazed & Confused*, September 2013: 139) – fashion insider exclusivity ahoy! But also the promise of a story of change and authenticity ('back to its roots').

3 Experiential

Travel, sport and adventure are all topics that can work extremely well with a strong injection of subjective experience. This kind of sell is good for action pieces, sport, adventure or active travel and experiential tests of cars, motorcycles, bikes, surfboards, fishing rods . . .

When Urban Cyclist heard about an alley cat race around city centre fish and chip shops we had to see it and ride it ourselves (*Urban Cyclist*, Winter 2012: 69); good atmospherics but as with the earlier example from this magazine, could be put through the wash one more time to rinse out extra words.

Kitesurfing is becoming one of the most-talked about extreme sports around, so we decided to give it a try (and get a little wet) (*easyJet*

Traveller, September 2011: 76) – if the reader has been wondering what it's like, here's an answer. Not sure about the positioning of the hyphen though.

Storyteller Martin Maudsley channels his inner wanderlust and explores leafy Lake District lanes in a horse drawn gypsy wagon (*Pretty Nostalgic*, July/August 2013: 65) – very efficient phrasing that pushes numerous buttons.

Improving on the 458 Italia is a fool's errand, so Ferrari decided that this hardcore version should be 'different, not better'. We're about to taste the difference . . . (*Car*, January 2014: 120) – see how we sacrifice ourselves to serve you better? Mixed with a healthy dose of Exclusivity (see above) and part of a bigger visual system that requires the headline and double page picture for maximum impact (see below).

4 Explainer/Statement

Sometimes a story lends itself to a straightforward introduction to the topic; sometimes the house style is to be plain and simple; and sometimes a production journalist runs out of inspiration and needs a ready-made solution for the blank space that faces him. The Explainer/Statement sell is tailor-made for these situations and can be found in almost every title, sooner or later.

As we have seen already (and will see again) *People's Friend* tends towards no-nonsense treatments on its pages, so it's no surprise to find the straightforward and explanatory **Great advice to keep you happy and healthy!** under the *Your Health + Wellbeing* header (31 August 2013: 18). Strange as it may seem, *Dazed & Confused* is a companion for *People's Friend* in this style: **Reclaiming the rag-and-bone trade; Inside the Brooklyn studio of a one-man art scene; The winning images in Dazed and D&AD's photo contest; Championing emerging filmmakers with Rankin and Nokia** – all taken from the front of book section of the September 2013 issue.

Perhaps *Dazed* believes that creative energy is better used in the rest of the content rather than page furniture but other titles manage to add a bit more pep to this kind of sell.

In the late 1940s, Britain's car industry went all out to attract essential overseas sales. We meet three survivors . . . (*Classics Monthly*,

Summer 2013: 106) is clear and straightforward but adds important historical context and makes a little promise (the meeting); 'survivors' is a good choice of word when used in conjunction with the double page photograph showing a trio of immaculate looking automobiles.

Towering above the Manchester skyline, this spectacular glass-walled penthouse is a tailor-made sanctuary for its architect owner (*Elle Decoration*, September 2013: 135) manages to encompass a physical reference (towering), a strong descriptor (spectacular), an aspirational location (glass-walled penthouse), a desirable state (sanctuary) and an aspirational and appropriate profession (architect owner). The same magazine also manages to incorporate scene-setting explanation into the piece about mirrors already cited in the previous chapter: Mirrors needn't be purely functional. Think of them as useful art for your walls and choose designs with striking shapes, facets or frames (op. cit.: 86). This is an incredibly condensed and elegant way to introduce what is essentially a combined consumer guide and how-to feature.

Creative Review sets a different kind of scene for a feature in its special issue to celebrate London underground's 150th anniversary: **The Underground's communications team has a harder job than its predecessors, but it is keen to build on past creative excellence** (March 2013: 56).

5 Hyperbole

In stark contrast to the category above, a hyperbolic sell will emphasise, or even over emphasise, the importance of the subject matter. The claims made can relate to the importance of the content matter and the effort that has gone into acquiring it, as with this example from *Men's Health*: **Now arriving: the future. MH has identified the key gamechangers that will revolutionise your health, work and play this year** (March 2014: 96). It starts with a claim of prediction (the future) and incorporates the button-pushing phrases 'key gamechangers' and 'revolutionise'. If you are concerned with improving your life why wouldn't you read it?

A hyperbolic sell can also be inspired by a person who is the subject of an interview or profile. The curatum might want to demonstrate its access to hard-to-reach figures (which overlaps with Exclusivity, as seen above) or it might be a verbal reproduction of the interviewee's persona, as in this example from *Shortlist*: **His films have won 75 Oscars, he's friends** with Obama and if he says jump, you get out the trampoline. Legendary film mogul Harvey Weinstein talks to Andrew Lowry (16 January 2014: 34)

Although the approach is justified for a larger than life figure such as Weinstein, it won't work for everyone no matter how hard you try by using phrases such as 'reveals all' and making connections with 'royalty': OK!'s Nicola Agius meets 'Daybreak' host Lorraine Kelly, who reveals all about her brush with royalty, recovering from her accident and what she'd be doing if she wasn't one of the nation's best-loved tv stars (OK!, 11 Feb 2014: 66).

High end consumer products or artefacts also lend themselves to a hyperbolic approach, especially if they are the latest, most exclusive, most expensive thing ever in the history of the universe. Or they could just be the best ever, as here: This JDM/Euro mash-up is, quite possibly, the best lovechild of all time (Fast Car, April 2014: 39) – even the apparently modest interjection 'quite possibly' could be seen as paradoxical thinking.[2]

By contrast, content that exhorts readers to excel through their own efforts, rather than by shopping for a status boost, can also be introduced with a bit of hyperbole. Turning again to Men's Health, we find that Kellan Lutz has pushed himself up into the A-list with his lead in The Legend of Hercules. If you want an epic upper body and the six-pack of a Greek god, this is how to expand your physical horizons (March 2014: 41).

6 Jeopardy

Reality makeover shows have given us a new and long-lived trope – the task that must be completed by a (usually arbitrary) deadline or within a strict time-frame. Challenge Anneka, Ground Force, Changing Rooms all popularised a televisual concept that is difficult to reproduce in a print publication, but car magazine Classics Monthly had a good shot at it: Delayed by major illness, this heroic restoration is being carried out by father and son with the strictest of deadlines to meet (Summer 2013: 32).

A variation on this is the sell that describes a difficult task or mission but leaves the reader uncertain as to whether it has been achieved or not (although the very fact that it has been written about might give a significant clue), as seen here: **When Anton Harnie considered modding his brand-new Beemer, he know he'd have to go hard or go home to pull it off** (*Fast Car*, April 2014: 45).

Features about transition and change naturally lend themselves to Jeopardy if they focus on personal development or an individual's quest for growth. *Psychologies* runs a lot of content of this type and leverages the danger well: **Documentary-maker Polly Morland has always felt that her timidity was holding her back. In a huge leap of courage, she left her job to pursue bravery and find out what it means to be courageous** (June 2013: 89).

Reality relationship shows (*TOWIE*, *Made In Chelsea*, *Celebrity Big Brother*, etc.) and celebrity magazines have given us another trope – the relationship in trouble. This staple has proliferated and often comes in pairs or triads, as in *OK!*'s 11 Feb 2014 issue: on page 51 we learn that **Danielle O'Hara steps out with hubby Jamie as she denies new rumours** and overleaf on page 53 that **Pop couple prove they're still together after recent split rumours**. A few pages later we learn that Peter Andre and his fiancée Emily MacDonagh are **'in a pickle' about their baby's name** – the very definition of jeopardy!

7 Oddball/Intriguing

An Oddball or Intriguing sell can be used to introduce content that is itself odd or intriguing, but at its more elevated end it shades into being thought provoking.

In the previous chapter I cited the oddball headline from a feature about a postwar British car by Jonathan Meades in *Intelligent Life*; its associated sell is a good way to start this section as it combines the odd and the intriguing: **From the side, it looked like a rocker with a mullet. From behind, like a dog squatting. Decades after its demise, the Jowett Javelin still intrigues** (46). The similes are taken from the body of the feature but have been skilfully adapted and condensed into a lyrical standfirst.

Sisters Cassie, Ellen and Lily Grist tell us how a random conversation at a bus stop evolved into a three year plan to open their own laundrette/café (*Pretty Nostalgic*, July/August 2013: 102) contains all the necessary ingredients – a random conversation, the important detail about the bus stop, an oddball combination of washing shop and tea room; mix in photographic evidence of the sisters in vintage clothing and cake stands next to tumble driers and you have a powerful attractor for the readers of this magazine.

One of the simplest and best sells of this type accompanied another headline I have already cited, from a story about a woman setting up a sex toy shop for women: **There's no stigma in buying a vibrator or a nice set of knickers, but selling them is a different matter** (*Oh Comely*, Sep/Oct 2013: 37). The key words in the first clause (stigma, vibrator, knickers) set up one set of associations, which are then challenged by the second clause in a way that encourages readers to reflect on why this should be so – and read on to find out.

8 Question

If a newspaper headline that contains a question mark can, according to Andrew Marr and others, always be answered 'No', what about sells? That's an easy one. Or is it? Sells have a different role to perform than headlines and there are different types of question, which means there is a different type of answer. The Question sell may have thrilling overtones of Jeopardy, an Intriguing mystery or a philosophical paradox as its driving force.

From the pages you see on Google to the choice of leading man in a movie, more and more of modern life is steered by algorithms. But what are they exactly, and who is behind them? Tom Whipple follows the trail (*Intelligent Life*, May/June 2013: 64) evokes a mystery in need of solving (follow the algorithm, rather than follow the money) with a distinct promise of investigative journalism.

With a model to suit all needs, the Peugeot 205 range provoked a sea change in the European hatchback market. The best supermini ever? (*Classics Monthly*, Summer 2013: 9) uses a 'backward' structure (starting with a subsidiary clause) to set up an apparently definitive statement that will be examined in depth over the next eight pages. It also encourages debate and engagement with readers who may believe otherwise ('No! The VW Polo is clearly superior [. . .]'). In the same issue we can find a slightly different use of a question to set the tone for a double road test of upmarket Mercedes and Jaguar models: **Both these cars promise blistering performance and a luxuriously appointed interior, all wrapped**

up in unassuming Q-car bodywork. How have these bankers' hotrods stood the test of time? (98). Some of the language here verges on cliché (blistering performance; luxuriously appointed) but 'banker's hotrods' is a phrase of genius.

Sometimes the question is answered immediately, which might be a high risk strategy if the content does not hold much promise. When the magazine is *Wired*, the writer is pre-scandal[3] Jonah Lehrer and social networks are namechecked, it seems worth the risk: **The secret to health and happiness? Healthy and happy friends. How half a century of medical data revealed the infectious power of social networks** (November 2009: 124).

Is next year's revolutionary Nissan taxi set to dethrone the traditional black cab? Richard Webber samples the New York and Japanese versions to find out (*Autocar*, 15 January 2014) seems at first sight to share some of the traditional newspaper-question DNA but it does set up the investigatory journey that follows. (The answer, by the way, is 'Don't know' rather than 'No'.)

Finally, a philosophical question – **Was there ever a greater contrast between a musician and the music he made? Andy Gill relives John Martyn's sublime performances and the "powerful bad voodoo" of his supercharged life** (*The Word*, March 2009: 84). This raises a perennially interesting question about artists as people compared with their creations in the first, interrogatory, sentence and then quantifies the binary opposition in the second. It also works superbly with the headline which is Born Under A Bad Sign, a song title that will ring bells with readers of *The Word* magazine. This is a good example of the Question, made more impressive by the fact that *The Word*, a monthly, had to react overnight to the news of Martyn's death, which came when the magazine was about to be sent to the printer as Mark Ellen explained in his editor's letter: 'Literally as I type this – Thursday 29 January, with five hours before we're due on press – the bitter news arrives of the death of John Martyn [. . .]' (op. cit.: 3).

9 Summary

The Summary sell is pretty much self-defining: a brief statement of the main points of an article. They are, as per definition, usually short and pertinent but can be used as a low key, non-controversial way to introduce material that might be seen as contentious by some readers.

The *Economist*, a curatum aimed at readers with busy lives and little time to waste, uses a lot of summary sells for its informative articles. A time-poor executive in need of facts about China will not have to think more than once about **The Communist Party calls for wide-ranging economic reforms and gives itself new tools to implement them** (16–22 November 2013: 63) or **One of the strongest storms ever recorded has devastated parts of the Philippines, and relief is slow to arrive** (op. cit.: 57). This kind of sell might look easy to create, but as with any form of précis writing the skill is concealed, like writing the perfect intro to a news story or condensing complex world events for *The Week*.

Converting a vast industrial dairy barn beside the River Stour in Suffolk has given the Fell-Clarks their dream home – and dramatic views (*Saga Magazine*, June 2012: 76) provides the reader with a clear indication of what lies ahead, as does **Urban Life is about to be transformed. Real-time data is teaching our towns How To Think – and that's reinventing everything from traffic to friendships** (*Wired*, Nov 09: 104), although including 'reinvention' holds out a promise too.

What do lorry drivers think about the civil war in Syria? This is an impossible question to answer – lorry drivers are not a homogeneous category of human being and will hold different opinions. Perhaps because of this *Truck & Driver* took the summary route to sell a possibly contentious story: **The conflict in Syria is practically on Europe's doorstep yet most countries appear to be ignoring the growing numbers of refugees. Now, a privately-organised convoy has brought around 300 tonnes of aid to the Turkish-Syrian border** (February 2014: 79).

10 Protracted

Some magazines use long sells as part of their house style, and in such cases the 'rule' about being brief and concise can be safely ignored. The words, however, still have to convey the right tone for the title and provide motivation to read on. Two examples from the American edition of *Vanity Fair* show how to find phrases and references that push the right buttons for an upmarket readership that is hungry for glamour with a frisson-inducing side serving of scandal.

In the 40s, 50s, and 60s, architect John Elgin Woolf and his partner, lover and, later, adopted son, designer Robert Koch Woolf, gave the Beverley Hills elite a new kind of home, as glamorous as any movie set. MATT TYRNAUER traces the star-studded rise of Woolf's "Hollywood Regency" style, and the unorthodox family he created.

(March 2009: 184)

It needs a lot of commas to accommodate all the names and details but the killer phrase 'partner, lover and, later, adopted son'[4] is surely enough to drive the reader through the traffic lights of punctuation.

Between World War II and the 60s, before bodyguards and gossip sites, Hollywood kids could grow up in a golden normalcy, combining the perks of movie royalty with small-town protections. From those who lived it, TODD S. PURDUM recaptures a world where Daddy's Oscar mattered, but not as much as being cool in school.

(op. cit.: 194)

It probably helps that these words sit on a page otherwise occupied by a colour photograph of a young Candice Bergen in swimwear and opposite a full page picture of Robert Wagner washing his Cadillac – shirt off.

For *Vanity Fair*, the action words (Hollywood, golden, movie royalty, small-town, Oscar, cool, etc.) are incorporated naturally but they can also be given added typographical emphasis. *Mojo* magazine's The Mojo Interview for March 2013 featured Adam Ant; the feature opened on a double page spread with a left hand portrait of Mr Ant (in moody mono-chrome) and a right hand of text, half of which was the sell, blown up large and emphasised as follows:

Punk survivor, **Dandy**
Highwayman, **tabloid**
spectacle, he saw both sides
of **fame**. Back on the road
and off the **meds**, can he thrive
again? "I had such a **public**
trauma," says **Adam Ant**

(op. cit.: 43)

Eagle-eyed readers will note not only that there is also a question posed in the sell, as well as a quote, but also that it is nowhere as long as the examples from *Vanity Fair*. However, as noted, it takes up a lot of space on the page and therefore becomes an important element in itself, as well as being emphasised internally.

A sell should always aim to abstract the essence of the story it accompanies but there are times when the concept cannot be summed up in a couple of sentences and needs to be more fully explained or put into context:

> **In 1550, Giorgio Vasari wrote one of art history's greatest ever works: Lives of the Artists, a journey into the minds of the greatest painters, sculptors and architects of the Italian Renaissance. Now, almost five hundred years later, a new feature-length documentary from Relentless takes the very same name. Its subjects? Artists. Not painters, sculptors or architects, but Artists no less: snowboarders, surfers and musicians who, like Vasari's revolutionaries, are driven to extremes in their search for fulfilment.**
>
> (*This Is The Order*, Issue 3, 2004: 70)

The first issue of *Riposte* ('A Smart Magazine For Women') adopted the idea of the sell as an important element of the page and treated it in two ways. The first was similar to the half page *Mojo* example above, using larger type than is normal but without the internal emphasis:

> **There are certain characters in the art and design world that you hear a lot about. There are some, though, that stand as quiet pillars in the creative world that, for one reason or another, are not as prominent considering their extraordinary importance. Françoise Mouly is one of these pillars.**
>
> (*Riposte* No 1: 37)

The second treatment sees the sell-and-headline system given a whole page, with the headline splitting the sell:

Some people have the good manners to arrive on the planet with an innate, lifelong desire to own beautiful things. If this rings even the slightest bell, head directly to the first floor of No 125 Charing Cross Road, London. There you'll find Claire de Rouen Books–reputedly described by David Bailey as "maybe the best photographic bookshop in the world".

The Grande Dame of Charing Cross Road

Different cities make different promises and London has long held a particular allure for the creatively inclined. It is a sprawling mass of commerce where artists are as abundant as economists. Like a flock of avant-garde swallows, creative minds migrate to London to make, to earn a crust and to emulate the kind of lives their idols live. In January 2012, the city suffered a great loss as one such idol passed on.

(op. cit.: 85)

It could be argued, however, that the words below the headline are from a different textual system and actually form the intro to the feature. This theory works with other content given the same treatment in the issue, and leads towards the creation of a new category of page furniture, one that is hybridised with other textual elements.

11 Hybrid/Systematic

Boneshaker is a magazine for bicyclists who like to do things a bit differently. Mixing leftfield cycling culture with oddball machines, art, poetry, it is one of the crop of hyper-niched indy print magazines that have flourished in the early part of the twenty-first century. It proudly claims, 'At present, we are committed to remaining free from advertisements and advertorial' (issue 11, 2013: 3^5). As you might expect, the design philosophy is far from formulaic but the magazine uses page furniture systematically to headline and sell features. Sometimes, however, it does something different – as on pages 20–1 of issue 11.

The headline is *Walls of Death, Wheels of Life* and the subject matter is pushbike walls of death. Don't know what that is? Try this sell, which is divided into three sections:

Picture yourself on a bicycle, the smell of sawdust and sweat in the air, the heat of the lights on your face. A blindfold

is fastened over your eyes. You lean down, grasp the handle-
bars and begin pedalling.

A hand on your shoulder guides you to the right, where
your front wheel meets an unseen incline. The hand is gone,
and you know you must pedal faster, even as you feel the
bike lurch toward the horizontal, perpendicular to the
ground. Pedal faster, or you will surely fall.

Pedal faster, and hear the tyres rumble around the near
vertical wall, the crowd gasp and whoop and holler. Feel
the track buck and roll beneath your wheels, gravity
wanting to take you down, your own speed keeping
you up. **Welcome to the Bomberdrome.**

Combined into a double page spread with six photographs this creates a
whole-page system that catches both eye and attention, and encourages
readers to turn the page, where they will find the intro proper.

If *Boneshaker* is at one end of the commercial scale, committed to not
taking advertising, *SportsDirect.com Magazine* is at the other, committed
to increasing sales at Mike Ashley's sports clothing business – but like
all customer magazines it can only do so by offering compelling content.
The launch issue did this well, showing good knowledge of magazine craft
(as it should, since British magazine design guru Andy Cowles was the
Launch Creative Director), including a good example of a whole-page
system on 80–1. A photograph of Sergio Aguero sucking on a sports
drink bottle runs across the spread, with a big headline asking *What's in
Aguero's bottle?* and a sell that refines the idea: **Ahead of the new football season, Mark Bailey reports on the science and technology behind
top players' preparations** (op. cit., August 2013). The first two paragraphs of the feature get the reader started, then below them there is
another element of the system, a caption that reads *Sergio Aguero takes
a sip from his tailor-made recovery drink*. In one way, it's a bit of a con –
Aguero is mentioned in a single sentence that virtually repeats the
caption – but taken overall it's a fair way of pulling readers into a very
interesting feature about modern training and nutrition. The point to be
made here is that each element of the system on the opening spread is
much stronger in combination with the other elements.

Occasionally a whole-page system will do away with one or more of the
elements listed above and still work brilliantly. The most commonly

retained part of the system is, unsurprisingly, the photograph – or, in the case of *Wired* October 2009: 84–5, the photo montage. Three images apparently show Peter Diamandis, the entrepreneur behind the X Prize Foundation,[6] floating in space. Four 'strips' of equally sized type announce the following:

> **Peter Diamandis plans to save Earth . . .**
> **. . . One competition at a time**
> **From cars to space: inside the X Prize**
> **By Matthew Honan Portraits Jill Greenberg**

A close analysis of those elements might find the first two lines to be the headline and the third the sell, but they are all given equal weight in the system, with the only extras being a small strap in the top right (X PRIZE) balanced by a page number in the bottom left (084).

Eighteen pages later there is another superb example of the whole-page system – at the centre of the spread is a photograph of five men standing outside a nondescript building in a place where palm trees grow. At the top of the page, in small type: '*In an era of financial scams and Ponzi frauds, it takes cunning, smart thinking (and a little luck) to nail the bad guys.*' Below the photograph, each of the men is identified by name and role (e.g. MARTIN KENNEY The asset-retrieval specialist); to the right of the spread, small photographs arranged vertically showing a man, a lakeside house, a stash of banknotes and a car, labelled underneath in the same type as the overline:

> *The fraudster*
> *The properties*
> *The haul*
> *The catch*

Below this, in the same font and point size, but set in bold:

FOLLOW THE MONEY

Linking all of these elements together, a silver line that runs through the main photograph, into a 'maze' on the left, comes out underneath, where it incorporates the text that identifies the team, and carries on to the right where it terminates next to the small photographs. This line carries a significant burden, being not just a semiotic representation of the feature to follow but also embodying the process that the five men went through in pursuit of the conman and his ill-gotten gains.

12 Irresistible fun/pun

Sometimes, when all is said and done, a sell becomes an opportunity to combine popular culture, wordsmithery and fun, such as this example from the *Ulster Gazette* (17/04/14). The story is about an expensive and complex rail project, it is headlined OVER £100M! and the sell runs like this:

> Is this the rail price?
> Is this just fantasy?
> Caught up in land buys
> No escape from bureaucracy!

Congratulations to deputy editor Richard Burden for his adaptation of Queen's *Bohemian Rhapsody* – although he thinks it's a headline, as he told the BBC: 'I just always liked to do that type of headline. If there's a film, a song, a lyric – anything that springs to mind and it lends itself, you'll try to fit the words in round it,' he says (bit.ly/beebquote).

Captions

This may sound both pretentious and portentous but the humble caption – those few words attached to an image – can have an effect on history. In a review of *Nature, Class, and New Deal Literature: The Country Poor in the Great Depression* (Fender 2011), a book that argues the usual narrative about malign nature (the 'Dust Bowl') forcing farmers and agricultural workers ('Okies') westward towards California should be expanded to include more socially constructed reasons such as bank foreclosures, Graham Barnfield notes: 'It became commonplace to recast 1930s rural economic problems as the products of an episodically hostile natural environment . . . Farm Security Administration photographers incorporated their own victim-centric political baggage into writing simple photo captions' (Barnfield, Graham, review on page 51 of THES, 22/29 December 2011).

When you consider how iconic some of those photographs by Paul Strand, Dorothea Lange and others have become, how often they have been reproduced and how readily the photographer's description of the subject matter has been accepted at face value, you begin to understand the power of a caption.

Not every caption has that potential, of course. Most captioning work will be run of the mill, but just imagine someone in 50 or 100 years clicking through an archive and coming across a picture that you have captioned – the power to influence immediate and future interpretation is there in every example.

Even without that in mind, the caption is a very powerful tool. Captions form an important part of a magazine's image and should be written in a consistent *style* and *tone* that can be traced through every single issue. Far from simply describing what the reader can already see, the caption can and should add information, explain an action, identify people and establish the *weltanschauung* of an entire publication. Take *Shortlist* as an example – some captions are strictly informative, such as those giving full details for fashion shoots, but otherwise the style is 'funny' in the mode of Gary Larson's absurd and much-copied Far Side cartoons. Sometimes this seems somewhat strained (it is, after all, difficult to be funny all the time) but it is a key identifier for the magazine, especially as the humour relies in part on a cultural understanding of the joke being essayed. Three examples from the 20 February 2014 issue:

A picture of a man skiing down a mountain, his long blond hair streaming behind him: JIMMY BULLARD BEGAN PRACTISING FOR THE JUMP 2018 EARLY (p50) – relies on readers knowing that Jimmy Bullard is a footballer with similar hair and that The Jump is a reality television programme featuring celebrities who have to learn various winter sports.

A picture of a well-equipped climber in snowy mountains, at the foot of a cliff: "WHAT DO YOU MEAN THE TUBE STRIKES ARE FINISHED?" (52) – the surrounding text is an advice piece about how to fight negative feelings in tough situations and the humour relies on juxtaposing the recent disruptive London Underground strikes, which caused much negative feeling but not much personal danger, with the climber's perilous mission. The advice comes from a mountaineer about to attempt a winter ascent of Nanga Parbat, the 'killer mountain', which adds to the irony.

A picture of Welsh rugby international Taulupe Falatau carrying the ball and attempting to side-step an Irish player: "WATCH OUT FOR THAT DOG TURD" (52). The humour (such as it is) comes from the Irish player's hand pointing to the pitch, where Faletau also appears to be looking. There might be a connotative link to the experience of amateur players among the readership who have to use less-than-perfect municipal pitches.

All three captions display *contextuality* as well as humour – that is, the caption text provides a context for the picture, just as the main text provides a context for the picture-caption unit. As a general rule, captions should be as contextual as possible: their content should be relevant to what the picture is showing and to what the main text is communicating. Captions must also add information or value to the image, not just describe it. The first caption quoted above could just be LONG HAIRED MAN SKIS DOWN MOUNTAIN but that doesn't tell us more than we can see for ourselves. In the context of the main text (which is essentially blurb for a competition) it is not necessary to know the name of the person in the picture, although it might be useful to know whether it was taken in Val d'Isere – which is the prize destination. The added value comes from the references to popular culture: the person in the picture is clearly a good skier and skiing is often thought of as an elite pastime but linking the image to football and a rather rubbishy television show demotes it from the elite and makes it commonplace.

Danielle Richardson, a subeditor on *Shortlist* who has stared at many a photograph waiting for inspiration to strike, has this to say about the process she goes through:

> Captions are one of the strongest ways you can get the tone of the magazine across, and therefore they're something most likely to get tweaked and changed to be as funny as possible and relevant to the readers – after a few months here I was happy to notice if even one on a page had survived as I'd written it! It can be disheartening when you think you've

managed to write something funny and it doesn't make it, but the occasional joy of someone tweeting in to say how funny your caption is makes up for it. It's an exercise that requires a level of imagination and lateral thinking; when faced with a daunting feature full of press shots of cars and told to 'go funny' on them, you've got to look at anything that might set them apart – does it look a bit like Darth Vader? Does it look a bit sleepy? Would James Bond drive it? It's the hotel room shots that are probably the biggest killer – there's only so many jokes about a room with a bed in it – in times of desperation, just pretend that inanimate objects are talking.[7]

A word of warning: always check how the image you are about to caption will be cropped. If it shows a number of people, will they all be visible in the final image? If it shows an artefact, will all of it appear or will the image zoom in on a particular spot? If your caption focuses on a subsidiary detail, will that detail make it through the design process? There's no point in spending hours straining after humour or poetry if the thing you are describing won't be seen.

A system of captions

As with headlines and sells, captions can be classified into a taxonomic system. It is not entirely scientific but when you are looking at a blank screen waiting for inspiration it might help to whittle down the possibilities.

1 Identifying merchandise

This is essentially a cataloguing job but as with all catalogues, it is only useful as long as it is accurate, so there will be lots of phoning suppliers to get prices and availability. There also needs to be a consistent house style developed for and strictly applied to punctuation, numbers, abbreviations and even referencing, as in this example from *Company*, April 2012:

> **Shirt**, **£39.99**, **Zara**. **Shorts**, **£283**, **American Retro at Harvey Nichols**. **Heels**, **£75**, **Office** (25, underlining in original)

Esquire has a different style for punctuation on its fashion pages:

> <u>LANVIN</u> Camel cotton blown volume parka, £2,470; midnight blue wool jacket, £1,830; black/green/red checked cotton shirt, £855; midnight blue wool trousers, £555 (September 2013, 158, underlining in original).

You can see why checking the prices is so important when they strain credibility so.

2 Augmented purchase information

Sometimes a list is not enough, either because the fashion editor wants to work a little extra magic or because an augmented description might help to shift a few more units. *Porter* was launched as a high-end customer magazine for online fashion retailer Net-A-Porter in Spring 2014, so there is probably a bit of both in their captions:

> THE EASE OF LOOSE, BUT IMMACULATE, PANTS CONVEY SERENE CONFIDENCE Pants by Hermès, £1,050; shoes by Dr. Martens, £140 (127)

> A MOMENT OF INTIMACY CAPTURED IN A FLASH OF SCARLET AND A SHEATH OF SATIN Cardigan by Chanel, £1,242; briefs by Gisele Bündchen Intimates, £18; ring, as before (131)

It is worth observing the tone and register of these captions. Yes, they work hand-in-glove with the photographs but the words and phrasing convey a distinct vibe that might even come down to the choice of key words in each case – 'serene confidence' in the first; 'flash' and 'sheath' in the second. This atmospheric crafting of *weltanschauung* is continued through the first issue. Note also the use of closed punctuation for 'Dr. Martens', which reflects that company's usage, and the American-English vocabulary – pants for trousers.

Glamour employs this type of augmented caption for some of its fashion pages. Text and image work closely together but the tone and register are completely different, as is the punctuation, which sometimes reflects social media usage:

Mannish sheeny jacket or girlie iridescent skirt? No contest – we're wearing both Silk Lurex and satin jacket £1,080, satin shirt £495 and cotton sateen skirt £995 **all Jonathan Saunders**; nappa leather and PVC brogues £292 **Stuart Weitzman**; Lurex socks £8 **Jonathan Aston at asos.com**

(March 2014, 198; emphasis reversed in original)

Twinkle, twinkle, little dress, how we want to. . . Wear. You. Now. Satin dress £555 **Marc by Marc Jacobs;** plastic sunglasses £65 **Sunpocket;** enamel and Swarovski crystal and silver-plated brass cuffs £225-£250 **mariafrancescapepe.com**

(200; emphasis reversed in original)

Using a full stop after every word is a relatively modern usage that seems common in both social media updates and short form fashion writing; its widespread adoption has been credited by some to Comic Book Guy[8] in *The Simpsons*.

3 Identification of people, things and context

In its December 2013 issue, music magazine *Uncut* ran features on Bon Scott, the original singer with Australian rockers AC/DC, and Joni Mitchell, the foremost singer-songwriter of the twentieth century. Both features were illustrated with multiple photographs of their subjects, who are so recognisable they hardly need to be identified, but they are pictured with different people and in different places at different stages of their careers and adding *that* information creates a lot of extra value.

Scott, for example, sang with a few bands that never made it to the big time; readers will want to know about them, and band members who contributed to the story or who went on to success in different circumstances need to be identified:

The Valentines in 1970 *(Scott second left, Vince Lovegrove third left)* (20)

Hard drinking hippies Fraternity circa '71 *(Scott, far right)* (20)

AC/CD in 1979: *(l-r)* Malcolm Young, Bon Scott, Angus Young, Cliff Williams and Phil Rudd (21)

This looks straightforward but pay attention to the detail of what is set in italics and what is put into brackets – there should be absolute consistency.

Joni Mitchell's career has encompassed many different styles of music on many different albums, relationships with prominent musicians (many of whom have have been inspired to write songs about her), expression in different art forms (she paints a lot), popularity, reclusiveness, rediscovery and veneration. A lot to sum up even in a nine page retrospective, which makes it doubly important that the captions establish context and personalities:

Joni Mitchell shot for Vogue magazine, November 20, 1968 (26)

Mitchell at a contract signing with, l-r, Elliot Roberts, David Crosby, and Warner Brothers executive Mo Ostin, 1967 (28)

Joni with the LA Express, Hollywood, October 1974: (l-r) Tom Scott, Max Bennett, Robben Ford, Larry Nash, John Guerin and Mitchell (33)

Note the way the components of her name are used to add variety. Plus, you have doubtless already noticed the inconsistent treatment of the small signifier 'l-r' in these examples from different features – does it take italics or not? Does it go in brackets or not? Back to the house style guide, please!

Uncut's readers may well recognise many of the people in the photographs without the captions to identify them but it is still important to do so. When *Saga*, the magazine for readers in the demographic captured by the insurance company that specialises in cover for the over-50s, profiled artist Sir Peter Blake it was pretty obvious who he was – the only figure in the two portraits that accompanied the piece – but he and his surroundings were identified in a caption with an overline:

STILL CUTTING EDGE Peter Blake at work in his light and spacious West London studio

(June 2012: 51)

This becomes more important when a cast of people are involved, perhaps in a story about a celebrity who has been connected with several partners or spouses. Keira Knightley has only married once but she had boyfriends before that, as *OK!* magazine pointed out courtesy of a triad of photographs:

Main: Keira married James Righton (far left) in May last year. Left: The star and former boyfriend Jamie Dornan

(11 Feb 2014: 63)

Once again, note the use of italics for directives (*Main*, *Left*), the separation of captions into discrete sentences and the capital letter after a colon. In this issue at least *OK!* seems to be much more consistent with the style for italics than *Uncut*.

Consistency and clarity becomes even more important when captions are used in a block that identifies several different photographs. *Vanity Fair*'s profile of film director John Ford focuses particularly on his use of Monument Valley, on the borders of Utah and Arizona, and his relationships with rancher Harry Goulding and movie star John Wayne. This caption block, with overline, describes a landscape on the left-hand page and people on the right-hand page:

THE DESERT STAGE A view of Monument Valley, on the Navajo Indian reservation, Arizona. *Opposite:* top, Harry Goulding (left) and the original guest rooms at the Gouldings' trading post, circa 1940; *bottom*, John Wayne (far left) and John Ford and Dolores del Rio (front) on the set of *The Searchers*, 1955.

(March 2009: 122–3)

There is an intricate style for italics and punctuation here that is used consistently throughout the issue. This might seem like a minor point but such consistency is a mark of professionalism that every production journalist should aim for.

4 Technical details

Curata that deal with content of a technical nature – machines, computers, gadgets – need a caption style that can incorporate the details that readers demand. At its most basic this could be a simple list but it does not have to be. This example from *Wired*, includes technical details that allow the reader to interpret the photograph of a man standing on the space frame of a tricycle that has an engine at the back and geared pedals at the front:

> **Jay Perdue, standing atop the Tri-Hybrid Stealth, his entry for the Automotive X Prize. It runs on a combination of diesel, electricity and pedal-power**
>
> (October 2009: 90)

Some, but not all, car magazines have to include a lot of technical details and using captions can add value to what might otherwise just be a picture of a new vehicle. This kind of use also allows the writers to demonstrate specialist knowledge and readers to absorb a lot of information very quickly:

> **Heavily revised suspension and a Torsen limited-slip diff help to give the RCZ R incisive handling and an abundance of steering feel**
>
> **Front seats are covered in leather and Alcantara in the RCZ R, complete with 'R' branding; fascia is starting to look dated**
>
> **Expert damper tuning means the ride retains just enough suppleness for comfort**
>
> (all *Autocar*, 15 January 2014: 27)

This style of caption is entirely appropriate for *Autocar*, which is relatively technical, or *What Car?*, which emphasises practical information over pure entertainment, but *Top Gear*'s priorities are the other way around, so its caption style tends to be entertainingly informative. Two examples from a comparison test of the BMW 4-series from the November 2013 iPad edition make the point about how language is used:

> **4-Series profile is purposeful but coolly attractive** (page 2/7)
>
> **Rumps in the night. The Merc's is the slimmest by far** (3/7)

In the first, the words 'coolly attractive' are crucial in representing the magazine's *weltanschauung*; in the second the jokey reference to 'rumps' (the photograph shows a back view of the cars) is the key.

A production journalist who does not have deep knowledge of the subject (or who has not driven the vehicle in question) will be dependent on the road tester for technical summaries such as those from *Autocar*, which makes clear and established channels of communication essential for the reputation of the magazine as well as the individuals working on it.

The production system must therefore specify the means by which information is gathered and passed from stage to stage of the production process, especially where photographs are concerned – between the photographer, the writer and the production journalist there are at least three procedural cracks into which vital information can disappear.

This also applies to features such as those found in *Classics Monthly* – a magazine that happens to deal with classic cars, but any subject matter dealing with repair or restoration techniques will require similar kinds of caption to these about repainting a classic Mini:

> **Initial flatting back was done by hand with 1500 grit wet and dry**
>
> **Windscreen scuttle repaired prior to paint**
>
> **Stonechip was applied to inside of the floorplan**
> (all from Summer 2013: 66)

5 Additional editorial information or augmented content

There are times when this type of caption comes quite close to **Augmented purchase information**, but the difference lies in the amount and importance of editorial content that is added. For example, the *high street edit* section of *Company* April 2012 opens with a single image of a model in a floaty, translucent dress. There is no copy apart from different elements of page furniture:

> Page identifier – **got to have it**
>
> Photo headline – **SHEER GENIUS**
>
> Photo standfirst – **Be seen in see-through with this season's sheer. It's a fashion tongue twister . . .**

Caption – **Mint sheer green dress with leaf appliqué, £59; peach sheer dress with leaf appliqué (underneath), £59, both Miss Selfridge. Printed cream court shoes, £39.99, New Look. Purple printed ankle socks, £8, Jonathan Aston**

Addition editorial information (emphasised with a hand drawn arrow pointing to the shoes) – **If you don't want to go too girlie, toughen up with a dark stained lip and points to match**

(all p. 23)

On page 40 there is a street-style vox pop called *you wear the trends*. Again, the format is mainly images and page furniture, and the predominant page furniture is captions:

Linda, fashion buyer at Net-a-porter.com Coat and shirt, Isabel Marant. Jumper, Acne. Jeans, Current/Elliott

Ceri Davies, writer Skirt from Brick Lane. T-Shirt and jumper, vintage. Shoes, H&M. Bag, Topshop

These are editorially informative rather than purchasing directive and the page is an important element of *printeractivity* for the physical magazine. Note yet again, the need for a consistent punctuation style and the capitalisation for T-Shirt.

One more example of editorially important captions from the same issue. The three page *running in high-tops* feature is like an extended version of the street-style vox pop, but with a single person's fashion choices on each page. Thus on page 79 Jaime Bradley shows off the wardrobe a band manager needs:

"I wear my letterman jacket from London Loves LA with EVERYTHING."

"This American Apparel bow tie and metallic jacket from Topshop perk up battered vintage band tees."

"Reebok high-tops = must-have shoe. This and every season" (full stop omitted in original)

"Not the most practical dog-walking shoes, but I adore these Jeffrey Campbell wedges."

These captions are presented as quotes (which they may well be) and because of this presentation they are granted a terminal full stop, which most captions do not have. 'High-top', 'must-have', 'dog-walking' – *Company*'s house style liked hyphenation but not all curata do: the *Guardian*, for example, avoids the use of hyphens wherever possible.

It is not just fashion-conscious young women who like captions to add editorial information, *Saga* readers do too. The piece (June 2012) referred to elsewhere about the dream home in Suffolk does a similar job with captions to photographs of the interiors:

> Contemporary comfort A classic Arco floor lamp arches elegantly over La Bambole armchairs (77)

> Industrial chic The teak dining-table top is supported by concrete drainpipes. Right: the main bedroom is in a 'hut' suspended from the ceiling (78)

One other subbing point worth noting there – *Saga*'s style is for a lower case letter after a colon; this is commonly regarded as the proper usage.

Travel features lend themselves to this style of caption as they can draw something extra out of the photography, changing them from happy snaps or PR handouts into elements that add value for the specific audience. *Esquire* wants its well dressed and suave men-about-town readers to enjoy the finest vodkas that St Petersburg can supply, so captions a picture of a swanky looking bar:

> **Hipster hangout Dom Byta, where vodka comes in birch sap flavour** (September 2013: 76)

And if they want to go somewhere a bit more culturally challenging:

> **Tsar trek: head to the Church of Our Saviour on the Spilt Blood, built in honour of Alexander II** (76). ('Tsar Trek' is an excellent touch.)

Our final example of this style of caption shows just how much extra editorial information can be conveyed. In its March 2009 issue, *The Word* ran a feature about protest songs and the effect they had (or didn't). The piece takes Bob Dylan's *The Lonesome Death of Hattie Carroll* as its starting point and there's a whole-page photograph of Carroll's killer in police custody and an inset of the songwriter:

William Zantziger is arrested, 9 February 1963, for the murder of a black waitress in Baltimore. Dylan (above, at Newport '65) distorted the facts but immortalised him in a song that was to haunt him until his death in January 2009. (77)

Shades of the Farm Security Administration photographers in there somewhere.

Captions have to be fashioned for different feature or reporting formats and there are times when the caption almost turns into a mini-feature. In its March 2014 issue, *Men's Health* ran a cut-out-and-keep Weekend Challenge (129) that incorporated four activities for four weekends, all aimed at improving running speed and mobility. Each activity was illustrated with a composited photograph, showing a trainer demonstrating two or three key points in the routine, that was:

- dated per weekend (in a roundel);
- headlined;
- annotated with letters;
- explained with a caption of around 50 words;
- graded with a box-out that gave target times.

Between them these elements had to capture the entire exercise, contextualise it within the four-week programme and authenticate each stage with quotes from the sporting star who was acting as an expert advisor (in this case American Football player LaMichael James). The work-out for the first weekend looked like this:

Date – 8TH–9TH **WEEKEND 01 STRAIGHT-LINE SPRINTING**

Headline – **40-YARD DASH**

Letters – **A, B**

Caption – **A straight, forward sprint might seem to be just that, but perfecting it will help you burst past defenders** (at Super Bowl or Sunday league). "Set two cones 40 yards apart," says James. "Start in a three-point stance (A). Be explosive in the first 10 steps (B) and stay low until you reach the cone."

Grade – *Average, 4.5 seconds; Excellent, 4.4 seconds, Elite, Sub 4.4 seconds*

Here, the caption is providing the main textual element of what is a visually led box-out feature. *SportsDirect.com* magazine did something very similar with its double page feature on **HOW TO PASS THE XAVI WAY**, using a combination of action illustrations, photographs and tightly written captions. Page 62 showed how to perfect the Xavi pass in five stages (**1 Xavi never tries to slow the play down – he maintains the flow of the game by always looking to keep the ball in motion.**) while on page 63 a coach explained the five steps to passing greatness: **DO YOU PASS TO THEIR FEET OR INTO SPACE? If you are making a pass to a player that has a good amount of space in front of them, passing the ball into that space makes it easier for them to move forward. This type of pass can release players down the wings, or even beat an offside trap.**

This type of super-condensed tutorial works very well for sports publications but it is not limited to them. The Fashion Insiders section of *Marie Claire Runway* (Spring/Summer 2014) had a format that gave each insider a series of Polaroid photographs (or photographs treated to look like Polaroids), identified with a key number and a keyed caption to explain the significance of the picture. Thus on page 112 Massimiliano Giornetti, designer for the fashion house Ferragamo, has eight pictures, the first of which is a fashion sketch. He explains the inspiration behind it by referring to the work of architect Miguel Angel Aragonés, whose work he finds particularly admirable and intriguing because of its clean geometrical shapes and the use of space and light. The other seven take us through make-up, snakeskin, backstage, nervousness, mood boards, models and the golden silk dress that was his favourite piece.

Intelligent Life, lifestyle offshoot of the *Economist*, revived the use of the photo-essay very effectively as one of its points of distinction; the May/June 2013 issue has a lovely example that focuses on weeds. Although there is accompanying text, written by Richard *Food For Free* Mabey, the beautifully composed photos by Ian Winstanley require captions to bring them fully to life and explain them individually. The style employed here harks back in mood to the *Porter* captions analysed above, invoking place and atmosphere:

Edge of darkness

In May, in a Birmingham subway, a solitary corn chamomile (Anthemis arvensis) gleans just enough light to straggle into flower (86)

The final example of this type of extended caption comes from *Creative Review*'s London Underground 150 commemorative issue (March 2013). A piece about the way brands and branding devices (such as the famous roundel) are exploited has text that explains the process and illustrations that show examples of posters, watches and other items, all of which need to be identified and explained. Thus on the opening spread (50–1), there is a caption that runs:

Facing page: Although travellers had been able to buy copies of tube posters from the 1920s onwards, it was not until the 1960s that merchandising began to be formalised. A range of posters and other items were available at the London Transport shop at Griffith House, here shown in 1975. Below, clockwise from top: London Transport Shops Catalogue, issued in 1978; 1970s panel poster I'd Be Lost Without It, designer unknown; Get Lost!, designer unknown.

It may seem odd that the caption bothers to state the designer is unknown, but look at the context – *Creative Review* is all about design and designers, so attribution is crucial. By including "designer unknown" the publication is explaining the reason for omission of this detail, which is particularly noticeable when the caption on the next spread namechecks all the designers.

6 Summary (Reportage format)

There are times in journalism when less has to be more. Times such as when you are trying to squeeze reports from 69 major fashion shows into 23 pages, as *Marie Claire Runway* did (Spring/Summer 2014). In what turned out to be a triumph of co-ordination between fashion editing, photo editing and caption writing, each design house show was given nine photographs and a caption of around 30 words that had to sum up the whole collection (I will repeat that, 30 words to sum up an entire fashion collection) and reflect what the photographs showed. Here is the first:

> **ALEXANDER MCQUEEN** Sarah Burton's sensational fashion warriors parade out in fierce, bondage-tinged strapped crop tops; artful tribal red, black and white prints; and tiered bold colour-blocked pony-hair and feather skirts.

And the last:

> **VIVIENNE WESTWOOD** Where to start with curve-cut plaid tops paired with sheer green lace maxis, jewelled jersey crop tops and a giant cat face? She is in her own fabulous style stratosphere.

7 Step by step/Instructional

The final example of augmented captioning comes from *Glamour* of March 2014 (the SuperSized edition) and the augmentation comes from the collective quantity of captions rather than the length of individual ones. The double page spread on 162–3 focuses on eye-liner; it is divided into three main styles (Flick, Graphic and Smoky), each illustrated with photographs of celebrities and models using variations on the style and identifying certain brands of liner that are particularly suited to that expression (a type of feature that could be categorised as products + personalities + practices). Each photograph is coupled with a caption that explains the what and how. There is a final row of images that identifies essential components for an eye make-up kit and a box-out that offers three colourful additions. It's a dense and complex page but looks packed with information rather than over-busy; it would not work without the captions, yet they are deceptively simple, ranging from:

> **Using a liquid liner, make a dot at the outer lashline to help draw the shape.**

to

> **Go sultry and wrap around** Le Crayon Khôl in Noir £16
> lancome.co.uk

8 Curt captioning

At the other end of the captioning scale from the long, detailed examples above lies the curt caption, as practised by *The People's Friend*. Take the feature *Exploring "Heartbeat" Country* from the 31 August 2013 issue. It is, as the headline makes clear, a travel piece about visiting the North York Moors, where the once-popular television series *Heartbeat* was filmed. On the first double page spread there are six photographs, each with a very brief caption:

> Photo of road signs showing gradient warnings: **Ups and downs**
>
> Photo of village nestling in valley: **Idyllic**
>
> Photo of a waterfall: **Mallyan Spout**
>
> Photo of a shop: **The "shop between bars"**
>
> Photo of an old Police car: **The famous Ford Anglia**
>
> Photo of a steam train: **Steam train**

Economical with words, certainly, perhaps even frugal – but given the magazine's continued success over the decades it must be a style the readers find acceptable, and in the end that's what matters most.

Notes

1   Standfirsts can have another useful function for writers, in that creating a sell before writing a feature can help to define the angle and keep the writing on target; this can be especially useful when a deadline is pressing.
2   In case you are wondering: JDM because the engine is from a Japanese Domestic Market model (Toyota Soarer) and Euro because the base car is a German Volkswagen Caddy.
3   In 2012 Lehrer was accused of, and admitted, both self-plagiarism and the fabrication of quotes. There is a summary on Wikipedia (to be taken with the usual caveats, etc., etc.): http://bit.ly/lehrerscandal.

4   It's enough to make you wonder whether Norman Tebbit had read the article before making his contribution to the Lords debate on gay marriage: www.bigissue.com/mix/news/2385/norman-tebbit-maybe-id-be-allowed-marry-my-son.

5   This is according to their own pagination system. Normal magazine pagination counts the front cover as 1, which would make this page 5.

6   http://bit.ly/xprizes.

7   Personal communication, 6/3/2014.

8   http://bit.ly/wordsentence.

8
Page furniture systems
Pull quotes, cross heads, tags

If sells and captions are the main building blocks of page furniture for features, there are other elements that have equally important roles in the eco-system of page furniture:

Pull quote (blown quote, display quote, call out) – short extracts from the feature displayed in large type on the page. Generally speaking, pull quotes that appear within a column of text should break a paragraph (i.e. be positioned between lines of text) not run in the space between paragraphs. If they are placed between paragraphs they can look like part of the text that has been enlarged for some reason, which is an amateurish mistake.

Subhead – a feature that deals with several disparate but associated topics may be written in chunks that cover the individual subtopics separately, rather than as a piece of continuous prose. Each chunk may be separated by a subhead set in type that is distinguished by size or emphasis (bold or italic or both).

Crosshead – a single word or short phrase used to break up long texts that might otherwise appear offputting to readers; was commonly used in newspapers but can be found online and performing a variety of functions in magazines.

Page livery – repeating graphic or textual elements that identify a section within the magazine or a regular feature; the magazine identification and page number (or folio) also count as page livery.

Box-out – a piece of text, generally additional to or reinforcing of, the main text, which may be accompanied by graphics, encased in a space defined by ruled lines or by colour (a *tint panel*). The space is usually rectangular and positioned within a normal column, but it may run across two or more columns and be designed in any shape the curatum's aesthetic and design software can accommodate. Box-outs may have their own headlines or subheads, thus adding a system within a system.

Pull quotes – the art of interest

The pull quote often has a complex part to play in page design, combining both graphic and textual elements; enhancing the design of the page and piquing interest in the story it accompanies. It has four distinct roles:

- temptation
- emphasis
- balance
- filler.

It is always worth looking closely at how pull quotes are used on the page – how many columns do they run across? How are the lines shaped and justified? Do they cut into the flow of text in a column? Do they take quote marks? Are they given extra lines or rules? Are they put into a tint box or panel of some kind? There are many possible creative treatments and even though execution is likely to be the province of a designer rather than a production editor, knowing what can be done to add interest is valuable.

Temptation

Pull quotes make strong entry points for a browsing reader. Pick out an unusual or intriguing phrase from the text – a quirky quote often works well – that will catch the browser's attention and that may make him or her stop to read the whole thing. The *Observer Magazine*'s interview

(2/6/13) with Felix Dennis, the publishing maverick who had recently been diagnosed with throat cancer (which sadly claimed his life in 2014), was peppered with them, each illustrating an aspect of his character – drugs, wealth and the creation of a national forest:

> On crack I didn't sleep for five years. You can get a lot done if you don't waste time sleeping (31)

> I've lived an unbelievable life, even if I did do my best to kill myself in order to live it (33)

> Will the trees make a difference? No! Nature doesn't care. She'll shrug once and we're gone (35)

The quote that illustrates an aspect of an interviewee's character, or highlights the ways in which they have changed or developed, is a staple. *Uncut*'s September 2014 issue had major interviews with Robert Plant, Richard Thompson and Tom Petty, all with pull quotes from the subjects:

> Now I don't lose my temper and, god, it's a lot better life
> (Petty: 59)

> Linda and I loved glum. Glum is the new glam . . .
> (Thompson: 47)

> I celebrate my gift . . . there's no point in fucking about and pretending
> (Plant: 33)

Using a direct quote as a pull quote is just about the only time when it is permissible to tinker with the words to get them to fit. There is no logical or ethical justification for this, unless you regard the pull quote solely as a graphical element – the words have to fill the lines in a particular way and swapping one word for another might be necessary from the designer's point of view. It's something that should only be done if absolutely necessary, it must retain the original meaning and there should be as little alteration as possible. On the other hand, pull quotes do not have to appear on the same page as where they occur in the story; they may be nearby or they can be on another page.

So far we have looked at the 'quote' side, but it is just as usual to see copy 'pulled' from a feature. This can work well in both entertaining and informative pieces. For its January 2014 issue, *Car* magazine pitted the Peugeot RCZ R against the VW Scirocco R to see which was the best hot coupé and used multiple pull quotes to highlight the contest:

> **It is the fastest Peugeot ever, and that includes the crazy 205 T16 from the 1980s** (85)

> **The Scirocco, one of our favourite real-world performance cars, is not as much of a giggle to hoon[1] about in** (89)

Emphasis

Pull quotes can be used to reinforce the main thrust of a story or bring out particular aspects. *Intelligent Life*'s profile of Ricken Patel (May/June 2013), executive director of idealistic campaigning group Avaaz, pulled key phrases from the copy to indicate the way he sets about defining his mission and also reveal the roots of his calling:

> **The theory of change justifies the campaign: why this, why now, how will it work, what will it achieve** (74)

> **His subject, really, is culture with a small c, starting with the beery work-shyness of his fellow students** (79)

Balance

If symmetry is an important part of the design aesthetic, pull quotes can be used as a graphic element on a page – for example, a block of photographs at the top right of a layout can be balanced by a pull quote in the bottom left. Decisions about this kind of use are likely to fall into the art editor's role (Figure 8.1).

Filler

The worst possible reason to use a pull quote is to fill a gap left because you have run out of text or images. This kind of use is unlikely to be

If symmetry is important, a pull quote block here can balance the picture block at top right

Figure 8.1 A simple example of symmetry in a double page spread.

Source: Courtesy of the author.

found in well designed or professionally published curata but it is common in amateur or learner-level work. Always look for ways to use pictures more effectively than trying to fix an unwanted space with pull quotes – it's a form of desperation that always shows.

Call out conundrum

Spotting a fake quote from a real person is relatively simple, as we saw in Chapter 6, but how should a real quote from a fake person be classified? This is the dilemma that faces us on p. 143 of *Esquire*'s September 2013 issue, where Alan Partridge (the radio presenter persona of Steve Coogan) is given a double page spread for a *This Much I Know* type of feature. At top right of the second page is this pull quote (reproduction of the interestingly varied typography is approximate):

"IT ABSOLUTELY STAGGERS ME THAT PEOPLE KEEP THEIR EGGS IN A FRIDGE"

Crossheads – another doorway

Crossheads are words or phrases placed at intervals between paragraphs in longer stories. The original intention was to break up blocks of text, introduce a bit of white space into columns and keep the reader moving along. Newspapers of the twentieth century used this device frequently, often selecting emotive words that had at least a vague connection with the story; for example, if you put the term 'newspaper crosshead' into a search engine, the results are likely to include images of columns broken by words such as:

Plagued
Begged
Smitten

However, as stories have become shorter and newspaper design has evolved into a more magazine-like state, broken up with images and graphics, the humble crosshead used this way has become a somewhat endangered species. In the *South Wales Evening Post* for 30 August 2013 only one single crosshead can be found in all 52 pages – on page 11 a tribute to Welsh rugby international and television personality Cliff Morgan is broken by the word

Contribution

The People's Friend has a typically curt variation on this theme by using crossheads in some of its short stories. In the issue for 31 August 2013,

Gold For A Princess ('Heather Pardoe's inspiring story, set in Wales in the 1880s [. . .]', p. 64) is punctuated with:

> **Impressed**
> **Hesitant**
> **Helpless**
> **Shock**
> **Courage** and
> **"What have I done?"**

The disparity in length and form of the final example is striking.

BBC News online still uses crossheads on some, but not all, of its stories. A court report of the trial of a former charity chief (http://bit.ly/bee bawema[2]) is punctuated by:

> **'Wanted money back'** and

> **Pre-signed blank cheques**

and a feature about the centenary of the Panama Canal (http://bit.ly/beebpanama[3]) with:

> **Game-changer**

> **Expansion needed** and

> **New rivals**

Portal

However, if a pull quote can be a main point of entry into a story, the crosshead can act as a minor portal, especially if treated with imagination. Take the story *Weaving the world together* (76–8) in the *Economist* for 19 November 2011. It's an examination of the ways in which mass migration is changing patterns of business, illustrated with two photographs, a table and an infographic; the text is broken up with five crossheads:

> **The immigrant song**
> **In through the out door**

Bringing it all back home
Going to California
Ramble on

In case you don't recognise them, the crossheads are all titles of Led Zeppelin songs. They fit the context of the story, so they work technically, and they also add a cultural resonance for people who get the references. This kind of thing is not restricted to the *Economist*'s production journalists, of course; a couple of years later I had an email correspondence with Rob Parr of *Times Higher Education* after spotting something similar:

> I wonder if the 10CC fan on your production team ("Godly and cream", Campus round-up; "They don't like cricket, oh no, they love it", News, 7 November) is the same person who ingeniously used Led Zeppelin song titles as the crossheads in an *Economist* article a couple of years ago?

> No, I'm not the source of the *Economist*'s Led Zep riffing, but the subs here do enjoy throwing in the odd pop-rock reference. There's a nice Bowie one in this week's Campus and a Survivor headline next week. Thanks for noticing!
> (Rob Parr, email correspondence 11/11/13)

Crossheads used this way can also be part of a design scheme, especially if the report or feature concerned is structured in the form of linked but discrete sections. A nicely 'designed' example of this way of using crossheadings can be found in the launch issue of *The Cleaver Quarterly* (May 2014: 46), an indy magazine dedicated to Chinese cuisine. David R. Chan has eaten at more than 6,500 Chinese restaurants and keeps track of them on a spreadsheet; the feature about his experiences takes a Q&A-like form, but the sections are introduced with phrases that all begin with 'On . . .':

On why he started his database
On the "aha" moment
On how he scouts out restaurants

The typeset phrases are set on irregularly shaped blocks of colour that give the impression of having been picked out with a somewhat muted highlighter pen.

New Scientist's collection of essays on *The Big Questions* (Volume 1/Issue 1, 2014) draws on the power of a good phrase to act as an attractor for readers. Celeste Biever's piece about artificial intelligence (pp. 60–1) sports the crossheads:

Nitty-gritty
Brain in a vat

while Emma Young's article about biodiversity in equatorial tropics (pp. 68–71) has just a single culturally referent crosshead:

Some like it hot

Pseudo-crossheads

Sometimes it is possible to have something that looks like a crosshead but is actually part of the body copy. *Red* magazine for November 2014 employs this technique for an article that sports the highly intriguing headline 'My husband granted me a one-night stand' (129–30). The body text runs across two columns and on both pages is interrupted by text that performs the function of a crosshead – it is typeset in an upper case red sans serif face that contrasts strongly with the black serif body face. The four headers and the lines that follow run:

'BE THERE IN 10. CAN'T WAIT TO SEE YOU XX'

I had a sudden urge to vomit, to purge myself of the nerves,

INSTEAD, I FOUND WAYS TO FURTHER INVITE

Tom's attention. I started wearing more body-conscious

I FELT STRANGELY, SHAMEFULLY ELATED.

Andy was offering me my cake and the chance to eat it.

THINGS FINALLY CAME

to a head on a family weekend in

Sectional subheads

The hundredth edition of *Psychologies* magazine (January 2014) has a number of features that work on a sectional structure – they are written in continuous prose but lend themselves to being broken up into linked themes: on pages 30–1 Suzy Greaves asks *What can you learn by looking back?*, a piece that advocates personal reflection, broken up with the following crossheads:

PRESS PAUSE
WHAT DID YOU SEE?
IF IT DIDN'T WORK . . .

Further into the magazine (p. 52) Katy Regan asks another question – *Are your friends making you single?* – and proceeds to offer advice in sections crossheaded with:

Married to your mates?

The surrogate

Being 'too good' a friend

The group of friends

Hanging out with couples

The textless crosshead

Calling something a textless crosshead sounds paradoxical, but it is a way to categorise what seems to be an increasingly popular way to break up longer features. It takes the form of a simple space, usually a single line, between paragraphs, with the subsequent paragraph picked up with a full out drop cap (a capital letter that drops down three or four lines and no indentation). Two new-for-2014 magazines to use the textless crosshead are Team Rock's *Country Music Magazine* (see the Dolly Parton interview, pp. 36–44 of issue 2) and *Forever Sports* (launched for retailer Sports Direct by Haymarket Network as an evolution of the SportsDirect.com magazine) in its feature about Michael Sam, the first openly gay American Football player to be drafted to the NFL (July 2014: 72–7). The typeface of the drop cap can also add to the publication's identity

– *Country Music* uses a folksy, loopy, brush-style script while *Forever Sports* goes for an elegant, thin sans-serif.

The reader's digest crosshead

Nothing to do with the troubled magazine of the same name,[4] the reader's digest crosshead category sits at the opposite end of the scale of text-heaviness and it's only used in particular circumstances. For example, *Country Music* secured the right to run a selection of extracts from Buck Owens's memoirs, covering the years between 1958 and 2006. Each selection needed to be put into context and was introduced with a very well-summarised paragraph, such as this from p. 48 of Issue 2:

> **It's February of '64. Buck Owens and His Buckaroos are top of the country charts with *Love's Gonna Live Here*. Over on the pop charts a young band from Liverpool are kicking off a seven-week sit-in at The No.1 spot with a little something called *I Want To Hold Your Hand*.**

Box outs – additional interest

Box outs perform several functions within a layout. They can be used to add information to a story, to highlight an important aspect of the story that may not fit easily into the main narrative or to tell a related but subsidiary story. They can also be used to add visual interest to a page by breaking copy and images into discretely consumable chunks.

Their shape is often quadrilateral – a square or rectangle – but there is nothing to stop the art editor specifying circular, oval, compound curve, triangular or polygonal shapes. Sometimes there will be a repeating motif – *Country Music Magazine*, for example, draws on a Wild West saloon bar poster vibe for its feature box outs.

A taxonomy of box outs

- Additional info – issue one of *New Scientist*'s *The Collection* looked at the 'big questions', one of which was how it benefits humans to be conscious (as opposed to being in a zombie-like state of uncon-sciousness). There is, it turns out, no easy or obvious answer to this age-old quiz, but a simple box out (white type in a red tint panel) in the rightmost column of the double page spread allows the author to add related information about the causes of anarchic hand syndrome – the condition that caused Peter Sellers's eponymous character in *Dr Strangelove* to struggle with his right arm – a result of *unconscious* decision making.

- Additional narrative – *Glamour* magazine's March 2014 issue ran a feature called *War vs Wedding*, looking at how Avine, a Syrian woman who owned a successful bridal salon, managed to rebuild her business within a refugee camp. The main story is augmented by box outs containing narratives about two of the brides who Avine has helped to prepare for their wedding days. This allows the main story to be told while separately highlighting the human interest stories that surround it.

- Endorsement – Dolly Parton is probably the biggest star that country music has ever seen and she has worked with, influenced, or written songs that have been covered by innumerable other artists. What better way for *Country Music Magazine* to reflect this in its long exclusive interview with her than to garnish the copy with small box outs of endorsements from the likes of Norah Jones, Kenny Rogers, Mindy Smith and Pam Tillis; add in a box giving the background to Dolly's classic *Jolene* and another recommend-ing six essential albums and you have nine zinging pages (36–44, January 2014).

- Minimalist – a box out does not have to be in a box. For an example of this look at *Wired*'s June 2014 issue. A feature called *Ask A Better Question* is embellished not just with a trio of strikingly appro-priate commissioned illustrations but also with five examples of 'smart questions' that delivered results for a variety of enterprises. The questions can clearly be categorised as box outs, but they are set in a sans serif typeface at a smaller point size that contrasts with the serif body copy, situated within the wide central gutter of a two column layout; the space is given definition by thin rules either side but there is no 'box' and each question is accompanied with an appropriate graphic. Taken all together, this is a very creative use of page furniture within a coherent design scheme.

- Maximalist – if the *Wired* example above demonstrates a minimalist approach, *Forever Sports* of July 2014 goes to the other extreme in its feature *Do Movie Training Montages Really Work?* (88–96). The whole structure is a 'box out feature' pegged on Tyson Fury's then-forthcoming fight with Derek Chisora, taking various improvisational training sequences from the *Rocky* films and analysing whether they would be effective in real life. Six exercises are tried by Fury, described, commented on and given a 'glove rating' of between one and five, the boxed text being set in white type on a black panel. In addition to the main copy, there are two further box outs, one a wry look at training routines in four more films (*Batman Begins, Team America: World Police, The Karate Kid* and *The Kickboxer*), the other giving Tyson Fury's vital statistics.

• Photo – box outs are not restricted to words. When *Mojo* interviewed a revivified Adam Ant in its March 2013 issue (42–7), the bottom half of the second spread was a box out of nine photographs (from 1960s school days to a 2002 court appearance on firearms charges) and captions – a very effective way of encapsulating and illustrating the rise and fall of Antmusic. In addition, the first spread has a boxed endorsement from Duff McKagan of Guns'N'Roses and the third spread a boxed recommendation of essential albums.

Page livery – adding identity

This term is used by some print publishers and designers to refer to repeating elements of page furniture. Strap lines or identity blocks to identify content that appears regularly – news pages, a particular type of feature, a section of the curatum – fall into this category, as do page numbers, names, repeating graphics or small reproductions of the logo.

The design and usage of page livery depends entirely on the overall design template for each curatum; some will use a lot, some will be more minimal and sometimes it varies as a title evolves. The pre-launch Issue Zero of indy motorcycle magazine *Esses* just used a small version of the logo at the top of each left and right hand page, with the page numbers set in white type in a black roundel at bottom left and right, whereas Issue One identified each feature with a strap line at the top of each left and right page, just one or two words set very small in upper case linked over the spread by a dotted line: WORTH MOTORCYCLES ....., ILLUSTRATION ....., LEWIS LEATHERS ....., CULTURE .... At the bottom of each page was the page number, white type in a black roundel, and a miniature of the *Esses* logo.

The Cleaver Quarterly, an indy magazine about Chinese cuisine, set the page number and issue date at the bottom left of left hand pages and the title name and page number top right of right hand pages. The alternating placement brought a touch of 'design' to what was otherwise straightforward type and numbers.

By contrast, *The People's Friend* identifies sections or stories with a dual-coloured box. On page five of the 31 August 2013 issue, we have **The People's Friend 5** set in serif white type (the name in italics, the number in roman) on a red panel immediately above romantic story set in larger sans serif white type on a dark blue background. The health section has the logo and folio in white on purple above your health in white on green. Left hand editorial pages usually just have the page number at top left.

Page livery that is used frequently can be stored in what page make-up software such as InDesign calls a 'library', ready to be pulled out and deployed where necessary. The subeditor or production journalist with layout responsibilities must remember what goes where and, most importantly, must check that the page number corresponds with the latest version of the flat plan. If there is an issue date incorporated in the livery, it must show the right week, or month, and year. It is easy to overlook such details in a rush to deadline but this is another place where a checklist of the type followed by pilots before take-off can prove invaluable. If you have such a list of all the production jobs that have to be completed, the task is taken out of memory and into a systematic process – you don't have to remember, you just check the list.

Meta tags – descriptive indexing

When it comes to material that will be published digitally, meta tags can be considered elements of page furniture even though they will not usually be visible to readers.

A meta tag is a special HTML tag that provides information about a web page. However, where normal HTML tags determine how the page is displayed (position, font, size, colour), meta tags provide information that defines what the page content is about, and which keywords represent its content. There is some debate about whether meta tags are still relevant to SEO as the major engines constantly improve their algorithms to rank pages by relevance and reputation rather than by elements that can be gamed, but it is generally accepted that well chosen meta tags can help with the classification of pages, so they still have a role to perform.

According to internet marketing experts Hobo:

> Your tags should be accurate, relevant and descriptive, and be careful focusing them all unnecessarily on just one keyword, but don't think "meta tags" until you have thought "topic" and "user experience". Satisfying both is key to building reputation, in Google, and on social channels. If you are optimising for Google, don't think page or article, think "topic" or "subject" or information "hub".
>
> (www.hobo-web.co.uk/definitive-guide-
> to-using-important-meta-tags/)

Google itself has a useful page that explains how to create and where to place meta tags – the emphasis is on description rather than keywords: https://support.google.com/webmasters/answer/79812?hl=en. However, it is important to remember that Google and other search engines change the way they work, so this advice will not be an eternal verity and sub-editors with digital responsibilities should check Google's support pages regularly.

Alt tags

Alt tags (properly called alt attributes) are textual descriptions attached to a digital asset (such as an image) that appears when the asset cannot be rendered in a browser – but they are also an important element in making web pages accessible to people with impaired vision as screen reader software interacts with the alt element. Most operating systems come with a screen reader built in, or with downloadable elements such as VoiceOver for MacOSX (which also works with braille displays).

An alt attribute attached to an image allows the screen reader to 'describe' the image, so it is important to focus on the important elements of the image – what does it show and why is it showing it? The size and shape of the image are probably not important in this context. If it is providing additional information that augments the text, summarise that succinctly; if it is more generally illustrative, perhaps a more lyrical approach would work better. WebAIM, an organisation whose mission is to expand the potential of the web for people with disabilities, has a useful and informative tutorial about how to write good alt attributes on its site: http://webaim.org/techniques/alttext/.

Page furniture in social media

It might seem strange to think of a tweet or Facebook update having page furniture, but a little lateral thinking will show that they do. What is a hashtag in a Twitter update if not furniture? A subeditor with social media responsibilities can either latch on to an existing hashtag, especially one that is trending at the time of the update, or compose an appropriate new one, assuming that there are any permutations left. Twitter handles can also be considered furniture, but only relevant ones should be included – i.e. those addressing people or organisations involved in the subject matter or discussion.

Likewise, Facebook updates that tag people who have an involvement or interest in the content may help to spread awareness or create a network effect.

Notes

1   If you are not familiar with this word, the online Urban Dictionary has a useful definition.
2   www.bbc.co.uk/news/uk-wales-south-west-wales-28808548; accessed 15/8/14.
3   www.bbc.co.uk/news/world-latin-america-28798310; accessed 15/8/14.
4   In February 2014 Better Capital sold *Reader's Digest* to media entrepreneur Mike Luckwell for £1. http://bit.ly/rdsold.

9

Legal and ethical problems for subeditors

This book is not about the law or ethics but those topics are of such importance to journalism that no book about subediting would be complete without considering them. That said, a single chapter should not be considered a replacement for a full length book such as the latest edition of *McNae's Essential Law for Journalists* or, best of all, a proper training course run by an accredited organisation.

The subeditor (or person performing that role) is in a position of great, and probably increasing, importance when it comes to legal and ethical matters. 'Subs are the last line of defence', according to Jessany Marsden, former editorial training manager at IPC Media. Her colleague Peter Genower (whose CV includes being editor-in-chief of *TV Times* and chairman of the Periodicals Training Council's training committee) reinforced her opinion by observing that knowledge of the law had become much more important in an age when people – and readers – have become more litigious and more aware of their rights.

In *Law For Journalists* (2013), lawyer Rod Dadak, a specialist in defamation cases, notes: 'Mistakes can be introduced during the subbing process, and a headline or caption can make a piece defamatory even if the original text was not' (231). This is not news. Peter Mason and Derrick Smith wrote, 'Sub-editors must have an even sharper knowledge than writers of the laws that influence what magazines can and cannot publish' in their book *Magazine Law: A Practical Guide* (1998: 90). The lesson still applies to print media, and digital media face further difficulties. Because they are 'published' internationally, they may be subject to different interpretations of the law: this is discussed further below.

The subeditor should not, however, be acting alone. Every curatum should have access to a lawyer's opinion, either before publishing something that may be contentious or after receiving a complaint, threat of action or writ following publication. In practice, newspapers are most likely to call upon this service most frequently, but it should be noted that any periodical, even the most obscure hobby magazine, can find itself on the wrong end of a legal action, and digital publishing being a global phenomenon is open to all kinds of issues. The sub should therefore know what to do and who to call on in case of doubt. As Dan Bourke, assistant night editor of the *Daily Mirror*, states, 'If you have a legal question, go to the lawyers instantly. It's not your job to make things legally sound, it's your job to recognise when a story needs a legal opinion.'

However, even the most expert legal opinion is no guarantee of protection. Colin Myler, former editor of the *Sunday Mirror*, discovered this in April 2001 when his paper published an interview with the father of an alleged assault victim while the court case was still in progress (discussed further below). A sub with even the most rudimentary knowledge of the law should have had the phrase 'contempt of court' going off like an alarm clock, but editors have a habit of pushing at the boundaries of what is acceptable, and this story was run after legal advice had been taken.

A subeditor can get a publication into trouble passively, by not picking up a dubious statement in a piece of copy, or actively, by changing copy so that it becomes defamatory, by attaching a libellous headline or sell to the copy, or by captioning a picture badly. A photograph can, in itself, be libellous. Cover lines on a magazine can also lead to trouble, as can poor punctuation. Even if all of the above are legally sound, there may be questions of ethics surrounding them.

Know the law

A subeditor should at the very minimum have a working knowledge of the laws governing defamation, reporting restrictions, honest opinion, privacy/confidentiality, copyright and, even though they occur infrequently, malicious falsehoods. A fully trained sub, and certainly anyone dealing with news, must also know about the absolute or qualified privilege of reporting courts, tribunals, company meetings and government (local, regional and national), contempt of court and trademarks.

The Defamation Act of 2013, which came into force in January 2014, was intended to address the so-called 'chilling' effect that existing libel laws had had on freedom of expression and public debate. It also attempts to clear up some of the issues surrounding internet publishing.

Professor Duncan Bloy, who lectures in media law at Cardiff University, summarises the major changes thus:

- There is a new negative statutory definition of defamation (discussed below).
- Operators of websites will have a defence to an action for defamation if the operator can show it did not post the statement on its own website, that is, the operator is simply the facilitator permitting others to add content.
- However, if the claimant cannot identify the person who posted the statement then the website operator will not have a defence if the claimant has given notice of complaint and the operator has failed to respond by taking down the offending material within a reasonable time.
- There are changes to legal privilege (discussed below).
- A single publication rule, which means that a claimant can only sue once on the content of the publication. Previous rules meant there was potentially a new cause of action every time the offending statement was published or accessed. The new rules 'prevent an action being brought in relation to publication of the same material by the same publisher after a one year limitation period from the date of the first publication of that material to the public or a section of the public' (Section 8, explanatory notes, Defamation Act 2013).
- Section 9 of the Act seeks to limit so-called libel tourism – England and Wales must be shown to be the most appropriate place in which to bring an action against someone who is not domiciled in the UK.
- Defamation actions are brought against someone who is the author, editor or publisher of a statement.
- Jury trials for defamation are abolished.

There is also specific protection for scientists and academics publishing peer-reviewed material in scientific and academic journals and a new process aimed at helping potential victims of defamation online, by resolving the dispute directly with the person who has posted the statement.

Another key change is the replacement of the 'Reynolds defence' – a ten point schema that aimed to provide protection for 'responsible journalism' that was reporting matters of public concern – with a defence of public interest that states:

> It is a defence to an action for defamation for the defendant to show that—
>
> (a) the statement complained of was, or formed part of, a statement on a matter of public interest; and
> (b) the defendant reasonably believed that publishing the statement complained of was in the public interest.

The complete 2013 Act and all accompanying material can be accessed online at: www.legislation.gov.uk/ukpga/2013/26/contents

1 Defamation: unwarranted badmouthing as understood by Joe Public

The legal systems of the UK are based on case law, that is, on how judges interpret the statutes for specific court actions, and those interpretations can change or evolve over time. Thus the definition of what constitutes a defamatory statement has moved on since it was outlined in 1840: 'A publication . . . which is calculated to injure the reputation of another by exposing him to hatred, contempt or ridicule.' Subsequent judgements added that a defamatory statement was one that might cause a person to be shunned or avoided; disparaged a person in their office, profession or trade; tended to make right-thinking people think less of a person.

The Defamation Act of 2013 clarified many of these elements into a new code. The Act's first section states clearly that:

> (1) A statement is not defamatory unless its publication has caused or is likely to cause serious harm to the reputation of the claimant.
> (2) For the purposes of this section, harm to the reputation of a body that trades for profit is not "serious harm" unless it has caused or is likely to cause the body serious financial loss.
>
> (http://bit.ly/DefAct2013)

This is a 'negative' definition, and the claimant – the person or organisation making the claim – has to prove that there has been serious harm to their reputation (or revenue) as a direct result of what was published or broadcast.

The clause about 'Right-thinking people' (a term for which there was no statutory definition, but which was in practice taken to mean the members of the jury who heard a case for defamation) has also been overtaken by the 2013 Act. Juries have been abolished for defamation cases and the 'right thinking person' has been replaced with the 'hypothetical reader or viewer'. Professor Duncan Bloy explains:

> The judge will ask whether the hypothetical reader or viewer would on the ordinary meaning of the words used consider that the words might be defamatory. The word used is whether the words are 'capable' of conveying the interpretation alleged by the claimant.

Furthermore, the hypothetical viewer or reader is assumed to have certain characteristics against which the words in question are judged. These characteristics were set out in the judgment of *Jeynes vs News Magazines Ltd* (2008):

> (1) The governing principle is reasonableness. (2) The hypothetical reasonable reader is not naïve but he is not unduly suspicious. He can read between the lines. He can read in an implication more readily than a lawyer and may indulge in a certain amount of loose thinking but he must be treated as being a man who is not avid for scandal and someone who does not, and should not, select one bad meaning where other non-defamatory meanings are available. (3) Over-elaborate analysis is best avoided. (4) The intention of the publisher is irrelevant. (5) The article must be read as a whole, and any "bane and antidote" taken together. (6) The hypothetical reader is taken to be representative of those who would read the publication in question. (7) In delimiting the range of permissible defamatory meanings, the court should rule out any meaning which, "can only emerge as the produce of some strained, or forced, or utterly unreasonable interpretation [. . .]"
>
> (http://bit.ly/jeynes2008)

The reference to 'bane and antidote' in point (5) simply means that if, for example, a headline makes an exaggerated claim that could be defamatory but the body of the article that follows corrects the misleading impression created by the headline, the chances of a successful action are significantly reduced.

At the same time, the law (in its concrete expression as pronouncements by judges over the years) recognises that a free press must be allowed to report wrongdoing and that such reports may damage the reputations of individuals. The key point is that such reports must be accurate, fair, justified – and provable. There are three levels of seriousness attributed to defamation, known as the Chase levels from the case of *Chase vs News Group Newspapers* (2002). They are, in decreasing order of gravity:

1   where there is no ambiguity in the allegation;
2   where there are reasonable grounds to believe that the allegations might be true;
3   where there could be grounds for investigating whether the claimant was responsible for the acts being alleged.

As Professor Bloy explains, 'The higher the level, the stronger the evidence needed if the media group is to succeed with a truth defence', which is defined in the 2013 Act thus: 'It is a defence to an action for defamation for the defendant to show that the imputation conveyed by the statement complained of is substantially true.'

Subeditors cannot be expected to re-research stories and, as the old phrase has it, stand them up, but they must know when a story may be defamatory. Subs should also be aware that injudicious copy editing may cause a story to become defamatory, particularly if the fairness and balance are affected, or if evidence that justifies the claims being made against a person is cut.

Defamation can take the form of libel or slander. A libel is a defamatory statement that is published in permanent form (such as print, broadcast or online journalism), whereas a slander is transitory, for example if it is spoken or if it is an internet posting. The latter ruling was made by Mr Justice Eady, who decided:

> When considered in the context of defamation law, therefore, communications of this kind are much more akin to slanders

(this cause of action being nowadays relatively rare) than to the usual, more permanent kind of communications found in libel actions. People do not often take a "thread" and go through it as a whole like a newspaper article. They tend to read the remarks, make their own contributions if they feel inclined, and think no more about it.

(*Smith vs ADFVN Ltd*, 2008;
http://bit.ly/slanderrule)

Libel is therefore the most prevalent concern, although journalists (in interviews or even in phone conversations) may lay themselves open to charges of slander.

Inept use of a photograph may also be defamatory. The news editor of a top selling weekly title recalled: 'A man being circled in a photo as the paedophile referred to in the story – wrong guy was circled, lawsuit, big money paid out.' That's a fairly obvious example, but subs responsible for layout should also beware the perils of juxtaposing the innocent and the guilty: running a big picture of a local worthy next to a headline that screams 'My Sex-change Hell' might just be funny but it might just be defamatory, too.

Think twice about reusing photos commissioned for one story to illustrate another. The person who posed for a heart-warming tale of selfless charity might not care to be used to stand for something less salubrious. Mason and Smith cite a library picture of a lorry being used to illustrate a story about the mistreatment of livestock in transport; wrong lorry shown, wrong company clearly identified in the signwriting, wrong side of the law.

Mr Justice Eady, in his ruling on the case of *Mosley v News Group*, decided that images could be assigned a higher degree of intrusion into privacy than words, another factor to bear in mind (Bloy and Hadwin, 2011: 268[1]).

And if a photo can do it, so can a caption. The weekly's news editor again:

Another story was about swingers and we had to run a panel of people's comments next to it. One was a guy who ran swinging nights at a club but he was labelled by subs in the caption as 'committed swinger' – he wasn't and threatened to sue.

Finally, note that the humble comma can be a powerful force for good or evil. Used incorrectly it can make an apparently innocuous sentence into a costly libel. Indeed, punctuation can completely change the meaning of a sentence (which is why lawyers are so sparing with it). To illustrate the point have a go at punctuating this old chestnut: 'Woman without her man is nothing.' (Answer at end of chapter.)

2 Malicious Falsehoods: knocking copy

Pushed for space and up against a deadline, a subeditor working on the *Scotsman*'s TV listings cut four words in the description of a programme and inserted three others. The copy now fitted perfectly.

Unfortunately the words he used altered the meaning of the description, so that the show changed from a tribute to a singer 'who was struck down by a brain tumour last year' to one 'who died of a brain tumour last year'. The singer had not died and was understandably upset. Had he been sufficiently upset to believe that the change was made deliberately and with the intention of harming his earnings, he could possibly have sued for malicious falsehood.

Like many words used in a legal context, 'malice' carries more meaning than its general usage. Certainly it refers to spite and ill-will but journalists who publish something they know to be untrue, or which they have been told is untrue, or who don't care whether it is true or not are held to be acting maliciously. If untrue information is published for personal gain or some other dishonest motive then that is a malicious falsehood.

Actions for malicious falsehood are quite rare and there is not much a subeditor can do about the origination of potentially malicious copy but it should be considered a duty to catch it before publication. This will probably require some checking back with the writer or editor.

3 Honest opinion

Pay particular attention to reviews of products or services; a critical review or test is not in itself malicious but there must be a clear delineation between fact and comment. Harsh and negative comments may be used as the basis for an action for defamation, which may be why Belfast restaurateur Ciaran Convery sued the *Irish News* after their food critic wrote an unfavourable review of his pizzeria, Goodfellas. The jury in the case found in Convery's favour and awarded £25,000 damages.[2]

A year later, however, the appeal court overturned the decision on the grounds that 'the original trial jury had been misdirected, with confusion between fact and comment in the article'. Lord Chief Justice Sir Brian Kerr said: 'Only if the jury has a clear understanding of what is capable of constituting comment, can it address the thorny issue of whether the facts on which comment is based are capable of justifying the comment made.'[3]

So it's not necessarily a cause for panic if a reviewer gets a bit caustic. The following comes from a restaurant review Marina O'Loughlin wrote for *Metro* (23/7/2009):

> And the food: crikey. A catalogue of hideousness washed down with the kind of rosé that costs three for a tenner at a petrol station. Prawn cocktail: spermy little frozen prawns awash with astringent, Pepto Bismol-coloured Marie Rose. But it comes in a groovy glass cone set into a groovy scarlet glass cube, so that's OK!

> Seafood risotto ('the squid's like chewing a foreskin,' says pal; no, I don't ask) is sickly with cheese, that Italian seafood solecism, and too much tarragon. There are tomato skins swimming in its depths.[4]

O'Loughlin's right to publish such views was, in a different context, defended by Lord Nicholls of Birkenhead who stated 'a critic need not be mealy-mouthed in denouncing what he disagrees with. He is entitled to dip his pen in gall for the purposes of legitimate criticism' (cited in Bloy and Hadwin, 2011: 47).[5]

The defence of honest opinion has been incorporated in the 2013 Act, section 3 of which outlines the conditions that have to be met:

> The first condition is that the statement complained of was a statement of opinion.

> The second condition is that the statement complained of indicated, whether in general or specific terms, the basis of the opinion.

The third condition is that an honest person could have held the opinion on the basis of:

(a) any fact which existed at the time the statement complained of was published; (b) anything asserted to be a fact in a privileged statement published before the statement complained of.

(http://bit.ly/DefAct2013)

When in doubt, however, these four guidelines should see you safe:

- always test the product according to the manufacturer's instructions for use;
- if conducting a comparison test, make sure you compare like with like;
- have evidence of the accuracy of your facts;
- always give the manufacturer the opportunity of responding to poor results before publication.

The subeditor does have the power to make matters worse by presenting critical copy in a way that draws special attention to it. A sensational headline in huge type, or an unwarrantedly prominent position on the page might be used as evidence of ill-intention.

4 Copyright: whose line is it anyway?

It is unlikely that a subeditor will run much risk of falling foul of the copyright laws as far as copy is concerned. Unless you deliberately insert great chunks of copyright material (novels, plays, song lyrics, film dialogue, other journalism, etc.), most quotes will come under the heading of 'fair dealing'. You may use other people's words in a report of current events or in a review, provided that the source is acknowledged and that they do not form a 'substantial part' of the copy. How much is a 'substantial part'? There is no legal definition, but if it is enough to lower the commercial value of the work in question then the author might have a claim for infringement of copyright and damages.

Pictures are what the subeditor should beware of. As Bloy and Hadwin (2011) explain: 'The leeway of fair dealing does not extend to photographs except where they are used, with appropriate acknowledgement and where already made public, to illustrate a review of work' (314).

Before using any picture or photograph – including those that arrive with press releases – you should check your publication has the right to use it. Even if it comes out of the archive (be that physical or digital) because it has been used before, it may be that copyright reverted to the creator after the first use. Although it is not uncommon for newspapers to 'grab' pictures from broadcast material, this is not legally condoned and such material should be acknowledged and paid for.

Perhaps the reporter has persuaded someone to take a photograph from their photo album to illustrate a piece about a family member in the news. If the picture was taken by a commercial photographer, it is likely that the copyright remains with them, especially if the picture was taken after the Copyright Designs and Patents Act 1988 came into force in 1989.

The reverse of that is where a commercial photographer (who has retained the copyright) offers your publication a picture of someone in the news. There is no copyright problem here but there may be an infringement of the family's right to privacy; the person who commissioned the picture usually controls the right to distribution even if they don't own the copyright.

Images found on social media are subject to the same restrictions, as Quinn (2013) notes: 'it can be risky to lift pictures from social networking sites such as Facebook, if you do not know who owns the copyright' (377). The terms and conditions of use of social media networks may state that copyright remains with the person who owns it, but there is a counter-argument that images without any clear attribution of copyright and nothing explicitly saying the image cannot be reproduced may be fair game under the concept of Implied Consent.

Subs working for local newspapers, news agencies and magazines specialising in human interest stories should pay particular attention to the use of pictures for all these reasons. Those employed on celebrity magazines should note the increasing tendency to litigation by stars and near-stars who feel their privacy – or exclusivity – has been invaded. In July 2001 the Press Complaints Commission rejected a claim by Anna Ford that pictures which the *Daily Mail* and *OK!* had published, of her on a public beach, invaded her privacy. Ford applied to the High Court for a judicial review of the ruling but her challenge was not allowed. More recently (April 2014), Paul Weller took action on behalf of three of his children after paparazzo snaps of them out on a shopping trip in LA with him were published in the *Mail Online*. Mr Justice Dingemans ruled that by not blurring the children's faces, the *Mail Online* had breached their rights to privacy under article 8 of the European Convention on Human Rights and also breached the conditions of the Data Protection Act.[6]

Michael Douglas and Catherine Zeta-Jones, on the other hand, were able to obtain an interim injunction in November 2000 against *Hello* magazine publishing photographs from their wedding, the rights to cover which had been sold to *OK!*. In all eight court cases arose from this event, but those of 2001, 2003 and 2005 provide useful reference points:

- the initial injunction, which was granted but then overturned on appeal;
- an action by the Douglases and *OK!* against *Hello* for breach of confidence, which was successful;
- an action that confirmed the Douglases' right to confidentiality, which was appealed. The Court of Appeal and then the House of Lords upheld the decision in 2007 and *OK!* was awarded just over £1m in damages.

These actions helped to establish precedents for how the European Convention on Human Rights should be interpreted within British law but there have been many developments since then, so this is an area in which all journalists, including subeditors and production people, must keep up to date. In a situation where one curatum is trying to scoop another, it is likely to be the editor who decides which pictures to run at what risk but given the increased responsibility on subs to source and deploy images, it is a crucial area of the law.

It is not only the selection of images that may lead to litigation, the way a picture is cropped (or pixellated, as we have seen) can also lead to trouble. When three newspapers ran pictures of JK Rowling on a beach in Mauritius she decided not to complain. *OK!* used the same picture but did not crop out Rowling's eight-year-old daughter and the Press Complaints Commission upheld the author's complaint that the magazine had breached the rule that children must not be interviewed or photographed with out the consent of a parent.

The internet is a massive source of photographs but it must be stressed that a photograph on the internet is still likely to be subject to copyright restrictions. Photo sites such as Flickr are an astonishingly good resource but it is essential to check the conditions of licensing for every image you might want to use. The copyright in images may belong to the original photographer, to an organisation or business for whom the photographer works or to another party to whom the photographer has assigned copyright (perhaps an agency or a publisher).

Some photographers, and many on Flickr, choose to license their work under the Creative Commons system. This is less formal than a 'normal' copyright licence, with seven categories that range from putting the material into the public domain (least restrictive) to 'CC Attribution-NonCommercial-NoDerivs', which prohibits commercial use or any amendment to the original material. Whether you pay for use or not, the photographer is likely to ask for a credit and/or a link back to her or his Flickr stream; this might be a condition of the licence but it should also be an ethical decision. The Creative Commons website offers plentiful advice for licensees and licensors: http://creativecommons.org/.

Of course it is not only photographs that the subeditor may have to source – multimedia elements such as video and audio clips are increasingly expected and they are likely to be copyrighted too, whether they are user generated content or commercially produced. UK copyright law has undergone two major reviews in the last decade, first with the Gowers Review of 2006,[7] then the Hargreaves review of 2011.[8] Both reports aspired to make the regulations surrounding intellectual property and copyright fit for purpose in an age when digital technology allows instant, infinite and practically no-cost reproduction of a work of art.

Professor Ian Hargreaves, CBE, chair of Digital Economy at Cardiff University, aimed to bring the rules surrounding copyright, which had been left behind rather badly by technological developments, up to date. 'The core aim of the review with regard to copyright was to strengthen it by making it fit for purpose in a digital world,' he explains.

> It can't make sense to have laws which say that it's illegal to do routine file-shifts of songs or vital copying by archivists to preserve cultural heritage.

> The reforms in the review, now adopted by Government and approved by Parliament in late 2014, provide a new level of digital opportunity for everyone; they amount to the most ambitious reform of copyright for decades and open up new forms of online licensing and access to previously hidden 'orphan'[9] works.

The spirit of the UK debate has now been picked up across the European Union, which sets the main framework for this type of law. A modernised copyright system will strengthen the law because digital consumers will have more confidence in it and the law will focus more precisely upon its true purpose: to ensure a reasonable expectation of financial reward for creative people.[10]

For subeditors and production journalists one of the most important changes to the copyright laws concerns the right to use 'quotations'. Formerly this was restricted to reviews, criticism or news reporting but as a report in the *World Intellectual Property Review* states, there is now 'a more liberal approach to the use of quotes such as text extracts, hyper-links, tweets, video clips or music samples',[11] provided that such use is fair (another term that will doubtless be defined more exactly by case law over the course of time).

One extremely useful outcome of the Hargreaves Report has been the establishment of the Copyright Hub, a sort of one-stop shop for licensing and permissions. According to its manifesto:

The Copyright Hub aims to make the licensing of content easier. We want to increase the relevance of copyright to everyone who creates and everyone who makes use of content. Copyright says that creators own their work and can decide what happens to it. It says that you need permission to use someone else's work. The Copyright Hub helps make both things work the way the internet works.[12]

The hub should be a resource for every subeditor. It can be accessed at www.copyrighthub.co.uk.

Another useful site is the Copyright Licensing Agency, which is jointly owned by the Authors' Licensing and Collecting Society and the Publishers' Licensing Society: www.cla.co.uk.

5 Privilege and qualified privilege: the right to report

Even in these days of small staff it is unlikely that the person who reports court or other quasi-legal proceedings will be the same person who subedits the copy. The prime responsibility for submitting a report that will not get the publication into hot water must rest with the reporter. Nevertheless the subeditor must have a keen awareness of what can and cannot be published and the form that such reports should take. Perhaps because of the small staff, court reports might be submitted by an enthusiastic but inexperienced freelance or by a news agency reporter who could be a student on work experience. In such cases, the subeditor really is the last line of defence. And don't think that if you work on a magazine this doesn't apply to you; all sorts of magazines, business and consumer, use court-based copy or run features based on or around court cases or tribunals. The same applies to websites.

In a nutshell, the press is allowed to give a full and fair report of proceedings in court without being open to an action for defamation, even if what was said in court was defamatory. This right, known as *privilege*, was established by the Law of Libel Amendment Act 1888, which stated: 'A fair and accurate report in any newspaper of proceedings publicly heard before any court exercising judicial authority shall, if published contemporaneously with such proceedings, be privileged.' The Defamation Act of 1996 (see above for the Defamation Act 2013) confirmed this and made it clear that the privilege is *absolute*, which means it is not open to challenge.

Provided, that is, the report meets the criteria specified below.

It must be *fair* – both sides in the case must be treated equally. This does not mean that each must be allocated the same number of words in the report, but that allegations and rebuttals must be reported fully. A subeditor cutting copy must therefore be careful to maintain that balance. Allegations must not be reported as fact, and must be attributed to the person who made them.

It must be *accurate* – the facts must be correct. Did the defendant plead guilty or not guilty – and to what charge? Was the defendant acquitted or convicted – and of what charge? If these are not reported correctly then an action for defamation could be brought. It goes without saying that names, ages and addresses must be correct – if they are allowed to be reported.

It must be published *contemporaneously* – that is, in the very next issue of the newspaper or magazine, or straightaway on a website. A morning paper will carry the previous day's cases, an evening paper those from the morning or previous afternoon, a weekly those from the previous week.

Proceedings must be *in public* – most are, but evidence that is heard 'in camera' cannot be reported, nor can evidence that has been ruled inadmissible.

It must be the *proceedings of the court* that are reported – comments from the public gallery are not covered by privilege, nor are interviews with people connected with the trial, such as a police officer, a lawyer or a relation of the defendant.

The sub should be particularly careful to ensure that headlines and intros connected with court reports are *fair and accurate*. Watch out for headlines based on sensational allegations; until they have been proved to be true or false they remain allegations and readers must understand them to be such. Page furniture can be just as defamatory as copy.

Absolute privilege is attached to reporting 'any court established under the law of a country or territory outside the United Kingdom, and any international court or tribunal established by the Security Council of the United Nations or by an international agreement,'[13] but newspapers and magazines can claim *qualified privilege* when providing 'fair and accurate reports of proceedings in public, anywhere in the world, of legislatures (both national and local), courts, public inquiries, and international organisations or conferences, and documents, notices and other matter published by these bodies' and:

> copies of or extracts from information for the public published by government or authorities performing governmental functions (such as the police) or by courts; reports of proceedings at a range of public meetings (e.g. of local authorities) general meetings of UK public companies; and reports of findings or decisions by a range of associations formed in the UK or the European Union (such as associations relating to art, science, religion or learning, trade associations, sports associations and charitable associations).

(See Section 7[14] of the explanatory notes attached to the 2013 Defamation Act for the full definitions, which amend sections 14 and 15 of the 1996 Act.)

Privilege in these circumstances is *qualified* not because it affords less protection but because a judge must decide whether any published item comes within this legal protection. The item must not only be fair and accurate, it must also be published without malice and must be of and in public interest, as defined in section 4 of the 2013 Act. This section also abolishes the previous defence known as the Reynolds defence.

Comments made outside the circumstances defined in Section 7 are not covered, so beware of follow-up quotes or interviews.

6 Contempt of court: speaking out of turn

It is a widely quoted axiom that in English law, a person is innocent until proved guilty. This principle provides a rough and ready guide to the boundaries of contempt: is this material likely to sway a juror's mind or otherwise prejudge the outcome of the trial? However, it is impossible to give a clear cut definition of what will or will not be judged to be in contempt of court. In a classic example of this matter, the *Sunday Mirror*'s legal advisors thought that an interview with Muhammad Najeib published on 8 April 2001 was acceptable. The judge presiding over the trial of Leeds footballers Jonathan Woodgate and Lee Bowyer (and two of Woodgate's friends) thought otherwise. His opinion was that the interview would prejudice the case, in which the four were accused of beating Sarfraz Najeib, Muhammad's son. The jury was discharged and the trial halted. The paper's editor, Colin Myler, resigned, and the Attorney general decided to apply for contempt proceedings against the publisher, Trinity Mirror.

Mirror Group Newspapers were involved in another significant contempt case in 2011 when, along with the *Sun*, the *Daily Mirror* was sanctioned by Lord Justice Thomas for publishing material about Christopher Jefferies that could have prejudiced a fair trial. Jefferies had been arrested on suspicion of murdering Bristol student Joanna Yeates but was released two days later and his absolute innocence established when Vincent Tabak confessed to the killing. In the meantime, however, the *Mirror* and the *Sun* had run news reports and features that made or implied all sorts of accusations against Jefferies. The case for contempt was unusual because Jefferies was innocent and would never have had to face trial, but as Lord Justice Thomas pointed out, when the material was published, neither newspaper knew this would be the outcome. He found both publications to have committed contempt.[15] They were fined £55,000 and £18,000 respectively. In addition, eight newspapers – the *Sun*, *Daily Mirror*, *Sunday Mirror*, *Daily Record*, *Daily Mail*, *Daily Star*, the *Scotsman* and *Daily Express* – apologised to Jefferies and agreed to pay him substantial libel damages.

It was not subediting problems that caused this; the decision to run the pieces was taken at the highest level, and the publications paid the price. It is, however, illustrative of the kind of problem that a subeditor can help to avoid. Contempt of court can arise from a simple error, such as reporting that someone has *committed* a crime rather than that they have been *accused of committing* it, or disclosing an accused person's previous convictions, or even publishing a picture of the accused if identification is to be an issue in the trial. It can also arise from publishing interviews with witnesses or, as we have just seen, relations.

The Contempt of Court Act 1981 establishes when and how a person or publication may be in contempt and every subeditor should know the main clauses off by heart. This Act comes into play once proceedings against a person are *active* – that is to say when there has been:

- an arrest without warrant;
- the issue of a warrant for arrest;
- the issue of a summons to appear;
- service of an indictment or other document specifying a charge;
- an oral charge.

Once proceedings are active, media outlets must not publish anything that 'creates a substantial risk that the course of justice in the proceedings in question will be seriously impeded or prejudiced'.[16] As we have seen with the Jefferies case, the proceedings do not have to result in an actual court case for the Act to apply.

7 Trade names: Hoovering up Sellotape

It is not a crime to use a registered trade name without capitalising the first letter, or to use a specific name in a generic sense. It is, however, poor subediting and if the company or its lawyers spot such a use you can expect a letter demanding that in future the name is used correctly. In effect, the registration of a trade name gives its owner copyright protection and if it is not defended the owner can lose the exclusive right to its use.

This can affect journalists and advertising personnel. Some years ago a newly established motorcycle manufacturer bought the rights to a very old-established and well known marque name that had been in limbo for some time. The marque logo had been adopted by many different companies without redress; it was found on tee-shirts, mugs, advertisements for spare parts and so on. The new owner's first course of action was to contact everyone discovered to be using the logo, telling them to cease and desist, including magazines running copy which made reference to the (unauthorised) use and advertisements that depicted the logo or name.

A subeditor must be aware of trade names and registered brands and use the correct spelling and punctuation. For example, the well-known British cross country vehicle used to be a Land-Rover while its more sophisticated sister was a Range Rover, but both are now hyphenless. An American might dress a wound with a Band-Aid when a British person would prefer Elastoplast.

Pay particular attention to trade names that have become generics. It seems quite natural to use Hoover when we mean vacuum cleaner and Sellotape when we mean transparent sticky tape but making the specific stand for the general is inaccurate and unprofessional (even if everyone does it).

What, though, of the four letter word that describes both unwanted email and pork luncheon meat? Spam the former can hardly be described as a generic use of Spam the latter, and that capital letter is very important. This is the kind of question that twentieth century subeditors used to discuss at length and with some heat. Fortunately, the twenty-first century subeditor can refer to the online trademark register at www.gov. uk/search-for-trademark.

8 Letters: the dangers of green ink

A subeditor in charge of a curatum's communications pages should not make the mistake of thinking that a reader's letter, email, tweet, Facebook posting or forum comment cannot be defamatory. If it contains defamatory statements and you publish it, it is subject to exactly the same laws as any other published material and your publication could be put in the position of having to prove the writer's claims to be true. Always check the accuracy of facts stated in communications, especially if a controversial view is being put forward.

Subs should also be careful about cutting letters. The balance of a writer's argument, or the overall meaning, should not be substantially altered.

A letter, social media posting or online comment may also contravene the Public Order Act of 1986 if it is likely to arouse racial hatred, making active moderation of comments and forums essential. Most profession-ally produced newspapers, magazines and digital curata will have a code that commentators are required to observe, and comments that breach the code should be removed, with a standard explanation given. The *Guardian* uses the wording: 'This comment was removed by a moderator because it didn't abide by our community standards. Replies may also be deleted' and includes a link to the community standards page.[17] There may be community moderators or social media community managers whose job it is to look after this, but it is also possible that the task may fall to a subeditor or production journalist.

However, an increasing number of curata are closing their comments sections because they have become 'negative spaces'. The problem was highlighted at the 2012 South By South West Festival when Nick Denton, founder of the successful online entity Gawker Media, said the idea behind comment sections, originally envisioned as a way to capture the wisdom of the readership community, was now 'laughable'.

'It didn't happen,' *CNN* reported Denton as saying. 'It's a promise that has so not happened that people don't even have that ambition anymore.

'The idea of capturing the intelligence of the readership – that's a joke.'[18]

By September 2013, *Popular Science* was agreeing with him. The maga-zine stopped publishing comments because they had found research that showed 'even a fractious minority wields enough power to skew a reader's perception of a story'.[19]

Pando Daily, which aims to be the site-of-record for digital startups, also reported in September 2014 that, 'time has shown that comment sections often create a negative space and provide a negative experience – to the reader, the writer, and to the publisher.'[20]

In the same month PewDiePie, the enormously popular games blogger otherwise known as Felix Arvid Ulf Kjellberg, closed comments on his YouTube channel (the most subscribed in the world, with over 34 million video gamers signed up). According to gamespot.com, 'he no longer saw the value in user comments as they were plagued by spam and argu-ments' but would still be communicating with subscribers via Twitter and Reddit.[21]

Permanently closing comments sections and relying on social media to facilitate the conversations around a topic spread to the mainstream in November 2014 when Reuters Digital removed commenting from its news stories. In a statement via the organisation's blog, executive editor Dan Colarusso explained:

> We value conversation about the news, but the idea of comments on a website must give way to new realities of behavior in the marketplace. The best place for this conversation is where it is open to the largest number of participants possible.[22]

The common thread running through this list of closures is that readers who want to discuss ideas around the published content now have to do so via third party platforms, a move that will only increase the importance of social media community management. In turn, those who perform that management role must understand not only the necessary mix of psychology and technology, but also the continued need for legal and ethical vigilance. Just one example will suffice to show how seriously courts take abuse on social media – when Swansea University student Liam Stacey posted offensive tweets about footballer Fabrice Muamba, who had collapsed on the field of play with a heart problem, he began a chain of events that eventually saw him jailed after pleading guilty to charges under the Racially Aggravated s4A Public Order Act 1986.[23]

There is, of course, much more to the law as it affects journalists and it should be stressed again that this chapter is no substitute for a proper training course.

Ethics

If the law defines what a newspaper, magazine or website may safely publish without running the risk of being taken to court, journalists' ethical codes help them to make decisions that will keep their consciences clear and allow them to sleep soundly. In other words, just because you can legally get away with saying something about someone that may hurt or damage them doesn't mean you should. That makes it sound easy and clear cut, but in the fast moving, messy, commercial world of journalism knowing the right thing to do and making sure it's done are two different things, and decisions may be affected by a range of external factors.

Every journalist's organisation that has ever existed has devised a code of conduct. In the UK, the National Union of Journalists and the Institute of Journalists have codes, and you can examine the NUJ's at http://bit.ly/nujcode. If you would like to put this in a wider context, look at the Ethicnet site; here the University of Tampere in Finland has amassed the codes of journalist organisations from all round the world, together with academic papers about the ethics of journalism: http://bit.ly/ethicnet.

When the Press Complaints Commission was active and extant (before evidence presented at the Leveson Inquiry demolished its reputation) British publications operated under its Code of Practice. The code was perhaps the best part of the organisation, and even if PCC members were found to have breached it repeatedly the principles were sound. Although the organisation has gone, its website was still extant at the time of publishing: http://bit.ly/pcccode.

The PCC has been replaced, to some extent and for some publications, by the Independent Press Standards Organisation (IPSO), which launched on 8 September 2014. IPSO also has an editors' code (http://bit.ly/ipsocode). The new organisation did not come into the world fully formed, as its website makes clear: 'Over the coming months, we will continue to build the new standards-raising functions that will enable us to implement the full system of independent regulation that the newspaper and magazine industry has agreed to establish and support.'

This statement overlooks the fact that, at the time of publication, major news organisations such as the *Guardian* group, the *Financial Times* and the *Independent* (which includes *i* and the *London Evening Standard*) had not signed up to IPSO, with the FT preferring to appoint its own editorial complaints commissioner.[24]

IPSO also faced competition from the Impress Project, which aimed for complete independence from both press organisations (IPSO is financed by those it seeks to oversee) and politicians. Its prospectus can be read at http://bit.ly/impresscode.

There is also the matter of the royal charter on press regulation. This was a consequence, perhaps not entirely intended, of the Leveson Inquiry's recommendation that 'it is essential that there should be legislation to underpin the independent self-regulatory system and facilitate its recognition in legal processes' (Paragraph 70 of the Leveson Report; the executive summary is available at http://bit.ly/levsum). Leveson's proposal caused an extensive ruckus among news organisations and defenders of unfettered free speech, who characterised it as an attack on the freedom of the press. Sadly, the argument has not given rise to anything as inspiring as John Milton's defence of the 'liberty of unlicenc'd printing', *Areopagitica* of 1644[25] and despite media opposition the Press Recognition Panel was established as a legal body on 3 November 2014. Its website is available at http://pressrecognitionpanel.org.uk.

Codes are all well and good if you think that the world is a black-and-white kind of place, but there are many shades of grey that even the best intentioned set of guidelines cannot illuminate. What is the ethical situation when a sensitively written piece about a difficult subject is undermined by a subeditor's jokey or insensitive headline or cover-line? 'I did a story about a bus driver who cheated on his wife', a feature writer for a woman's weekly recalls.

> The woman was happy with her story but not at all happy with the sub's headline 'The driver on the bus goes bonk, bonk, bonk'. She thought it belittled her sad tale. Another headline was 'www.cheatingsod.com' about a woman whose husband left her for an internet lover. These things happened every week and I often felt uncomfortable.

Ethical issues of a different sort are raised when companies or organisations publish their own magazines (or have them published by a third party). Sometimes this might be a consumer matter such as pushing the company's product when a different product is known to be better, but if the organisation is concerned with politics, the law or medicine it could be a matter with more philosophical weight behind it. In this situation a subeditor could find him or herself trying to defend the freedom of the press.

Law and ethics: specific subediting issues

Subeditors should be particularly aware of the following points:

- juxtaposition – make sure that layouts do not juxtapose elements that may lead to a picture or story becoming defamatory;
- malicious falsehood – if you're going to say someone's dead, make sure they are;
- honest opinion – if a product test is negative, make sure you can stand up the findings;
- subbing court reports – must be fair and accurate for absolute privilege. Headlines and introductory matter must not exaggerate;
- contempt of court – nothing in the report must be capable of causing serious risk of prejudicing the outcome of a trial, and that includes pictures;
- defamatory pictures – when using library shots to illustrate a story make sure there's nothing defamatory to the subject depicted;
- headlines – legally, they can be defamatory, as can standfirsts, captions and other page furniture; ethically, think about the overall effect. If your clever headline undermines a sensitively written story, is it worth using? On the other hand, remember the injunction that 'bane and antidote' must be taken together;
- punctuation – can lead to trouble if used incorrectly.

Answer to punctuation riddle:

An English professor wrote the words, "Woman without her man is nothing" on the blackboard and directed the students to punctuate it correctly.

The men wrote: "Woman, without her man, is nothing."

The women wrote: "Woman! Without her, man is nothing."

Resources

The British and Irish Legal Information Institute holds an ever expanding database of 'British and Irish case law & legislation, European Union case law, Law Commission reports, and other law-related British and Irish material': www.bailii.org/.

Legislation.gov.uk is managed by the National Archives and publishes all Government legislation.

Notes

1   Duncan Bloy and Sara Hadwin (2011, 2nd edn), *Law and the Media*. London: Sweet & Maxwell, 268.
2   http://bit.ly/goodfellas01, accessed 27/11/14.
3   http://bit.ly/goodfellas02, accessed 27/11/14.
4   http://bit.ly/mol22, accessed 27/11/14.
5   Bloy and Hadwin, 47.
6   http://bit.ly/wellerkids, accessed 27/11/14.
7   http://bit.ly/gowersreview, accessed 21/11/14. Andrew Gowers was editor of the Financial Times from 2001 to 2006.
8   http://bit.ly/hargreavesIP, accessed 21/11/14. Ian Hargreaves, CBE, was director of News and Current Affairs at the BBC, editor of *The Independent* and *New Statesman*.
9   Defined as works that are covered by copyright but for which the rights owners cannot be found by those seeking permission to reproduce them. The new arrangements allow the Copyright Hub to hold licence fees in trust for such rights holders.
10   Personal communication, 25/11/14.
11   http://bit.ly/worldipr, accessed 21/11/14
12   http://bit.ly/chubmanifesto, accessed 21/11/14.
13   http://bit.ly/absoluteprivilege, accessed 21/11/14.
14   http://bit.ly/absoluteprivilege, accessed 21/11/14.
15   http://bit.ly/jefferiescontempt, accessed 28/11/14.
16   http://bit.ly/CoC1981, accessed 28/11/14.
17   http://bit.ly/commstand, accessed 21/11/14.
18   http://bit.ly/dentoncomments, accessed 25/11/14.
19   http://bit.ly/popscicomments, access 25/11/14.
20   http://bit.ly/pandocomments, accessed 25/11/14.
21   http://bit.ly/pewdiecomments, accessed 25/11/14.
22   http://bit.ly/reuterscomments, accessed 25/11/14.
23   http://bit.ly/staceytweets, accessed 28/11/14.
24   http://bit.ly/ftcomplaints, accessed 21/11/14.
25   http://bit.ly/areopagitica, accessed 21/11/14.

10

Covers, splash pages and landing zones

It is quite unlikely that a subeditor will have a great deal of influence over the original creation of a magazine front cover, a newspaper front page, a website splash page or the 'cover' of an app. Nevertheless, subs are likely to have to work on those pages at some point and an understanding of how they function and what can make them more effective will help to produce a better end product.

Specifics differ but the main purpose of all these pages is to attract and retain attention and, if the curatum has a cover price, encourage purchase. In the post-Gutenberg age, increasing significance has been attached to the attention economy. Back in 1997 Michael Goldhaber's conference paper *The Attention Economy and the Net* outlined the principles of a new aspect of the political economy of media products. As I noted in *Promotional Culture And Convergence* (Holmes 2013: 186):

> if information is ubiquitous, getting people to spend their limited amount of attention on any particular piece of information becomes increasingly important because, 'economies are governed by what is scarce, and information, especially on the Net, is not only abundant, but overflowing' whereas 'Attention, at least the kind we care about, is an intrinsically scarce resource'.
>
> http://bit.ly/goldhaber

Attention may lead to direct or indirect financial advantage – either a purchase by the consumer or revenue from advertisers who wish to reach the consumer or the creation of a relationship with the consumer that may result in commercial exchange via a brand extension. But even leaving financial considerations aside, there are a lot of professional craft skills involved in making great covers, some very traditional, others that have had to evolve to suit changing technological circumstances.

Magazines: print

The cover is the hardest working page in a print magazine. There are, at the time of writing, still over 8,000 magazines published in the UK, and even a small branch of WH Smith will have a large range on display. This means that for titles in well populated sectors, such as women's or craft magazines, there may be dozens of rivals surrounding the one you work for. Add to this the hard fact that even a person who considers him- or herself a regular and loyal reader may in reality only buy every other issue and it should start to become obvious why the cover is always given so much attention. As an attractor it has about two seconds to make an impact – David Hepworth, the pandit of publishing, once said, 'A cover must appeal to a moron in a hurry'. This is not to suggest that anyone should think of their readers as morons; it's a way of expressing how simple and clear the message(s) promoted by the cover must be – there is no room for ambiguity in this crowded and competitive marketplace.

The cover must encapsulate the hopes, fears and aspirations of the magazine's readers – it must encourage their hopes, combat their fears and offer them help in realising their aspirations. This might sound like a ludicrous ambition to place on a printed sheet but look analytically at the cover of *any* issue of *Men's Health* and the hopes, fears and aspirations being addressed will become obvious: readers hope to develop a lean, fit and muscular body (with a particular emphasis on acquiring a six-pack, or washboard abs); they fear ageing or becoming saggy; they aspire to a better quality of life, including promotion at work, a higher salary and better sex with hotter women. Similarly, the cover of a title such as *PhotoPlus Canon Edition* (April 2014) addresses fears such as not being able to work your expensive new single lens reflex digital camera effectively, leading to a main cover line of 'Master your SLR in 48 hours' (meaning – see, that money wasn't wasted!); hopes of being able to take better pictures ('How to use a polariser'); aspirations of reaching a more professional understanding of photography ('Get creative indoors with a macro lens').

When you see a strong cover line like those quoted above, it looks both natural ('Of course that's the way to phrase it') and simple ('What's so difficult about putting six words together?') but as with headlines, getting it right – and getting it right issue after issue – takes focus, concentration and graft. It must start with a clear understanding of what the readership wants, how the editorial content can address those information needs and then how to summarise that content in a short clause that can be understood by 'a moron in a hurry', without insulting or patronising potential readers. It has been claimed that coverlines are the most intensely worked on copy in any magazine and they probably do, or should, have the most attention lavished on them. When Kate White, editor in chief of *Cosmopolitan* in the USA, addressed an international magazine congress on the subject of covers she told the audience she spent around 80 per cent of her time working on covers; for the June 2005 issue she recalled: 'I worked on the cover lines every single day for two weeks, for about an hour or two a day.'[1]

If you have already been involved in creating headlines (see Chapter 6) and captions (Chapter 7), you should already be able to capture the curatum's tone of voice; there will be a natural overlap of craft skills but always bear in mind a successful cover needs lines that:

- are pointed and succinct;
- make a promise – that the content must keep; no-one will buy twice if the first time disappoints. As legendary *Esquire* cover designer George Lois told *Gym Class*, 'My covers promised a shit hot magazine. If you bought it and you said, dull, boring, dull, as you turned the pages, the cover would have been ludicrous.' (Issue 07: 36);
- offer the reader a benefit, preferably immediate or achievable within a definite time limit (using words such as 'now', 'tonight', 'this weekend', 'in six weeks');
- demonstrate value ('365 fashion tips for tomorrow').

John Morrish, the creator and warden of journalist.com and a former editor of *Time Out*, wrote: 'There is magic in cover design. It can never be "just a picture". The best covers bring together an image and words to express an idea, using such strength and economy that the reader has to know more.' But he also pointed out that a cover must appeal to a reader's self-interest, 'A consumer's automatic response will be, "What can reading this do for me?"'[2] Coverlines are the magazine's way of promising to give the readers something in return for the investment of their money and attention. Barry McIlheney, a vastly experienced editor who is now chairman of the Professional Publishers Association, once told a development seminar there were six types of cover line:

- We'll change your life
- We'll solve your problems
- We'll tell you a secret
- We'll make you feel better
- We'll make you laugh
- We'll take you somewhere amazing.

Once the initial interest has been sparked, the ignition process must be continued by engineering smooth navigation for readers; the subeditor or production team need to create links between the cover and the contents page by using the same story names or descriptions and repeating key words; similar links should be maintained between the contents page and the actual feature. Careful planning will be needed at all stages and clear, continuous communication between individuals and teams working on the curatum is essential. Unless everyone knows exactly how all the content fits together there will be numerous cracks for good intentions to fall between.

As far as organising the visual elements of the cover is concerned, the magazine logo must be visible on a crowded shelf, the coverlines must read out clearly from three metres and the most important coverline should go in the hotspot (which is normally defined as the top left corner of the cover; the spot that is most likely to be clearly visible no matter how the news stand shelves are organised).

The cover is also the 'face' of your magazine and, as J. William Click and Russell N. Baird say in their classic work *Magazine Editing and Production* (1986), 'Like a person's face it is the primary indicator of a personality' (198). The picture chosen for the cover can make a difference of thousands, even tens of thousands, to sales, up or down as Mark Ellen found to his discomfort. *Word* (later *The Word*) had been founded as an independently published music and culture magazine in February 2003 and established its credentials as a Nick Cave-Ray Davies-Lucinda Williams kind of scene from the off. Imagine the shock, then, when loyal readers, including myself, looking for the September 2003 issue found the queen of bland herself on the front cover – Dido. I can still remember it literally stopping me in my tracks and although I had gone to the mag racks specifically proposing to buy *Word* I could not bring myself to do so. My new friend's face had suddenly changed and I didn't recognise it any more. I wasn't the only one; editor Ellen later recalled that edition remaining 'both nailed and glued to the shelves ... metric tonnes of unsold copies were recycled to make confetti, the rest bulldozed into giant landfills all over Kent and Suffolk'. It must have caused a huge financial setback to the relatively young curatum.

By contrast, *People* magazine in the USA knew exactly who its readers wanted to see on the cover – Princess Diana: 'There was just constant demand,' said Landon Y. Jones, who recently stepped down after eight years as managing editor of *People*, which put Diana on its cover 43 times. No other personality comes close: Elizabeth Taylor is a distant second with 14 *People* covers.

It is vitally important, therefore, to know exactly who or what interests your readers right now. Contrariwise, who or what must you never, ever use? If you are in a market sector with a lot of competition, and those competitors are likely to want to use the same people on their covers, how can you get a better picture than your rivals? If you use a poorly lit, opportunistic pap photo of a celebrity that makes them look less than gorgeous, will that affect your magazine's relationship with them later?

Sometimes using the wrong picture can have worse results than poor sales, as *Rolling Stone* discovered when it tried to launch in China. Commercial and political regulations mean that overseas publishers are not permitted direct ownership there but can form joint ventures with, or license their titles to, Chinese publishers – who must be in possession of a valid *kanhao* (publishing licence). Jan Wenner's long established rock magazine formed an alliance with the publishers of *Music World*, so that issue 240 of the Chinese magazine became the first issue of *Rolling Stone China*. On its cover they put Cui Jian, a popular but slightly subversive performer well suited to the mag's almost-edgy vibe. Sadly, the debut issue also became the finale as the authorities clamped down on the Sino-American title, a fate many attribute to the choice of cover star, although the excessive prominence of the *Rolling Stone* logo has also been blamed (Yuan, 2009).[3]

Rolling Stone also experienced an interesting reaction when it put Dzhokhar Tsarnaev on the cover of its August 2013 issue – Tsarnaev was the surviving brother of the pair that set off a bomb near the finish of the Boston Marathon (his brother Tamerlan was shot dead by police). The photo showed a young man with longish curly hair in what appeared to be a slightly soft-focus selfie; he looked a little bit like Jim Morrison. The immediate reaction was largely outrage – how could *Rolling Stone* give this suspected killer the oxygen of publicity and with such an attractive, almost iconic, image?[4] Longer term, the magazine claimed an uptick in newsstand sales with this issue,[5] although a later analysis showed that even quite a large sounding percentage increase actually translated into a relatively small number as the bulk of magazine sales in the USA are subscriptions.

Even though established subscribers are not going to be influenced by what appears on the news stand (although a great series of covers may persuade a regular purchaser to take out a subscription), some magazines create special covers for subscribers once a year. For a title such as *Men's Health*, which tends to run very similar covers month after month, this allows the art team to flex its muscles with a special illustration or a completely different treatment and it also helps to make subscribers feel valued.

Magazines: digital replicas, websites, apps

Digital replicas of magazines are exact copies of the print version, digitised and uploaded to a hosting site such as issuu. A lot of indy mags (but also best sellers such as Glamour) are uploaded to issuu because it is free and simple; it takes pdf copies of pages made in Quark or InDesign and therefore what is uploaded will normally be identical to what appears in print – although it is possible to create different covers or other pages for the uploaded version.

Zinio looks similar to issuu, but it is a commercial operation that provides a rival service to Apple's Newsstand or Google Play Newsstand, but instead of delivering only app-based publications, it also delivers browser-based versions, so the magazine is available on mobile, tablet, laptop or desktop and the service's library can be accessed from any of those devices in iOS, Android and web. Magazines in a Zinio subscriber's library can also be accessed offline for consumption where there is no WiFi or mobile network – on an aeroplane or a train, for example.

Many people think Zinio's 'catalogue' is better and more clearly organised than the Apple or Google newsstands, but it is very important to remember the size at which a magazine's cover will be displayed. On a smartphone it may be smaller than a normal postage stamp, on an iPad it's about the same as a commemorative postage stamp and it will not be very much bigger on a computer screen. This means that instead of being able to use an area of 210×297mm (A4) or 148×210mm (A5 – roughly 'handbag' size) to catch the attention of the 'moron in a hurry', the message has to be condensed into a single overriding shout. Have a good look at Zinio and both versions of Newsstand and note which covers deliver the strongest messages – inevitably it will be those that use a powerful image and a single clear statement. For this reason it is definitely worth considering, if at all possible, a different, extra-simplified, cover for digital editions.

One advantage of getting readers to download the app for a magazine is that it puts them in a similar position to a subscriber, although there is no obligation to buy every issue, and they can therefore be marketed to more easily. But just putting a magazine on Newsstand won't by itself bring either exposure or sales – there are over 10,000 titles for browsers to choose from, which is the most over-stocked branch of WH Smith imaginable – so it is important to understand the elements other than just cover design that will make it stand out. This topic is beyond the remit of the current book but some idea of the possibilities can be found in Allison Reber's *How to get the best out of digital publishing on Apple's Newsstand*, written for the Guardian.[6] Bear in mind that all digital services and platforms change regularly, so the best way to 'surface' your publication will always be a work in progress.

Print newspapers

Deciding what goes onto the front page of a newspaper lies far beyond the remit of a subeditor, but the treatment and execution may be passed down the chain of responsibility. The editor, night editor or news editor are most likely to be the judges of what story or stories are most newsworthy and also their hierarchy on the page; one or more of them may also decide the headline(s), certainly of the splash (or main) story.

The guidelines for writing news headlines and supporting systems covered in chapters 4 and 5 apply here, but as with magazine coverlines, front page headlines need to be as sharp and pointed as possible. There is still a tendency for print newspapers, especially the tabloids, to turn to pun-based or referential headlines. Newspaper headlines can also address the hopes, fears and aspirations of the readership. These are likely to be more generalised and less specific than magazine communities but it still leaves some substantial targets – see if you can:

- identify the correct newspaper for each of these headlines (all taken from the week Monday 24 to Saturday 29 November 2014; use of upper and lower case as original);
- identify some of the major hopes, fears and aspirations of their readerships;
- identify the subject of the story:

Monday 24/11

A)   GAZZA: I HAVE TO SAVE MYSELF
B)   Rigby inquiry 'failed to seek out witnesses'
C)   VEG DIET WILL BEAT DIABETES
D)   JIHADI ATTACK ON UK 'INEVITABLE'
E)   Coalition abandons target to reduce migration

Tuesday 25/11

A)   SHUT UP! YOU STUPID SWEATY LITTLE GIT
B)   Labour's assault on private schools
C)   STATINS FOR ALL OVER-60s
D)   OVER 40? YOU CAN'T HAVE A MORTGAGE
E)   Labour 'class war' on private schools

Wednesday 26/11

A)   Facebook ACCUSED
     Lee Rigby family fury as net giant failed to report murder threat
     BLOOD ON THEIR HANDS
B)   Web firms accused over Rigby
C)   'HIDDEN' MIGRANT MILLIONS
D)   FACEBOOK KEPT QUIET ABOUT RIGBY KILLER'S PLOTTING
E)   Fury at Facebook over terror note left by Lee Rigby's killer

Thursday 27/11

A)   ENDERS SHIRL RACE HATE RAP
     'Hurled abuse' outside Jamie restaurant

B)   Scotland to be given control of income tax
C)   COFFEE FIGHTS ALZHEIMER'S
D)   2M ELIGIBLE FOR GASTRIC BANDS
E)   Jihadists funded by welfare benefits

Friday 28/11/14

A)   RIGHT SAID PLEB
      Tory Mitchell DID insult cop, rules judge
B)   He did say 'pleb': judge's ruling leaves Mitchell's career
      in ruins
C)   MIGRANTS: FOUR YEAR BENEFITS BAN
D)   MIGRANTS: AT LAST PM ACTS
E)   I'm ready to lead Britain out of Europe if migrant reform
      fails
      (above photo of David Cameron looking shouty)

Saturday 29/11/14

A)   DOUGH HO HO!
B)   Merkel forces Cameron retreat
C)   MIGRANT CONTROLS OR WE'LL QUIT EU
D)   SHOPPING MADNESS (re: Black Friday)
E)   Police checks for migrants

Answers at the end of the chapter.

As you can see from that small selection, the guidelines for writing news headlines apply to newspaper front covers, especially as regards using punctuation to distance the newspaper from the statement or to disguise the fact that there is no source for a 'quote'. Several of the headlines would be indecipherable without their accompanying pictures of former cabinet ministers or *East Enders* actresses. The use of puns, or pun-like devices, is also consistent although not quite as widespread as might be imagined[7] and there is one classic example of the 'headline vocabulary' that Keith Waterhouse deprecated; like many such examples, it is so blatantly 'tabloid' that it is not hard to imagine it as an act of irony – and possibly also an act of contempt for the readership.[8]

There are some consistently expressed concerns about health (perhaps the sign of an ageing readership), immigrants, the EU and terrorism, from which clues we may be able to hazard a guess as to the fears, at least, of the readerships, although the similarity between B and E on Tuesday may be slightly surprising when you know where they come from. In John Dale's e-book *24 Hours In Journalism*[9], the editor of the *Daily Express*, Hugh Whittow, makes many cameo appearances, including one where he is trying to decide the front page splash for the next day's edition:

> What he's got in mind is cheap and easy and you can't get sued for it. The worst the *Express* will suffer is a few elitist comments on the BBC's *Today* for being a tad alarmist. He gets touchy about that but those snobs don't bother the self-acclaimed 'World's Greatest Newspaper'. They're not his readership.
>
> Yes, he's made his choice . . .
>
> He will splash with the nation's favourite conversational opener.
>
> The weather.
>
> Again . . .
>
> Now the weather copy is being prepared and when it's ready he's got just the headline to grab the attention of his ageing, undemanding audience:
>
> 8 INCHES OF SNOW IN NEXT 24 HOURS . . .
> (Chapter 9, location 4269/7382)

Studying front page headlines as they are used – and that includes the typographical treatment, combination with pictures and additional decks – is a very good way to get a feel for how to create them. If you don't want to hang about in a newsagent or take a trip to the library, there are a couple of very useful websites to visit, both of which reproduce front covers every day:

> www.thepaperboy.com/uk
> http://en.kiosko.net/uk/

Both also display an excellent selection of newspapers from around the world, which might spark a few new ideas.

Newspapers: digital replicas, websites, apps

Digital replicas such as those offered by *Metro* (http://bit.ly/digimetro, free) and the *Guardian* (http://bit.ly/digiguardian, paid) are facsimiles of the printed versions and the same rules apply.

Newspaper apps are strange beasts that, in my opinion, combine the worst aspects of print and digital: they are largely static and may only be updated once a day but can only be accessed where there is WiFi or a mobile data network. The idea is perhaps to offer a highly curated take on world events for a readership without the time or inclination to faff about but even the combined might of Rupert Murdoch and Steve Jobs could not make News Corp's *The Daily* a success. It was attractively designed and looked very slick on the iPad's high resolution screen but failed to convince sufficient numbers of people that it was worth paying for when similar content, and all the news, could be read for free, and without having to wait for the daily update, on the open web. At the time of writing (November 2014), Jeff Bezos, the man behind Amazon and owner of the *Washington Post*, was about to launch an app version of the newspaper for the Kindle Fire e-reader. The plan was to update content twice a day, at 5 am and 5 pm, and to push it for free to Fire owners for the first six months. Versions that would work with iOS and Android were also under development, as explained by the Post's rival *New York Times*.[10] In terms of the front cover, *The Daily* ended up going for a single image and a strong single message but because the app was subscription-based it had very little influence on purchasing decisions; it swill be interesting to see how the Bezos-Kindle *Washington Post* tackles front pages.

Not all newspaper websites are freely available – the *Times*, the *Sun* and the *Financial Times* all currently live behind paywalls and readers are in essence subscribers – but even committed readers appreciate good sign-posting and clear navigation on the splash or landing page, and effective use of SEO technique in headlines may bring more potential subscribers to the site.

These considerations are probably even more important for newspaper sites with open access. The *Telegraph* (no 'Daily' online) has what can be considered quite a traditional home page in web design terms – that is to say, it picks up the visual cues expected on a print front page but carries many more stories and incorporates links to multimedia; indeed, the second item on the navigation top bar is 'Video'. The *Guardian*'s main site looks similar in concept but at the time of writing there was an alternative in Beta testing that looked a lot more like a 'native web' site than a traditional newspaper site – that is, it bore more resemblance to *Buzzfeed*, *Mashable* or the *Huffington Post* than to an entity with nearly 200 years of print tradition behind it. The *Mirror* (again, no Daily online) has looked this way for some time and the *Independent*'s site was redesigned in 2011 to capture a similar effect.

Headlines, decks and sells for news stories have been discussed in chapters 4 and 5 and all the advice given there applies to splash or landing pages. There is no magic formula for success online and what formulae there are will evolve with the new medium. The only lesson is to expect change and learn to work with it effectively.

Magazine cover exercise

This four-stage exercise can be done for any title in any sector. It depends on having a clear understanding of the subject matter and the information needs of the readership. It would also work for newspapers and online curata that have a defined cover.

Stage 1: What has changed?

What has changed in your readers' lives? Are they feeling a financial pinch or is life easy? Are they likely to have developed new interests as a result of social, cultural or technological developments? Will they have bought a house? Moved to a bigger or smaller house?

If you are covering a particular field (a hobby, a technology sector, a sport), what has changed in that field? Has it expanded or contracted. Is there more or less overlap with other fields than there used to be?

There may be significant global events that have had far reaching effects – very few people escaped at least some consequences of the financial meltdown of 2008 and economic politics of austerity are still commonplace; climate change is affecting everything from gardening through surfing to fishing.

Write down as many changes as you can think of and although it might seem Micawberishly optimistic, remember that every negative has a positive – if people can't afford to move, they are more likely to do up their current house; if less rainfall means drier gardens, people can plant Mediterranean flora.

Stage 2: Hopes, fears and aspirations

This focuses more closely on the readers – how does what has changed impact their hopes, fears and aspirations? If you have been working on a set of assumptions, are they still valid or have developments left you behind? Think about how you can address the current hopes, fears and aspirations in content; be specific about the form and format of that content. If your magazine has relied on a certain mix of content, is it time to review and refresh that mix? Does the overall angle and tone need to be updated?

Stage 3: Perfect coverlines

Now express those specific new content ideas as coverlines. You will not be able to do it if you have come up with general concepts but this is an exercise, so you can be as expansive as you like. Then try to make your blue-sky concepts more realistic or practicable. How close could you get to achieving them in real life?

Stage 4: Digital focus

Finally, take the strongest, most appealing story (you can assume that you have a great image to go with it) and sharpen the cover line even more, so that when potential readers are looking at the postage stamps on Zinio or Newsstand they are a) left in no doubt about the subject matter of the story and the general thrust of the magazine and b) are tempted to read on.

Newspaper headline answers

The selections all ran – A) *Sun*, B) *Guardian*, C) *Daily Express*, D) *Daily Mail*, E) *Daily Telegraph*. Tuesday's *Sun* headline was allegedly a quote from David Mellor as he abused a London cabbie; Thursday's concerned an East Enders actress; Saturday's a 'Dole family's luxury splurge'. The *Mail*'s Saturday headline was a comment on what is now called 'Black Friday' – the day when pre-Christmas sales start.

Notes

1 *Magazine World*, August 2005: 20.
2 *m.real magazine*, issue 4: 7.
3 Zhiyi Yuan (2009), The surviving conditions of Chinese alternative magazines, unpublished MA thesis, Cardiff University.
4 http://bit.ly/magblogRS, accessed 29/11/14.
5 http://bit.ly/RSsales, accessed 29/11/14.
6 http://bit.ly/rebertips, accessed 30/11/14.
7 On the very day that I wrote this, *the Guardian* carried a report about China banning puns to protect the integrity of Mandarin: http://bit.ly/chinapuns, accessed 30/11/14.
8 Read Marina Hyde's personal experience of this: http://bit.ly/suncontempt, accessed 30/11/14.
9 http://bit.ly/dale24hours.
10 http://bit.ly/kindledaily, accessed 30/11/14.

Glossary of terms used in journalism

Journalism is rich in jargon. Some of it comes from printing (book for magazine); or survives from the pre-computer age (spike for rejected copy); or is imported from the United States (clippings for cuttings). It is often punchy and graphic (ambush, bust, fireman). But if it crops up in copy (e.g. in stories about the media), the sub will usually have to change it (replace 'story' by 'report'), or explain it (after 'chapel' insert 'office branch' in brackets). The obvious exception is in publications for journalists such as *Press Gazette* and the *Journalist*.

ABC   Audit Bureau of Circulation – source of independently verified circulation figures

ad   advertisement

add   extra copy to add to existing story

advance   1 text of speech or statement issued to journalists beforehand; 2 expenses paid before a trip

advertorial   advertisement presented as editorial (see also **native advertising**)

agencies   news agencies, e.g. PA and Reuters

agony column   regular advice given on personal problems sent in by readers; hence agony aunt

ambush   journalists lying in wait for unsuspecting, unwilling interviewee

ampersand   & – symbol for 'and'

angle   particular approach to story, journalist's point of view in writing it

art editor   visual journalist responsible for design and layout of publication

artwork   illustrations (e.g. drawings, photographs) prepared for reproduction

ascender   the part of a lower-case letter (e.g. b and d) that sticks out above the x-height in a typeface

attribution   identifying the journalist's source of information or quote

author's (corrections, marks)   proof corrections by writer of story

back of the book   second part of magazine (after the centre spread)

back number, issue   previous issue of publication

backbench, the   senior newspaper journalists who make key production decisions

backgrounder   explanatory feature to accompany news story

bad break   clumsy hyphenation at the end of a line

banner (headline)   one in large type across front page

basket   where copy goes – once a physical basket, now a digital folder

bastard measure   type set to a width that is not standard for the page

beard   the space between a letter and the edge of the base on which it is designed

beat   American term for specialist area covered by reporter (see also **patch**)

bill(board)   poster promoting edition of newspaper, usually highlighting main news story

black   duplicate of written story (from colour of carbon paper once used with typewriter)

bleed   (of an image) go beyond the type area to the edge of a page

blob   solid black circle used for display effect or to tabulate lists

blob par   extra paragraph introduced by blob

blow up   enlarge (part of) photograph

blown quote   another term for pull quote

blurb   displayed material promoting contents of another page or future issue

body copy   the main text of a story, as opposed to page furniture

body type   the main typeface in which a story is set (as opposed to display)

bold   thick black type, used for emphasis

book   printer's (and so production journalist's) term for magazine

bot   black on tone

box   copy enclosed by rules to give it emphasis and/or separate it from the main text

breaker   typographical device, e.g. crosshead, used to break up text on the page

brief   1 short news item; 2 instruction to journalist on how to approach story

bring up   bring forward part of story to earlier position

broadsheet   large-format newspaper such as the *Telegraph*

bromide   photographic print

bullet (point)   another term for blob

bureau   office of news agency or newspaper office in foreign country

business-to-business (b2b)   current term for what were once called 'trade' magazines, i.e. those covering a business area, profession, craft or trade

bust   (of a headline) be too long for the space available

buy-up interview   exclusive bought by publication

byline   writer's name as it appears in print at the beginning of a story

c and lc   capital and lower-case letters

call out   another term for pull quote

calls (also check calls)   routine phone calls made by reporters to orga-nisations such as police and fire brigade to see if a story is breaking

camera-ready   (e.g. artwork) prepared for reproduction

caps   capital letters

caption   words used with a picture (usually underneath), identifying where necessary and relating it to the accompanying story

caption story   extension of picture caption into a self-contained story

cast off   estimate amount of printed matter copy would make

casual   journalist employed by the shift

catch(line)   short word (not printed) identifying different elements of a story in the editorial process

centre   set type with equal space on either side

centre spread   middle opening of tabloid or magazine

chapel   office branch of media union (the shop steward is the father, FoC, or mother, MoC, of the chapel)

character   unit of measurement for type including letters, figures, punctuation marks and spaces

chequebook journalism   paying large sums for stories

chief sub   senior subeditor in charge of the others

city desk   financial section of British national newspaper (in the US the city desk covers home news)

classified advertising   small ads 'classified' by subject matter, grouped in a separate section

clippings/clips   American term for cuttings

close quotes   end of section in direct quotes

close up   reduce space between lines, words or characters

CMYK   cyan, magenta, yellow and black, the process (basic printing) colours

col   column

colour piece   news story written as feature with emphasis on journalist's reactions

colour sep(aration)s method by which the four process colours (CMYK) are separated from a colour original

column 1 standard vertical division of page; 2 regular feature by journalist often encouraged to be opinionated and/or entertaining

column rule light rule between columns of type

conference meeting of editorial staff to plan current/next issue

consumer magazines the category includes specialist titles (e.g. *Angling Times*), women's magazines and those of general interest

contact sheet photographer's sheet of small prints

contacts book a journalist's list of contacts with details of phone, fax, email etc

contents bill *see* bill

controlled circulation free distribution of specialist title to target readership by geography (free newspapers) or interest group (business-to-business magazines)

copy text of story

copy taster *see* taster

copyright right to reproduce original material

copytaker telephone typist who takes down copy from reporter

corr correspondent

correction published statement correcting errors in story

correspondent journalist covering specialist area, e.g. education

coverlines selling copy on front cover

credit (line) name of photographer or illustrator as it appears in print next to their work

Cromalins the Dupont system of glossy colour proofs

crop cut (image) to size or for better effect

crosshead line or lines, taken from the text, set bigger and bolder than the body type and inserted between paragraphs to liven up page

curatum a curated body of work such as a newspaper, magazine or website

cut shorten or delete copy

cut-out illustration with background masked, painted or cut to make it stand out on the page

cuts cuttings

cuttings stories taken (originally cut) from newspapers and filed electronically under subject

cuttings job story that is over-dependent on cuttings

dateline place from which copy is filed

deadline time story (or any part of it) is due

deck originally one of a series of headlines stacked on top of each other; then usually used to mean one line of a headline; now revived for website decks as used by, e.g., *Mail Online*

delayed drop device in news story of delaying important facts for effect

delete remove

descender the part of a lower-case letter (e.g. g and j) that sticks out below the x-height in a typeface

desk newspaper department, e.g. picture desk

deskman American term for male subeditor

diary, the list of news events to be covered; hence an off-diary story is one originated by the reporter

diary column gossip column

direct input transmission of copy direct from the journalist's keyboard to the computer for typesetting (as opposed to the old system in which compositors retyped copy)

disclaimer statement explaining that a particular person or organisation was not the subject of a previously published story

display ads ordinary (not 'classified') ads which appear throughout a publication

display type   type for headlines etc.

district reporter   one covering a particular area away from the main office

doorstepping   reporters lying in wait for (usually) celebrities outside their homes

double   a story published twice in the same issue of a publication

double-column   (of text, headline, illustration) across two columns

double (page) spread   two facing pages in a magazine, whether advertising or editorial

downtable subs   those other than the chief sub and deputies

drop cap, letter   outsize initial capital letter used to start story or section; it drops down alongside the text which is indented to accommodate it

drop quotes   outsize quotes used to mark quoted matter

dummy   1 pre-publication edition of new publication used to sell advertising and experiment editorially; 2 blank version of publication, e.g. to show quality and weight of paper; 3 complete set of page proofs

edition   version of newspaper printed for particular circulation area or time

editor   senior journalist responsible for publication or section

editorial   1 leading article expressing editorial opinion; 2 content that is not advertising

editor's conference   main planning meeting for next issue

em, en   units of measurement for type – the width of the two letters m and n

embargo   time before which an organisation supplying material, e.g. by press release, does not want it published

ends   the story ends here

EPD   electronic picture desk

EPS file   Encapsulated PostScript file

exclusive   claim by publication that it has a big story nobody else has

exes   journalists' out-of-pocket expenses

face   type design

facing matter   (of advertising) opposite editorial

facsimile   exact reproduction, as with electronic transmission of pages

feature   article that goes beyond reporting of facts to explain and/or entertain; also used of any editorial material that is not news or listings; hence feature writer, features editor

fifth colour   a colour additional to CMYK, usually a special finish like metallic or fluorescent

file   transmit copy

filler   short news item to fill space

fireman   traditional term for reporter sent to trouble spot when story breaks

fit   (of copy etc.) to occupy exactly the space available

flannel panel   magazine's address, contact information and list of staff

flash   brief urgent message from news agency

flatplan   page-by-page plan of issue

flip   (of picture) transpose left to right

flush left or right   (of type) having one consistent margin with the other ragged

fold, the   centre fold in a newspaper so that only the upper half of the paper ('above the fold') is visible at the point of sale

folio   page (number)

follow up   take published story as the starting point for an update

format   1 size, shape or style of publication or section; 2 computer instruction; hence to format

fount (pronounced font and now often spelt that way)   typeface

free(sheet)   free newspaper

freebie   something useful or pleasant, often a trip, supplied free to journalists

freelance   self-employed journalist who sells material to various outlets

freelancer   American term for freelance

fudge   another term for stop press

full out   (of type) not indented

galley proof   typeset proof not yet made up into a page

gatefold   an extra page which folds out from a magazine

ghost writer   journalist writing on behalf of someone else, often by interviewing them; hence to ghost (e.g. a column)

gone to bed   passed for press so too late for corrections

grams per square metre (gsm; g/m^2)   the measure used to define the weight of paper

graphics   visual material, usually drawn

grid   design skeleton specifying (e.g.) number and width of columns

gutter   space between two facing pages; can also be used of space between columns

H & J   (of copy on screen) hyphenated and justified, so in the form in which it will be typeset

hack, hackette   jocular terms for journalist

hair space   thinnest space between typeset letters

half-tone   illustration broken into dots of varying sizes

handout   printed material, e.g. press release, distributed to journalists

hanging indent   copy set with first line of each paragraph full out and subsequent ones indented

hard copy   copy on paper, e.g. printout, rather than screen

head, heading   headline

heavy   broadsheet newspaper

heavy type   thicker than standard

hold (over)   keep material for future use

hot metal   old typesetting system in which type was cast from molten metal

house ad   publisher's advertisement in its own publication

house journal   publication for employees of a particular organisation

house style   the way a publication chooses to publish in matters of detail

imposition   arrangement of pages for printing

imprint   name and address of publisher and printer

in-house   inside a media organisation

in pro   in proportion (used of visual material to be reduced)

indent   set copy several characters in from left-hand margin

input   type copy into computer

insert   1 extra copy to be included in existing story; 2 printed matter inserted in publication after printing and binding

intro   first paragraph of story; also used (confusingly) in some magazine offices to mean standfirst

ISDN   integrated services digital network – a means of transmitting editorial material between offices, to printers etc.

italics   italic (sloping) type

jack-line   another word for widow

journo   jocular term for journalist

justified   type set with consistent margins

kern   reduce the space between characters in typeset copy

keyword   specific words or phrases used in copy to make it visible to a search engine; important for **SEO**

kicker   introductory part of caption or headline

kill   drop a story; hence kill fee for freelance whose commissioned story is not used

knocking copy   story written with negative angle

label   (of headline) without a verb

landscape   horizontal picture

layout   arrangement of body type, headlines etc. and illustrations on the page

lead   1 main story on a page; 2 tip-off or idea for story (in the US the intro of a story is called the lead or lede)

leader   leading article expressing editorial opinion

leader dots   three dots used to punctuate (aka ellipsis)

leading (pronounced 'ledding')   space between lines (originally made by inserting blank slugs of lead between lines of type)

leg   column of typeset copy

legal   send material to be checked for legal problems, e.g. libel

legal kill   lawyer's instruction not to use

lensman   American term for male photographer

letter spacing   space between letters

libel   defamatory statement in permanent or broadcast form

lift   1 use all or most of a story taken from one newspaper edition in the next; 2 steal a story from another media outlet and reproduce it with few changes

ligature   two or more joined letters

light face   type lighter than standard

linage (this spelling preferred to lineage)   payment to freelances by the line; also refers to classified advertising without illustration

line drawing   drawing made up of black strokes

listings   lists of entertainment and other events with basic details

literal   typographical error

lobby, the   specialist group of political reporters covering parliament

local corr   local correspondent

logo   name, title or recognition word in particular design used on regular section or column; also used of magazine's front-page title

lower case   ordinary letters (not caps)

make-up   assembly of type and illustrations on the page ready for reproduction

mark up   specify the typeface, size and width in which copy is to be set

masking   covering part of photograph for reproduction

masthead   publication's front-page title

measure   width of typesetting

medium type   between light and heavy

merchandising   details of stockists and prices in consumer features

mf   more copy follows

model release   contract signed by photographic model authorising use of pictures

mono(chrome)   printed in one colour, usually black

more   more copy follows

mug shot   photograph showing head (and sometimes shoulders)

must   copy that must appear, e.g. apology or correction

mutton   old name for an em

native advertising   an online form of **advertorial** that uses content to build trust and engagement with potential customers; if successful may go **viral**

neg   photographic negative

news agency   supplier of news and features to media outlets

news desk   organising centre of newsroom

newsman   American term for male reporter

newsprint   standard paper on which newspapers are printed

newsroom   news reporters' room

nib   news in brief – short news item

night lawyer   barrister who reads newspaper proofs for legal problems

nose   intro of story; hence to renose – rewrite intro

NUJ   National Union of Journalists

nut   old name for an en; hence nutted, type indented one en

obit   obituary

off-diary   *see* diary, the

off-the-record   statements made to a journalist on the understanding that they will not be reported directly or attributed

on spec   uncommissioned (material submitted by freelance)

on-the-record   statements made to a journalist that can be reported and attributed

op-ed   feature page facing page with leading articles

open quotes   start of section in direct quotes

originals   photographs or other visual material for reproduction

orphan   single word or part of word at the end of a paragraph on a line by itself

out take   another term for pull quote

overlay   sheet of transparent paper laid over artwork with instructions on how to process it

overline   another word for strapline

overmatter   typeset material that does not fit the layout and must be cut

overprint   print over a previously printed background

PA   Press Association, Britain's national news agency

package   main feature plus sidebars

page furniture   displayed type, e.g. headlines, standfirsts and captions, used to project copy

page plan   editorial instructions for layout

page proof   proof of a made-up page

pagination   the number of pages in a publication; also a newspaper system's ability to make up pages

panel   another word for box

paparazzo/i   photographer(s) specialising in pursuing celebrities

par, para   paragraph

paste-up   page layout pasted into position (pre-digital)

patch   specialist area covered by reporter

pay-off   final twist or flourish in the last paragraph of a story

pdf   portable document format, Adobe's open standard for electronic document exchange, now much used by printers

peg   reason for publishing feature at a particular time

photomontage   illustration created by combining several photographs

pic, pix   press photograph(s)

pica   unit of type measurement

pick-up (of photographs)   those that already exist and can therefore be picked up by journalists covering a story

picture desk   organising centre of collection and editing of pictures

piece   article

plate   printing image carrier from which pages are printed

point   1 full stop; 2 standard unit of type size

pool   group of reporters sharing information and releasing it to other media organisations

PostScript   Adobe's page description language

PR(O)   public relations (officer); hence someone performing a public relations role

press cuttings   *see* cuttings

press release   written announcement or promotional material by organisation sent to media outlets and individual journalists

production hub   a centralised office for subbing and designing a range of newspapers or magazines

profile   portrait in words of individual or organisation

proof   printout of part or whole of page so it can be checked and corrected

proofread   check proofs; hence proofreader

publisher   1 publishing company; 2 individual in magazine publishing company with overall responsibility for title or group of titles

puff   story promoting person or organisation

pull   proof, to pull is to take a proof

pull (out) quote (blown quote, call out, out take)   short extract from text set in larger type as part of page layout

pullout   separate section of publication that can be pulled out

pyramid   (usually inverted) conventional structure for news story with most important facts in intro

query   question mark

queue   collection of stories held in a computer

quote   verbatim quotation

quotes   quotation marks

ragged   (of type) with uneven margin

raised cap   outsize initial capital letter used to start story or section; it is raised above the text

range left or right   (of type) have one consistent margin with the other ragged

register   alignment of coloured inks on the printed page

rejig   rewrite copy, particularly in the light of later information

renose   rewrite intro of a story

reporter   gatherer and writer of news

repro house   company that processes colour pictures ready for printing

retainer   regular payment to local correspondent or freelance

retouch   alter photograph to emphasise particular feature

Reuters   international news agency

reverse indent   another term for hanging indent

reversed out   (type) printed in white on black or tinted background

revise   extra proof to check that corrections have been made

rewrite   write new version of story or section as opposed to subbing on copy

ring-round   story based on series of phone calls

river   white space running down a column of type, caused by space between words

roman   plain upright type

rough   sketch for layout

round-up   gathering of disparate elements for single story

RSI   repetitive strain injury, attributed to overuse and misuse of computer keyboard, mouse etc.

rule   line between columns or round illustrations

run   period of printing an edition or number of copies printed

run on   (of type) continue from one line, column or page to the next

running foot   title and issue date at the foot of the page

running head   title and issue date at the top of the page

running story   one that is constantly developing, over a newspaper's different editions or a number of days

running turns   pages with no paragraph breaks on first and last lines; also used of columns

rush   second most urgent message from news agency (after flash)

sans (serif)   plain type (*see* serif) – this is an example

scaling (of pictures)   calculating depth

schedule   1 list of jobs for (e.g.) reporters; 2 publication's printing programme

scheme   make a plan of page layout

scoop   jocular word for exclusive

screamer   exclamation mark

screen   the number of dots per square inch of a half-tone

section   1 separately folded part of newspaper; 2 complete printed sheet making up part of magazine

sell   another word for standfirst, often used in women's magazines

SEO   search engine optimisation; refining copy to make it visible to search engines (see **keyword**)

serif   decorative addition to type – this is an example

set and hold   typeset and keep for use later

setting   copy set in type

shareable   content that is likely to be shared on social networks and thus go **viral**

shift   daily stint worked by staff journalists and casuals

shoot   a photographic session

shy   (of headline) too short for the space available

sidebar   subsidiary story or other material placed next to main story, usually in box

sidehead   subsidiary heading, set flush left

sign-off   writer's name as it appears in print at the end of a story

sketch   light-hearted account of events, especially parliamentary

slip   newspaper edition for particular area or event

small caps   capital letters in smaller size of the same typeface

snackable   bite-sized chunks of information that can be consumed quickly and shared easily on social networks; once described as the 'fast food of the content world'

snap   early summary by news agency of important story to come

snapper   jocular term for press photographer

snaps   press photographs

solid   (of type) set without extra leading

spike   where rejected copy goes (originally a metal spike)

splash   newspaper's main front-page story

splash sub   subeditor responsible for tabloid's front page

spoiler   attempt by newspaper to reduce impact of rival's exclusive by publishing similar story

spot colour   second colour (after black) used in printing publication

spread   two facing pages

s/s   same size

standfirst   introductory matter accompanying headline, particularly used in features

stet   ignore deletion or correction (Latin for 'let it stand')

stone   bench where pages were made up; hence stone sub – subeditor who makes final corrections and cuts on page proofs

stop press   small area on back page of newspaper left blank for late news in days of hot metal

story   article, especially news report

strap(line)   subsidiary headline above main headline

Street, the   Fleet Street, where many newspapers once had their offices

stringer   local correspondent; freelance on contract to a news organisation

style   house style

stylebook/style sheet   where house style is recorded

sub   subeditor

subhead   subsidiary headline

subtitle   another word for standfirst

tabloid   popular small-format newspaper such as the *Sun*

tagline   explanatory note under headline

take   section of copy for setting

take back   (on proof) take words back to previous line

take over   (on proof) take words forward to next line

taster   production journalist who checks and selects copy; also cover-line

think piece   feature written to show and provoke thought

tie-in   story connected with the one next to it

tint   shaded area on which type can be printed

tip(-off)   information supplied (and usually paid for) whether by free-lance or member of the public

titlepiece   traditional term for name of magazine as it appears on the cover – now replaced by masthead and logo

TOT   triumph over tragedy, feature formula particularly popular in women's magazines

tracking   space between characters

trade names   product names (e.g. Hoover, Kleenex, Velcro)

tranny   transparency – photograph in film form

trans(pose)   reverse order

turn   part of story continued on a later page

typeface   a complete range of type in a particular style, e.g. Times New Roman

typescale   measuring rule for type

typo   American term for typographical error

typography   craft of using type

u/lc   upper and lower case

underscore underline

unj(ustified) text set flush left, ragged right

upper and lower case mixture of capitals and ordinary letters

upper case capital letters

vignette illustration whose edges gradually fade to nothing

viral usually "going viral" – indicates material that is spread very rapidly via digital networks (see **snackable** and **shareable**)

vox pop series of street interviews (Latin: *vox populi* – voice of the people)

weight thickness or boldness of letters in a typeface

white space area on page with no type or illustration

widow the last line of a paragraph at the top of a page or column

wire a means of transmitting copy by electronic signal; hence wire room

wob white on black – type reversed out

wot white on tone

x-height height of the lower-case letters of a typeface (excluding ascenders and descenders)

Appendix: Copy editing and correction marks

COPY EDITING & CORRECTION MARKS
For use on printouts, typescripts, manuscripts, etc.

These are the most commonly used standard copy correction and editing marks. Use them to show where corrections are to be made. Is it still worth learning them? I believe so as they provide a universal system that many people still use.

Write directly in the (double-spaced) copy. If there is any doubt about what you mean or intend, make a brief comment in the (wide) margin.

Text to be inserted (small changes)

Example: Oh dear I have let a letter out of a word.

Delete character   / through the character

Drat, there are too many letters in one word.

Delete text   — through the text

Sometimes writers repeat ~~themeselves~~ themselves.

Delete character and close space   through the character

Use this when there is a misstake in the middle of a word or an unwanted space.

Delete text and close space   through the text

Similarly, if a writer has repeated herself ~~repeated herself~~ in the middle of a sentence.

Transpose characters

My figners got a bit scrabmled heer.

Transpose words

This in is completely the order wrong.

Put this in italics _____ under the characters to be changed

The name of this book is Lord of the Rings.

Put this in bold ∿∿ under the characters to be changed

Example: I cannot stress this enough.

Put this in capitals ≡ under the characters to be changed.

Example: london is the capital city.

Change to lowercase ◯ circle round character(s) to be changed

Example: London is the Capital City.

Make more space between characters or words   Y

Example: I was typing so fast I forget to use the spacebar

Make less space between characters or words

Example: Oops, I overdid the spacing a bit.

To uncorrect a correction _ _ _ under the word(s) and above or in the margin.

Example: Sorry, I really didn't mean to change this at all.

Text to be inserted (only use for major changes and additions**)**

(The letter in the diamond identifies the new text, which may be on a separate sheet.)

Example: There are several new paragraphs to be inserted. Please go to the section marked which is at the end of this document.

PUNCTUATION

Correct punctuation directly on the copy. Use the normal punctuation marks except for the following, which all go in a ring:

Full stop:

Colon:

Solidus (slash):

This mark is only to be used when there is a lot of material to be added – too much to fit into the space available on the manuscript. It may be one or more paragraphs, perhaps a new quote or some additional background.

The overall objective of all corrections is to make your meaning clear, so don't clutter up the copy with too much extra matter.

CORRECTING PROOFS – TYPESET MATERIAL

The marks used on proofs are the same, with a few additions (see below). Because there is very little room to show corrections, indicate *where* in the line the correction is to be made, then *confirm* the type of correction in the gutter or margin. You will need a fine-nibbed pen.

Additional marks to be used in the margin

Delete

Change to italic

Change to roman

Change to lower case

Punctuation

Insert a comma

Insert an apostrophe

Insert a full stop

Copy mark-up test

The changes or corrections to be made are indicated in square brackets. You can photocopy this page and compare your answers with the corrected version.

Join up letters in ba dly spaced wo rds.

Insert a word
[insert the word "new" between "a" and "word"]

Insert a phrase in this sentence
[insert: "that clarifies the meaning" between "phrase" and "in"]

Insert a mising letter

Change an incorrect lerter.

Change a bad word.
[change "bad" to "good"]

Transpose words two.

Transpose jumbeld letters.

Take out onne letter. Take out twowo.

Separate twowords.

Separate anbd correct wordswhere necesary.

Make these Upper Case letters into Lower Case.

Capitalise london.

capitalise this sentence.

Indicate bold face.
[make "bold face" bold]

Indicate italic.
[make "italic" italic]

Indicate that this sentence finishes with a full stop

And insert commas which are another form of punctuation in this sentence.

Sometimes a colon is needed sometimes not.

On other occasions a semi colon is more appropriate however, many people are unaware of the proper way to use this form of punctuation.

Where dashes have to be inserted like this use the insertion mark.
[put dashes where you think appropriate]

Copy mark-up test
The changes or corrections to be made are indicated in square brackets. You can photocopy this page and compare your answers with the corrected version.

Join up letters in ba|dly spaced wo⌐rds.

Insert a/word
[insert the word "new" between "a" and "word"]

Insert a phrase/in this sentence
[insert: "that clarifies the meaning" between "phrase" and "in"]

Insert a mis|ing letter

Change an incorrect le|ter.

Change a ~~bad~~ word.
[change "bad" to "good"]

Transpose |words|two|.

Transpose jumb|ed letters.

Take out on|e letter. Take out two~~wo~~.

Separate two|words.

Separate an|d correct words|where necesary.

Make these Upper Case letters into Lower Case.

Capitalise london.

capitalise this sentence.

Indicate bold face.
[make "bold face" bold]

Indicate italic.
[make "italic" italic]

Indicate that this sentence finishes with a full stop

And insert commas,which are another form of punctuation,in this sentence.

Sometimes a colon is needed/sometimes not.

On other occasions a semi colon is more appropriate/however, many people are unaware of the proper way to use this form of punctuation.

Where dashes have to be inserted/like this/use the insertion mark.
[put dashes where you think appropriate]

Proofing marks (for typeset copy)

Indicate *where* the correction is to be made in the copy; specify the exact *kind* of correction in the margin. If there is more than one correction in a line, note them in order and separate them with a solidus (/) or a caret mark (⁄)

Example

Wanted: subeditor. Must have traditionel subbing skills, excellent spelling and grammar, be great at rewrites and converting to house style, capable of coming up with creative headlines, smells and captions, generally computer literate but an expert at layout using Indesign, with management skills and the expertise to oversee the entire production process from raw copy to final pages. Experience of online journalism, web pages and content managment systems essential, as is the ability to write news and features and edit audio and video Must be fast, accurate, competent in Media Law and able to remain calm and positive under extreme presure.

A subeditor must certainly correct spelling and grammar, but must also check factual accuracy, rewrite copy to make it better or to conform with a house style, seek out potential libel libels or other legal pitfalls and remove them, fit copy into a layout, devise headlines, stand firsts (sells) and captions, and then, more than likely, lay that copy out in page templates for print and online editions, having selected, cropped and sized the illustrations or photographs *and* edited and uploaded audio or video files.

References

Barthes, Roland (1957), *Mythologies*. Paris: Editions du Seuil.

Bloy, Duncan and Hadwin, Sara (2011, 2nd edn), *Law and the Media*. London: Sweet & Maxwell.

Boyle, Raymond, 2006, *Sports Journalism: Context and Issues*. London: Sage.

Brett, Nicholas Brett and Holmes, Tim (2008), Supplements, in Bob Franklin (ed.), *Pulling Newspapers Apart: Analysing Print Journalism*. Abingdon: Routledge, 198–205.

Bruton, Finn (2013), *Spam: A Shadow History of the Internet*. Boston, MA: MIT Press.

Click, J. William and Baird, Russell N. (1986), *Magazine Editing and Production*. Dubuque, IA: W. C. Brown.

Conboy, Martin (2004), *Journalism: A Critical History*. London: Sage.

Dick, Murray (2013), *Search: Theory and Practice in Journalism Online*. London: Palgrave Macmillan.

Dicker, Brian (1950), *The Kemsley Manual of Journalism*. London: Cassell.

Dodge, John and Viner, George (1963), *The Practice of Journalism*. London: Heinemann.

Engel, Matthew (1996), *Tickle The Public: One Hundred Years of the Popular Press*. London: Phoenix.

Evans, Harold (1974), *Editing and Design Book 3: News Headlines*. London: Butterworth-Heinemann.

Evans, Harold (2000), *Essential English for Journalists, Editors and Writers*. London: Pimlico.

Fender, Stephen (2011), *Nature, Class, and New Deal Literature: The Country Poor in the Great Depression*. London: Routledge.

Goldman, William (1983), *Adventures in the Screen Trade*. London: Abacus.

Harris, Michael and Lee, Alan, eds, (1986), *The Press in English Society from the Seventeenth to Nineteenth Centuries*. London and Toronto: Associated University Presses.

Herd, Harold (1952), *The March Of Journalism: The Story of the British Press from 1622 to the Present Day*. London: George Allen & Unwin.

Holmes, Tim (2013), Magazines and Promotion, in Helen Powell (ed.), *Promotional Culture And Convergence: Markets, Methods, Media*. London: Routledge, pp. 173–90.

Holmes, Tim and Nice, Liz (2012), *Magazine Journalism*. London: Sage.

Holmes, Tim, Hadwin, Sara and Mottershead, Glyn (2013), *The 21st Century Journalism Handbook*. Harlow: Pearson.

Hutt, Allen (1973), *The Changing Newspaper*. London: Gordon Fraser Gallery.

Inwood, Stephen (1998), *A History of London*. London: Macmillan.

Lake, Brian (1984), *British Newspapers: A History and Guide for Collectors*. London: Sheppard Press.

Lee, Alan J. (1976), *The Origins of the Popular Press in England*. London: Croom Helm.

Leslie, Jeremy (2013), *The Modern Magazine: Visual Journalism in the Digital Age*. London: Laurence King Publishing.

McLuhan, Marshall (1964), *Understanding Media: The Extensions of Man*. New York: McGraw-Hill.

Mansfield, F. J. (1931), *Sub-editing: A Book Mainly for Young Journalists*. London: Sir I. Pitman & Sons.

Marr, Andrew (2005), *My Trade: A Short History of British Journalism*. Basingstoke: Pan Books.

Marsh, David (2013), *For Who The Bell Tolls*. London: Guardian and Faber & Faber.

Mason, Peter and Smith, Derrick (1998), *Magazine Law: A Practical Guide*. London: Routledge.

Moos, M. A., ed. (1997), *Media Research: Technology, Art, Communication: Essays by Marshall McLuhan*. Amsterdam: G+B Arts International.

Morrish, John (1996), *Magazine Editing, How to Develop and Manage a Successful Publication*. London: Routledge.

Nicol, Alexander (1950), *The Kemsley Manual of Journalism*. London: Cassell (p. 99).

Polkinghorne, Arthur (1965), *The Journalist's Craft: A Guide to Modern Practice*. Sydney: Angus & Robertson (p. 97).

Quinn, Frances (2013), *Law For Journalists*. Harlow: Pearson.

Rooney, Dick (2000), Thirty Years of Competition in the British Tabloid Press: The *Mirror* and the *Sun* 1968–98, in Colin Sparks and John Tulloch (eds), *Tabloid Tales: Global Debates over Media Standards*. Lanham, MD: Rowman & Littlefield, 91–110.

Sellers, Leslie (1968), *The Simple Subs Book*. Oxford: Pergamon Press.

Steinberg, S. H. (rev. John Trevitt) (1996), *Five Hundred Years of Printing*. London: British Library.

The Kemsley Manual of Journalism (1950). London: Cassell.

Tulloch, John (2000), The Eternal Recurrence of New Journalism, in Colin Sparks and John Tulloch (eds), *Tabloid Tales: Global Debates over Media Standards*. Lanham, MD: Rowman & Littlefield, 131–46.

Waterhouse, Keith (1989), *On Newspaper Style*. London: Viking.

Index

.